Wide Angle

KRISTIN DONNALLEY SHERMAN

GARY PATHARE

JAIMIE SCANLON

OXFORD

UNIVERSITY PRESS

OXFORD
UNIVERSITY PRESS

198 Madison Avenue
New York, NY 10016 USA

Great Clarendon Street, Oxford, OX2 6DP,
United Kingdom

Oxford University Press is a department of the University of Oxford. It furthers
the University's objective of excellence in research, scholarship, and education by
publishing worldwide. Oxford is a registered trade mark of Oxford University Press
in the UK and in certain other countries

ISBN: 978 0 19 452858 0   Wide Angle American 5 SB W/OP Pack
ISBN: 978 0 19 452834 4   Wide Angle American 5
ISBN: 978 0 19 454667 6   Wide Angle American 5 OP

Printed in China

This book is printed on paper from certified and well-managed sources

ACKNOWLEDGEMENTS

Back cover photograph: Oxford University Press building/David Fisher

Illustrations by: A. Richard Allen/Morgan Gaynin Inc pp. 50; Aaron Sacco/Mendola
artists pp. 16; Shaw Nielsen pp. 13, 25, 37, 49, 61, 73, 85, 97, 109, 121, 133, 145.

Video Stills, Mannic Productions: pp. 12, 24, 36, 48, 60, 72, 84, 96, 108, 120, 132, 144.
People's Television: pp. 55, 146.

*The Publishers would like to thank the following for their kind permission to reproduce
photographs and other copyright material:* **123rf:** p. 38 (Nazca Lines, Peru/Felix Lipov);
Alamy: pp. 7 (great barrier reef coral and fish/Steffen Binke), 10 (female make-up
artist/keith morris), 19 (grandparents & grandchildren on beach/MBI), 23 (white
sheep/Juice Images), (woman/Nano Calvo), 31 (giant tortoise/Arco Images GmbH),
(Greenland shark/Nature Picture Library), (Japanese koi in pond/Craig Russell),
(Kakapo parrot in nest/Frans Lanting Studio), 33 (African elephants at watering hole/
Cultura RM), 41 (lock and portion of URL/EggHeadPhoto), 46 (drone hovering near
window/dpa picture alliance), 52 (doctors using robots to perform surgery/JIRAROJ
PRADITCHAROENKUL), (group of children learning about robots/Lev Dolgachov),
(worker in Ford plant with co-bot/dpa picture alliance), 62 (tai chi in public park/
Design Pics Inc), 65 (soccer in parking lot/Dorothy Alexander), 67 (climbing indoor
bouldering wall/James Davies), 70 (male wheelchair basketball team celebrating
win/PJF Military Collection), 90 (old and modern/Christian Kober 1), 113 (clown/
OZSHOTZ), 125 (1980s family/ClassicStock), 127 (people meeting on or enjoying
The Highline/Gavin Hellier), 130 (gorillas/robertharding), 131 (flamingos/National
Geographic Creative), 136 (mother and daughter/Hero Images Inc.), (siblings/
Wavebreak Media ltd), 139 (business hotel room/f8 images), (shared hostel kitchen/
Archimage), (student dorm room/Glasshouse Images), 142 (detached wooden
cottage/Chris Lofty); **Bjarke Ingel:** p. 4 (Bjarke Ingel's 8-house project/Jens Lindhe);
BLINK: Cover, Quinn Ryan Mattingly, pp. 3 (organic farmer/Edu Bayer), 6 (traffic
scene/Quinn Ryan Mattingly), 15 (Spanish class/Edu Bayer), 18 (Guarani pray at
the prayer house/Nadia Shira Cohen), 27 (ship/Gianni Cipriano), 30 (The Swabian
castle of Augusta/Gianni Cipriano), 39 (restaurant window/Edu Bayer), 44 (tourist
sitting/Gianni Cipriano), 51 (tents/Nadia Shira Cohen), 57 (cowboy/Edu Bayer), 63
(dancing/Krisanne Johnson), 69 (soccer team/Edu Bayer), 75 (haircut/Edu Bayer), 81
(ID worker talks with rural women/Krisanne Johnson), 87 (men hangout in their car/
Krisanne Johnson), 92 (Egyptian protestors in Tahrir Square./Nadia Shira Cohen),
99 (water well drilling rig/Edu Bayer), 104 (sharing food/Nadia Shira Cohen), 111
(lemon field/Gianni Cipriano), 117 (post its/Edu Bayer), 123 (siblings/Edu Bayer), 129
(reading/Quinn Ryan Mattingly), 135 (high school students/Krisanne Johnson), 141
(home in Swaziland/Krisanne Johnson); **Getty:** pp. 7 (aerial great barrier reef/Felix
Martinez), (boats on the reef/David Wall Photo), 10 (white male lab rat researcher/D-
Keine), 11 (picking up litter on beach/SONNY TUMBELAKA), (teen girl texting/Fajrul

Islam), 14 (New York women in community garden/Michel Setboun), 19 (toddler
on tricycle/Allen Donikowski), 20 (reading/Godong), 28 (flood/wsfurlan), (volcanic
eruption/Stocktrek Images/Richard Roscoe), 29 (archaeologists on dig site Pompeii
or Herculaneum/AFP Stringer), 31 (chimpanzees in wild/USO), (immortal jellyfish/
Yiming Chen), 34 (sleeping/Dmitriy Bilous), 46 (NYPD sign camera surveillance NY
city/400tmax), 47 (hand swiping credit card machine close up/David Woolley), 64
(2-4 women ten pin bowling/Peter Cade), (group playing pictionary/Lucy Lambriex),
(person in 20s spinning plate or making balloon animal/Sandra Mu Staff), (three
people in 20s in a park/Ales-A), 67 (adults in ceramic class/Gary Burchell), (playing
Go outside/Tuul & Bruno Morandi), 70 (children competing in race/Dave Nagel),
(crowd reaction to their team winning/Scott Barbour Stringer), (latino male soccer
players arguing with referee/OMAR TORRES Staff), 76 (man or woman having reiki/
Dean Mitchell), 82 (2-3 designers/Thomas Barwick), (journalist with cameraman
interviewing someone/track5), (male band rehearsing/BJI Blue Jean Images), 88
(hammock/Colin Anderson), 98 (audience/RichLegg), (storyteller/kali9), 112 (spider/
David Alligood EyeEm), 124 (1/Steve Cole), (2/Hoxton/Ryan Lees), (3/Oliver Eitel),
127 (aerial view of people using The Highline to commute/Cameron Davidson),
(people relaxing on The Highline/Maremagnum), 136 (twins/Westend61), 142 (house
keys/PYMCA Contributor), **OUP:** pp. 23 (tree/Mike Richter), 28 (forest fire/Evgeny
Dubinchuk); **iStock:** p. xvi, (phone/lvcandy), (tablet/RekaReka); **Shutterstock:**
pp. 9 (Gadisar Lake in Jaisalmer city/pzAxe), 10 (doctor injecting child/Yusnizam
Yusof), 11 (vegan/pro-vegetarian food truck (no pigs or pork)/R.Bordo), 19 (4-5 girl
eating ice cream cone/photoiva), (happy 6-8 girls covering eyes/Andrew Angelov),
28 (earthquake/NigelSpiers), 32 (tennis player/sirtravelalot), 58 (Solar panel on a red
roof/Smileus), 58 (shipping container house with wind turbine/Paul Beentjes), 74
(cyclist/Roman Mikhailiuk), 76 (doctors in operating theatre/santypan), (drugstore
looking or buying medication/Tyler Olson), (male 30s in lotus position outside/
Zdenka Darula), 79 (coins/Tony Stock), 82 (female fashion designers assessing dress/
PR Image Factory), 94 (speech/hxdbzxy), 101 (stretching/wavebreakmedia), 106
(Adidas/Michael715), (Lego/ChameleonsEye), (Mcdonalds/LongJon), (Netflix/Faizal
Ramli), 112 (crowded public space/William Perugini), (lighting bolts/strikes/Darin
Echelberger), (perspective of height/Geraldo Ramos), 114 (obstacle course/BluIz60),
122 (parachute jumping/Germanskydiver), 130 (antelopes/Rachel Portwood), (lions/
Maggy Meyer), (penguins/Alexey Seafarer), (wild dogs/Simon Eeman), 131 (meerkats/
tratong), 142 (detached contemporary house/dotshock), (terraced brick townhouses/
Christine Bird), **Superstock:** p. 28 (tornado/Jim Reed).

Authentic Content Provided by Oxford Reference

The publisher is grateful to those who have given permission to use the following extracts and adaptations of copyright material:

p.4 adapted from Castree, Noel, Kitchin, Rob and Rogers, Alisdair. "moral geographies." In *A Dictionary of Human Geography*. : Oxford University Press, 2013. http://www.oxfordreference.com/view/10.1093/acref/9780199599868.001.0001/acref-9780199599868-e-1212

p.17 adapted from Reed, Graham F. "déjà vu." In *The Oxford Companion to the Mind*. : Oxford University Press, 2004. http://www.oxfordreference.com/view/10.1093/acref/9780198662242.001.0001/acref-9780198662242-e-239

p..29 adapted from Touchette, Lori-Ann. "Pompeii." In *The Oxford Companion to Western Art*. : Oxford University Press, 2001. http://www.oxfordreference.com/view/10.1093/acref/9780198662037.001.0001/acref-9780198662037-e-2093

p.41 adapted from Lannon, John, Hick, Steven F., and Halpin, Edward F. "Internet." In *Encyclopedia of Human Rights*. : Oxford University Press, 2009. http://www.oxfordreference.com/view/10.1093/acref/9780195334029.001.0001/acref-9780195334029-e-154

p.52 adapted from Collins, Harry M. "artificial intelligence." In *Science, Technology, and Society*. : Oxford University Press, 2005. http://www.oxfordreference.com/view/10.1093/acref/9780195141931.001.0001/acref-9780195141931-e-6

p.70 adapted from Tomlinson, Alan. "competition." In *A Dictionary of Sports Studies*. : Oxford University Press, 2010. http://www.oxfordreference.com/view/10.1093/acref/9780199213818.001.0001/acref-9780199213818-e-274

p.77 adapted from Humphrey, Nicholas. "placebo effect." In *The Oxford Companion to the Mind*. : Oxford University Press, 2004. http://www.oxfordreference.com/view/10.1093/acref/9780198662242.001.0001/acref-9780198662242-e-680

p.89 adapted from Garner, Bryan A. "Etymology." In *Garner's Modern English Usage*. : Oxford University Press, 2016. http://www.oxfordreference.com/view/10.1093/acref/9780190491482.001.0001/acref-9780190491482-e-2878

p.102 adapted from Walsh, Claire. "Retail Trade." In *The Oxford Encyclopedia of Economic History*. : Oxford University Press, 2003. http://www.oxfordreference.com/view/10.1093/acref/9780195105070.001.0001/acref-9780195105070-e-0629

p.113 adapted from McDonough, Michael. "phobias." In *The Oxford Companion to the Mind*. : Oxford University Press, 2004. http://www.oxfordreference.com/view/10.1093/acref/9780198662242.001.0001/acref-9780198662242-e-672

p.123 adapted from " Steve Jobs." In *Oxford Essential Quotations*, edited by Ratcliffe, Susan. : Oxford University Press, 2016, http://www.oxfordreference.com/view/10.1093/acref/9780191843730.001.0001/q-oro-ed5-00005922

p.131 adapted from Blumstein, Daniel T. "Group Living." In *Encyclopedia of Evolution*. : Oxford University Press, 2002. http://www.oxfordreference.com/view/10.1093/acref/9780195122008.001.0001/acref-9780195122008-e-180

p. 137 adapted from "nature or nurture." In *A Dictionary of Education*, edited by Wallace, Susan. : Oxford University Press, 2015. http://www.oxfordreference.com/view/10.1093/acref/9780199679393.001.0001/acref-9780199679393-e-685

p.147 adapted from "Auctoritates Aristotelis." In *Oxford Dictionary of Quotations*, edited by Knowles, Elizabeth. : Oxford University Press, 2014. http://www.oxfordreference.com/view/10.1093/acref/9780199668700.001.0001/q-author-00010-00000156

p. 148 adapted from "Memory." In *Oxford Essential Quotations*, edited by Ratcliffe, Susan. : Oxford University Press, 2016, http://www.oxfordreference.com/view/10.1093/acref/9780191826719.001.0001/q-oro-ed4-00007227

p.149 adapted from "Jean-Anthelme Brillat-Savarin." In *Oxford Dictionary of Scientific Quotations*, edited by Bynum, W. F., and Porter, Roy. : Oxford University Press, 2006. http://www.oxfordreference.com/view/10.1093/acref/9780198614432.001.0001/q-author-00007-00000189

p.150 adapted from "Ayn Rand." In *Oxford Dictionary of Quotations*, edited by Knowles, Elizabeth. : Oxford University Press, 2014. http://www.oxfordreference.com/view/10.1093/acref/9780199668700.001.0001/q-author-00010-00002720

p.151 adapted from "History." In *Oxford Dictionary of Humorous Quotations*, edited by Gyles Brandreth. : Oxford University Press, 2012. http://www.oxfordreference.com/view/10.1093/acref/9780199570034.001.0001/q-subject-00002-00000108.

p.152 adapted from "Paul A. Samuelson." In *Oxford Dictionary of Quotations*, edited by Knowles, Elizabeth. : Oxford University Press, 2014. http://www.oxfordreference.com/view/10.1093/acref/9780199668700.001.0001/q-author-00010-00002820

p153. adapted from "Paul Hawken." In *Oxford Essential Quotations*, edited by Ratcliffe, Susan. : Oxford University Press, 2016, http://www.oxfordreference.com/view/10.1093/acref/9780191826719.001.0001/q-oro-ed4-00017749

p.154 adapted from "Words." In *Oxford Essential Quotations*, edited by Ratcliffe, Susan. : Oxford University Press, 2016, http://www.oxfordreference.com/view/10.1093/acref/9780191843730.001.0001/q-oro-ed5-00011727

p.155 adapted from "Billy Rose." In *The Oxford Dictionary of American Quotations*, edited by Rawson, Hugh, and Margaret Miner. : Oxford University Press, 2006. http://www.oxfordreference.com/view/10.1093/acref/9780195168235.001.0001/q-author-00008-00001401

p.156 adapted from "Theory." In *Oxford Essential Quotations*, edited by Ratcliffe, Susan. : Oxford University Press, 2016, http://www.oxfordreference.com/view/10.1093/acref/9780191826719.001.0001/q-oro-ed4-00010851

p. 157 adapted from "St Edmund of Abingdon." In *Oxford Essential Quotations*, edited by Ratcliffe, Susan. : Oxford University Press, 2016, http://www.oxfordreference.com/view/10.1093/acref/9780191843730.001.0001/q-oro-ed5-00003968

p. 158 adapted from "Character." In *Oxford Essential Quotations*, edited by Ratcliffe, Susan. : Oxford University Press, 2016, http://www.oxfordreference.com/view/10.1093/acref/9780191826719.001.0001/q-oro-ed4-00002824

Cover photo by Quinn Ryan Mattingly. Halong Bay, Vietnam, September 2013.

A man swims in Halong Bay, Vietnam. Halong Bay is a UNESCO World Heritage Site consisting of hundreds of limestone peaks rising from the Gulf of Tonkin in northern Vietnam.

Contents

UNIT	READING	LISTENING	SPEAKING	WRITING
1 Values **3**	Recognizing scenarios · *Moral Geography*	Understanding opinions and speculation	Narrating experiences	Writing paragraphs and topic sentences · ▶ The Great Barrier Reef
2 Memory **15**	Recognizing and understanding chronology · *Memories...*	Understanding speaker's audience and purpose · ▶ A lecture about memorization techniques	Critiquing and reviewing	Discourse markers for time and sequence
3 Discoveries **27**	Previewing longer texts · *Finding the World's Lost Cities*	Dealing with unknown words while listening	Supporting opinions with evidence and examples	Summarizing
4 Privacy **39**	Understanding an argument and counterargument · *Use it and Lose It*	Listening for gist	Describing experiences	Using reason and result linking words
5 Alternatives **51**	Recognizing homographs · *Social Robots*	Making inferences	Making speculations	Introducing examples and explanations · ▶ A Part-time Job
6 Fun **63**	Recognizing and understanding tone: Humor · *Worth Playing For*	Understanding speaker's attitude and mood · *Competition*	Structuring a presentation	Phrases that signal similarity and difference

ENGLISH FOR REAL	GRAMMAR	VOCABULARY	PRONUNCIATION	REVIEW
▶ Starting a formal conversation	Dramatic present in narratives Present perfect versus present perfect continuous Question types: subject, direct/indirect, with preposition	Verb + preposition collocations with *for*, *on*, and *against* Values and ethics Social issues	Intonation: Showing interest	see page 147
▶ Listening and participating in a group discussion	Narrative tenses Past perfect simple versus past perfect continuous Habits and routines	Noun suffixes Emotions Memory	Word stress in longer words Using cadence (speaking speed) and intonation to express certainty or hesitation	see page 148
▶ Agreeing and disagreeing	Contrast clauses Articles Determiners and quantifiers: *each of/ every one of, either…or, neither…nor, either of/ neither of*	Phrasal verbs Disasters	Linking	see page 149
▶ Expressing regret	Models of necessity, obligation, and prohibition Modals of regret Past modals of deduction	Phrases for clarification Computing	Reduced form of *have* in past modals	see page 150
▶ Delivering bad news	Future forms Future perfect Present tenses for the future	Adverbs of probability Jobs and money	Compound nouns	see page 151
▶ Expressing sympathy	Verb + *-ing* or *to* infinitive (same or different meaning) Verb with *-ing* and *to* infinitive Other uses of *-ing* form	Intensifying adverbs Sports and competition	Stress and rhythm	see page 152

UNIT	READING	LISTENING	SPEAKING	WRITING
7 Solutions 75	Recognizing and understanding metaphors *The Placebo Effect*	Listening and note-taking	Evaluating and synthesizing	Checking your work: Audience and purpose
8 Words 87	Recognizing and understanding idioms *What's the Word?*	Recognizing paraphrase	Telling a story	Using reported speech
9 Investment 99	Recognizing and understanding generalizations *Invest in Yourself* Read about investment	Listening for main ideas and key details ▶ A talk about logos	Using data to support a point of view	Writing main and supporting arguments
10 Theories 111	Recognizing and understanding complex sentences with subordinate clauses *The Origins of Fear*	Listening for main ideas and supporting evidence	Expanding ideas with related points and examples	Including significant details
11 Lifestyle 123	Understanding reason and consequence *Lifestyle Choices*	Dealing with longer listening *Group life*	Talking about advantages and disadvantages	Using synonyms to avoid repetition ▶ The High Line
12 Character 135	Recognizing and understanding addition and contrast linking words *To Be or To Learn*	Recognizing and understanding vague language	Eliciting and making relevant comments on the opinions of others ▶ Finding a place to live	Using addition and contrast linking words

GRAMMAR FOCUS 159-170

ENGLISH FOR REAL	GRAMMAR	VOCABULARY	PRONUNCIATION	REVIEW
▶ Persuading	Defining and non-defining relative clauses Participle clauses *Would rather* + infinitive	Opposites Health and medicine	Focus words in chunks	see page 153
▶ Sharing news about yourself	Reporting verbs Reported questions Reported speech	Discussing a quotation or paraphrase Neologisms	Spoken punctuation	see page 154
▶ Complaining	Structures with infinitive Infinitive constructions Purpose clauses with infinitive	Collocations with *get*, *have*, *make*, and *take* Finance and business Advertising	Linking two consonants	see page 155
▶ Expressing reactions	Passive reporting verbs Passive future Passive voice	Alternatives for the word *thing* Words in context	Intonation for uncertainty	see page 156
▶ Giving and responding to compliments	*Have / get something done* Intensifying adverbs Conjunction clauses	Collocations for *lifestyle*: Verb + noun; adjective + noun Relationships	Using intonation to soften language	see page 157
▶ Giving criticism	Second conditional versus third conditional Mixed conditionals *I wish...*	Prefixes *inter-*, *pre-*, *trans-*, *pro-* Personal qualities	Sentence stress in conditional sentences	see page 158

Acknowledgments

AUTHOR

Kristin Donnalley Sherman holds an M.E. in TESL from the University of North Carolina, Charlotte. She has taught ESL/EFL at Central Piedmont Community College in Charlotte, North Carolina, for more than fifteen years and has taught a variety of subjects including grammar, reading, composition, listening, and speaking. She has written several student books, teacher's editions, and workbooks in the area of academic ESL/EFL. In addition, she has delivered trainings internationally in ESL methodology.

Gary Pathare has a Master's in Education in TESOL from Newcastle University, England. He has been teaching English at the Higher Colleges of Technology in Dubai since 2001, after ten years' teaching English and teacher training in Barcelona and Rome. Gary has spoken at international conferences on a wide range of topics including spelling, literacy, writing, reading, grammar, metaphor, original uses of technology, memorization, materials writing, teacher training, and innovation in ELT.

Jaimie Scanlon is a freelance ELT author, editor, curriculum designer, and teacher trainer. Over the past 20 years, she has taught English to learners of all ages and has trained English teachers in Asia, Eastern Europe, and the United States. Jaimie holds an M.A. in TESOL and French from the School for International Training in Vermont, where she currently lives with her husband and two children.

SERIES CONSULTANTS

PRAGMATICS Carsten Roever is Associate Professor in Applied Linguistics at the University of Melbourne, Australia. He was trained as a TESOL teacher and holds a Ph.D. in Second Language Acquisition from the University of Hawai'i at Manoa. His research interests include interlanguage pragmatics, language testing, and conversation analysis.

Naoko Taguchi is an Associate Professor of Japanese and Second Language Acquisition at the Dietrich College of Modern Languages at Carnegie Mellon University. She holds a Ph.D. from Northern Arizona University. Her primary research interests include pragmatics in Second Language Acquisition, second language education, and classroom-based research.

PRONUNCIATION Tamara Jones is an instructor at the English Language Center at Howard Community College in Columbia, Maryland.

INCLUSIVITY & CRITICAL THINKING Lara Ravitch is a senior instructor and the Intensive English Program Coordinator of the American English Institute at the University of Oregon.

ENGLISH FOR REAL VIDEOS Pamela Vittorio acquired a B.A. in English/Theater from SUNY Geneseo and is an ABD Ph.D. in Middle Eastern Studies with an M.A. in Middle Eastern Literature and Languages from NYU. She also designs ESL curriculum, materials, and English language assessment tools for publishing companies and academic institutions.

MIDDLE EAST ADVISORY BOARD Amina Saif Al Hashami, Nizwa College of Applied Sciences, Oman; **Karen Caldwell,** Higher Colleges of Technology, Ras Al Khaimah, UAE; **Chaker Ali Mhamdi,** Buraimi University College, Oman.

LATIN AMERICA ADVISORY BOARD Reinaldo Hernández, Duoc, Chile; **Mauricio Miraglia,** Universidad Tecnológica de Chile INACAP, Chile; **Aideé Damián Rodríguez,** Tecnológico de Monterrey, Mexico; **Adriana Recke Duhart,** Universidad Anáhuac, Mexico; **Inés Campos,** Centro de Idiomas, Cesar Vallejo University, Peru.

SPAIN ADVISORY BOARD Alison Alonso, EOI Luarca, Spain; **Juan Ramón Bautista Liébana,** EOI Rivas, Spain; **Ruth Pattison,** EOI, Spain; **David Silles McLaney,** EOI Majadahonda, Spain.

We would like to acknowledge the educators from around the world who participated in the development and review of this series:

ASIA Ralph Baker, Chuo University, Japan; **Elizabeth Belcour**, Chongshin University, South Korea; **Mark Benton**, Kobe Shoin Women's University, Japan; **Jon Berry**, Kyonggi University, South Korea; **Stephen Lyall Clarke**, Vietnam-US English Training Service Centers, Vietnam; **Edo Forsythe**, Hirosaki Gakuin University, Japan; **Clifford Gibson**, Dokkyo University, Japan; **Michelle Johnson**, Nihon University, Japan; **Stephan Johnson**, Rikkyo University, Japan; **Nicholas Kemp**, Kyushu International University, Japan; **Brendyn Lane**, Core Language School, Japan; **Annaliese Mackintosh**, Kyonggi University, South Korea; **Keith Milling**, Yonsei University, Korea; **Chau Ngoc Minh Nguyen**, Vietnam – USA Society English Training Service Center, Vietnam; **Yongjun Park**, Sangi University, South Korea; **Scott Schafer**, Inha University, South Korea; **Dennis Schumacher**, Cheongju University, South Korea; **Jenay Seymour**, Hongik University, South Korea; **Joseph Staples**, Shinshu University, Japan; **Greg Stapleton**, YBM Education Inc. – Adult Academies Division, South Korea; **Le Tuam Vu**, Tan True High School, Vietnam; **Ben Underwood**, Kugenuma High School, Japan; **Quyen Vuong**, VUS English Center, Vietnam

EUROPE Marta Alonso Jerez, Mainfor Formación, Spain; **Pilar Álvarez Polvorinos**, EOI San Blas, Spain; **Peter Anderson**, Anderson House, Italy; **Ana Anglés Esquinas**, First Class Idiomes i Formació, Spain; **Keith Appleby**, CET Services, Spain; **Isabel Arranz**, CULM Universidad de Zaragoza, Spain; **Jesus Baena**, EOI Alcalá de Guadaira, Spain; **José Gabriel Barbero Férnández**, EOI de Burgos, Spain; **Carlos Bibi Fernandez**, EIO de Madrid-Ciudad Lineal, Spain; **Alex Bishop**, IH Madrid, Spain; **Nathan Leopold Blackshaw**, CCI, Italy; **Olga Bel Blesa**, EOI, Spain; **Antoinette Breutel**, Academia Language School, Switzerland; **Angel Francisco Briones Barco**, EOI Fuenlabrada, Spain; **Ida Brucciani**, Pisa University, Italy; **Julie Bystrytska**, Profi-Lingua, Poland; **Raul Cabezali**, EOI Alcala de Guadaira, Spain; **Milena Cacko-Kozera**, Profi-Lingua, Poland; **Elena Calviño**, EOI Pontevedra, Spain; **Alex Cameron**, The English House, Spain; **Rosa Cano Vallese**, EOI Prat Llobregate, Spain; **Montse Cañada**, EOI Barcelona, Spain; **Elisabetta Carraro**, WE.CO Translate, Italy; **Joaquim Andres Casamiquela**, Escola Oficial d'Idiomes – Guinardó, Spain; **Lara Ros Castillo**, Aula Campus, Spain; **Patricia Cervera Cottrell**, Centro de Idiomas White, Spain; **Sally Christopher**, Parkway S.I., Spain; **Marianne Clark**, The English Oak Tree Academy, Spain; **Helen Collins**, ELI, Spain; **María José Conde Torrado**, EOI Ferrol, Spain; **Ana Maria Costachi**, Centro de Estudios Ana Costachi S.I., Spain; **Michael Cotton**, Modern English Study Centre, Italy; **Pedro Cunado Placer**, English World, Spain; **Sarah Dague**, Universidad Carlos III, Spain; **María Pilar Delgado**, Big Ben School, Spain; **Ashley Renee Dentremont Matthäus**, Carl-Schurz Haus, Deutch-Amerikanisches-Institut Freiburg e.V., Germany; **Mary Dewhirst**, Cambridge English Systems, Spain; **Hanna Dobrzycka**, Advantage, Poland; **Laura Dolla**, E.F.E. Laura Dolla, Spain; **Paul Doncaster**, Taliesin Idiomes, Spain; **Marek Doskocz**, Lingwista Sp. z o.o., Poland; **Fiona**

Dunbar, ELI Málaga, Spain; **Anna Dunin-Bzdak**, Military University of Technology, Poland; **Robin Evers**, l'Università di Modena e Reggio Emilia, Italy; **Yolanda Fernandez**, EOI, Spain; **Dolores Fernández Gavela**, EOI Gijón, Spain; **Mgr. Tomáš Fišer**, English Academy, Czech Republic; **Juan Fondón**, EOI de Langreo, Spain; **Carmen Forns**, Centro Universitario de Lenguas Modernas, Spain; **Ángela Fraga**, EOI de Ferrol, Spain; **Beatriz Freire**, Servicio de Idiomas FGULL, Spain; **Alena Fridrichova**, Palacky University in Olomouc, Faculty of Science, Department of Foreign Languages, Czech Republic; **Elena Friedrich**, Palacky University, Czech Republic; **JM Galarza**, Iruñanko Hizkuntz Eskola, Spain; **Nancie Gantenbein**, TLC-IH, Switzerland; **Gema García**, EOI, Spain; **Maria Jose Garcia Ferrer**, EOI Moratalaz, Spain; **Josefa García González**, EOI Málaga, Spain; **Maria García Hermosa**, EOI, Spain; **Jane Gelder**, The British Institute of Florence, Italy; **Aleksandra Gelner**, ELC Katowice, Bankowa 14, Poland; **Marga Gesto**, EOI Ferrol, Spain; **Juan Gil**, EOI Maria Moliner, Spain; **Eva Gil Cepero**, EOI La Laguna, Spain; **Alan Giverin**, Today School, Spain; **Tomas Gomez**, EOI Segovia, Spain; **Mónica González**, EOI Carlos V, Spain; **Elena González Diaz**, EOI, Spain; **Steve Goodman**, Language Campus, Spain; **Katy Gorman**, Study Sulmona, Italy; **Edmund Green**, The British Institute of Florence, Italy; **Elvira Guerrero**, GO! English Granada, Spain; **Lauren Hale**, The British Institute of Florence, Italy; **Maria Jose Hernandez**, EOI de Salou, Spain; **Chris Hermann**, Hermann Brown English Language Centre, Spain; **Robert Holmes**, Holmes English, Czech Republic; **José Ramón Horrillo**, EOI de Aracena, Spain; **Laura Izquierdo**, Univeristy of Zaragoza, Spain; **Marcin Jaśkiewicz**, British School Żoliborz, Poland; **Mojmír Jurák**, Albi – jazyková škola, Czech Republic; **Eva Kejdová**, BLC, Czech Republic; **Turlough Kelleher**, British Council, Callaghan School of English, Spain; **Janina Knight**, Advantage Learners, Spain; **Ewa Kowalik**, English Point Radom, Poland; **Monika Krawczuk**, Wyższa Szkoła Finansów i Zarządzania, Poland; **Milica Krisan**, Agentura Parole, Czech Republic; **Jędrzej Kucharski**, Profi-lingua, Poland; **V. Lagunilla**, EOI San Blas, Spain; **Antonio Lara Davila**, EOI La Laguna, Spain; **Ana Lecubarri**, EOI Aviles, Spain; **Lesley Lee**, Exit Language Center, Spain; **Jessica Lewis**, Lewis Academy, Spain; **Alice Llopas**, EOI Estepa, Spain; **Angela Lloyd**, SRH Hochschule Berlin, Germany; **Helena Lohrová**, University of South Bohemia, Faculty of Philosophy, Czech Republic; **Elena López Luengo**, EOI Alcalá de Henares, Spain; **Karen Lord**, Cambridge House, Spain; **Carmen Loriente Duran**, EOI Rio Vero, Spain; **Alfonso Luengo**, EOI Jesús Maestro Madrid, Spain; **Virginia Lyons**, VLEC, Spain; **Anna Łętowska-Mickiewicz**, University of Warsaw, Poland; **Ewa Malesa**, Uniwersytet SWPS, Poland; **Klara Małowiecka**, University of Warsaw, Poland; **Dott. Ssa Kim Manzi**, Università degli Studi della Tuscia – DISTU – Viterbo, Italy; **James Martin**, St. James Language Center, Spain; **Ana Martin Arista**, EOI Tarazona, Spain; **Irene Martín Gago**, NEC, Spain; **Marga Martínez**, ESIC Idiomas Valencia, Spain; **Kenny McDonnell**, McDonnell English Services S.I., Spain; **Anne Mellon**, EEOI Motilla del Palacar, Spain; **Miguel Ángel Meroño**, EOI Cartagena, Spain; **Joanna Merta**, Lingua Nova, Poland; **Victoria Mollejo**, EOI San Blas-Madrid, Spain; **Rebecca Moon**, La Janda Language Services, Spain; **Anna Morales Puigicerver**, EOI TERRASSA, Spain;

Jesús Moreno, Centro de Lenguas Modernas, Universidad de Zaragoza, Spain; Emilio Moreno Prieto, EOI Albacete, Spain; Daniel Muñoz Bravo, Big Ben Center, Spain; Heike Mülder, In-House Englishtraining, Germany; Alexandra Netea, Albany School of English, Cordoba, Spain; Christine M. Neubert, Intercultural Communication, Germany; Ignasi Nuez, The King's Corner, Spain; Guadalupe Núñez Barredo, EOI de Ponferrada, Spain; Monika Olizarowicz-Strygner, XXII LO z OD im. Jose Marti, Poland; A. Panter, Oxford School of English, Italy; Vanessa Jayne Parvin, British School Florence, Italy; Rachel Payne, Academia Caledonian, Cadiz, Spain; Olga Pelaez, EOI Palencia, Spain; Claudia Pellegrini, Klubschule Migros, Switzerland; Arantxa Pérez, EOI Tudela, Spain; Montse Pérez, EOI Zamora, Spain; Esther Pérez, EOI Soria, Spain; Rubén Pérez Montesinos, EOI San Fernando de Henares, Spain; Joss Pinches, Servicio de Lenguas Modernas, Universidad de Huelva, Spain; Katerina Pitrova, FLCM TBU in Zlin, Czech Republic; Erica Pivesso, Komalingua, Spain; Eva Plechackova, Langfor CZ, Czech Republic; Jesús Porras Santana, JPS English School, Spain; Adolfo Prieto, EOI Albacete, Spain; Sara Prieto, Universidad Católica de Murcia, Spain; Penelope Prodromou, Universitá Roma Tre, Italy; Maria Jose Pueyo, EOI Zaragoza, Spain; Bruce Ratcliff, Academia Caledonian, Spain; Jolanta Rawska, School of English "Super Grade," Poland; Mar Rey, EOI Del Prat, Spain; Silke Riegler, HAW Landshut, Germany; Pauline Rios, Rivers, Spain; Laura Rivero, EOI La Laguna, Spain; Carmen Rizo, EOI Torrevieja, Spain; Antonio F. Rocha Canizares, EOI Talavera de la Reina, Spain; Eva Rodellas Fontiguell, London English School; Sara Rojo, EOI Elche, Spain; Elena Romea, UNED, Spain; Ann Ross, Centro Linguistico di Ateneo, Italy; Tyler Ross, Ingliese for you, Italy; Susan Royo, EOI Utebo, Spain; Asuncion Ruiz Astruga, EOI Maria Molinar, Spain; Tamara Ruiz Fernandez, English Today, Spain; Soledat Sabate, FIAC, Spain; Maria Justa Saenz de Tejad, ECI Idiomas Bailen, Spain; Sophia Salaman, University of Florence, Centro Linguistico de ATENEO, Italy; Elizabeth Schiller, Schillers Sprachstudio, Germany; Carmen Serrano Tierz, CULM, Spain; Elizabeth R. Sherman, Lexis Language Centre, Italy; Rocio Sierra, EOI Maspalomas, Spain; David Silles McLaney, EOI Majadahonda, Spain; Alison Slade, British School Florence, Italy; Rachael Smith, Accademia Britannica Toscana, Italy; Michael Smith, The Cultural English Centre, Spain; Sonia Sood, Oxford School Treviso, Italy; Monika Stawska, SJO Pigmalion, Poland; Izabela Stępniewska, ZS nr 69, Warszawa / British School Otwock, Poland; Rocío Stevenson, R & B Academia, Spain; Petra Stolinova, Magic English s.r.o., Czech Republic; Hana Szulczewska, UNO (Studium Języków Obcych), Poland; Tim T., STP, Spain; Vera Tauchmanova, Univerzita Hradec Kralove, Czech Republic; Nina Terry, Nina School of English, Spain; Francesca R. Thompson, British School of East, Italy; Pilar Tizzard, Docklands Idiomes, Spain; Jessica Toro, International House Zaragoza, Spain; Christine Tracey, Università Roma Tre, Italy; Loredana Trocchi, L'Aquila, Italy; Richard Twiggl, International House Milan, Italy; Natàlia Verdalet, EOI Figueres, Spain; Sergio Viñals, EOI San Javier, Spain; Edith von Sundahl-Hiller, Supernova Idiomas, Spain;

Vanda Vyslouzilova, Academia, Czech Republic; Helen Waldron, ELC, Germany; Leslie Wallace, Academia Language School, Switzerland; Monika Wąsowska-Polak, Akademia Obrony Narodowej, Poland; Melissa Weaver, TLC-IH, Switzerland; Maria Watton, Centro Lingue Estere CC, Italy; Dr. Otto Weihs, IMC FH Krems, Austria; Kate Williams, Oxford House Barcelona, Spain; June Winterflood, Academia Language School, Switzerland; Ailsa Wood, Cooperativa Babel, Italy; Irene Zamora, www.speakwithirene.com, Spain; Coro Zapata, EOIP Pamplona, Spain; Gloria Zaragoza, Alicante University, Spain; Cristina Zêzere, EOI Torrelavega, Spain

LATIN AMERICA Fernando Arcos, Santo Tomás University, Chile; Ricardo Barreto, Bridge School, Brazil; Beth Bartlett, Centro Cultural Colombo Americano, Cali, Colombia; Julie Patricia Benito Lugo, Universidad Central, Colombia; Ana Luisa Bley Soriano, Universidad UCINF, Chile; Gabriela Brun, I.S.F.D N 129, Argentina; Talita Burlamaqui, UFAM, Brazil; Lourdes Leonides Canta Lozano, Fac. De Ciencias Biolgicas UANL, Mexico; Claudia Castro, Stratford Institute – Moreno-Bs.As, Argentina; Fabrício Cruz, Britanic, Brazil; Lisa Davies, British Council, Colombia; Adriana de Blasis, English Studio Ciudad de Mercedes, Argentina; Nora Abraira de Lombardo, Cultural Inglesa de Mercedes, Argentina; Bronwyn Donohue, British Council, Colombia; Andrea C. Duran, Universidad Externado de Colombia; Phil Elias, British Council, Colombia; Silvia C. Enríquez, Esculea de Lenguas, Universidad Nacional de La Plata, Argentina; Freddy Espinoza, Universidad UCINF, Chile; Maria de Lourdes Fernandes Silva, The First Steps School, Brazil; Doris Flores, Santo Tomás English Program, Chile; Hilda Flor-Páez, Universidad Catolica Santiago de Guayaquil, Ecuador; Lauriston Freitas, Cooplem Idiomas, Brazil; Alma Delia Frias Puente, UANL, Mexico; Sandra Gacitua Matus, Universidad de la Frontera, Chile; Gloria Garcia, IPI Ushuaia-Tierra del Fuego, Argentina; Alma Delia Garcia Ensastegui, UAEM, Mexico; Karina Garcia Gonzalez, Universidad Panamericana, Mexico; Miguel García Rojas, UNMSM, Peru; Macarena González Mena, Universidad Tecnológica de Chile, Inacap, Chile; Diana Granado, Advanced English, Colombia; Paul Christopher Graves, Universidad Mayor, Chile; Mabel Gutierrez, British Council, Colombia; Niamh Harnett, Universidad Externado de Colombia, Colombia; Elsa Hernandez, English Time Institute, Argentina; Reinaldo Hernández Sordo, DUOC UC, Chile; Eduardo Icaza, CEN, Ecuador; Kenel Joseph, Haitian-American Institute, Haiti; Joel Kellogg, British Council, Colombia; Sherif Ebrahim Khakil, Universidad Autonoma Chapingo, Mexico; Cynthia Marquez, Instituto Guatemalteco Americano, Guatemala; Aaron McCarroll, Universidad Sergio Arboleda, Colombia; Milagro Machado, SISE Institute, Peru; Marta de Faria e Cunha Monteiro, Federal University of Amazonas – UFAM, Brazil; Lucía Murillo Sardi, Instituto Británico, Peru; Ricardo A. Nausa, Universidad de los Andes, Colombia; Andrea Olmos Bernal, Universidad de Guadalajara, Mexico; M. Edu Lizzete Olvera Dominguez, Universidad Autonoma de Baja California Sur, Mexico; Blanca Ortecho, Universidad

Cesar Vallejo Centro de Idiomas, Peru; **Jim Osorio**, Instituto Guatemalteco Americano, Guatemala; **Erika del Carmen Partida Velasco**, Univam, Mexico; **Mrs. Katterine Pavez**, Universidad de Atacama, Chile; **Sergio Peña**, Universidad de La Frontera, Chile; **Leonor Cristina Peñafort Camacho**, Universidad Autónoma de Occidente, Colombia; **Tom Rickman**, British Council, Colombia; **Olga Lucia Rivera**, Universidad Externado de Colombia, Colombia; **Maria-Eugenia Ruiz Brand**, DUOC UC, Chile; **Gabriela S. Eguiarte**, London School, Mexico; **Majid Safadaran**, Instituto Cultural Peruano Norteamericano, Peru; **María Ines Salinas**, UCASAL, Argentina; **Ruth Salomon-Barkmeyer**, UNILINGUAS – UNISINOS, Brazil; **Mario Castillo Sanchez Hidalgo**, Universidad Panamericana, Mexico; **Katrina J. Schmidt**, Universidad de Los Andes, Colombia; **Jacqueline Sedore**, The Language Company, Chile; **Lourdes Angelica Serrano Herrera**, Adler Schule, Mexico; **Antonio Diego Sousa de Oliveira**, Federal University of Amazonas, Brazil; **Padraig Sweeney**, Universidad Sergio Arboleda, Colombia; **Edith Urquiza Parra**, Centro Universitario México, Mexico; **Eduardo Vásquez**, Instituto Chileno Britanico de Cultura, Chile; **Patricia Villasante**, Idiomas Católica, Peru; **Malaika Wilson**, The Language Company, Chile; **Alejandra Zegpi-Pons**, Universidad Católica de Temuco, Chile; **Boris Zevallos**, Universidad Cesar Vallejo Centro de Idiomas, Peru; **Wilma Zurita Beltran**, Universidad Central del Ecuador, Ecuador

THE MIDDLE EAST Chaker Ali Mhamdi, Buraimi University College, Oman; **Salama Kamal Shohayb**, Al-Faisal International Academy, Saudi Arabia

TURKEY M. Mine Bağ, Sabanci University, School of Languages; **Suzanne Campion**, Istanbul University; **Daniel Chavez**, Istanbul University Language Center; **Asuman Cincioğlu**, Istanbul University; **Hatice Çelikkanat**, Istanbul Esenyurt University; **Güneş Yurdasiper Dal**, Maltepe University; **Angeliki Douri**, Istanbul University Language Center; **Zia Foley**, Istanbul University; **Frank Foroutan**, Istanbul University Language Center; **Nicola Frampton**, Istanbul University; **Merve Güler**, Istanbul University; **H. Ibrahim Karabulut**, Dumlupınar University; **Catherine McKimm**, Istanbul University; **Merve Oflaz**, Dogus University; **Burcu Özgül**, Istanbul University; **Yusuf Özmenekşe**, Istanbul University Language Center; **Lanlo Pinter**, Istanbul University Language Center; **Ahmet Rasim**, Amasya University; **Diana Maria Rios Hoyos**, Istanbul University Language Center; **Jose Rodrigues**, Istanbul University; **Dilek Eryılmaz Salkı**, Ozyegin University; **Merve Selcuk**, Istanbul Kemerburgaz University; **Mehdi Solhi Andarab**, Istanbul Medipol University; **Jennifer Stephens**, Istanbul University; **Özgür Şahan**, Bursa Technical University; **Fatih Yücel**, Beykent University

UNITED KINGDOM Sarah Ali, Nottingham Trent International College, Nottingham; **Rolf Donald**, Eastbourne School of English, Eastbourne, East Sussex; **Nadine Early**, ATC Language Schools, Dublin, Ireland; **Dr. Sarah Ekdawi**, Oxford School of English, Oxford; **Glynis Ferrer**, LAL Torbay, Paignton Devon; **Diarmuid Fogarty**, INTO Manchester, Manchester; **Ryan Hannan**, Hampstead School of English, London; **Neil Harris**, ELTS, Swansea University, Swansea; **Claire Hunter**, Edinburgh School of English, Edinburgh, Scotland; **Becky Ilk**, LAL Torbay, Paignton; **Kirsty Matthews**, Ealing, Hammersmith & West London's college, London; **Amanda Mollaghan**, British Study Centres, London; **Shila Nadar**, Twin ECL, London; **Sue Owens**, Cambridge Academy of English, Girton, Cambridge; **Caroline Preston**, International House Newcastle, Newcastle upon Tyne; **Ruby Rennie**, University of Edinburgh, Scotland; **Howard Smith**, Oxford House College, London; **Yijie Wang**, The University of Edinburgh, Scotland; **Alex Warren**, Eurotraining, Bournemouth

UNITED STATES Christina H. Appel, ELS Educational Services, Manhattan, NY; **Nicole Bollhalder**, Stafford House, Chicago, IL; **Rachel Bricker**, Arizona State University, Tempe, AZ; **Kristen Brown**, Massachusetts International Academy, Marlborough, MA; **Tracey Brown**, Parkland College, Champaign, IL; **Peter Campisi**, ELS Educational Services, Manhattan, NY; **Teresa Cheung**, North Shore Community College, Lynn, MA; **Tyler Clancy**, ASC English, Boston, MA; **Rachael David**, Talk International, Miami, FL; **Danielle De Koker**, ELS Educational Services, New York, NY; **Diana Djaboury**, Mesa Community College, Mesa, AZ; **Mark Elman**, Talk International, Miami, FL; **Dan Gauran**, EC English, Boston, MA; **Kerry Gilman**, ASC English, Boston, MA; **Heidi Guenther**, ELS Educational Services, Manhattan, NY; **Emily Herrick**, University of Nebraska-Lincoln, Lincoln, NE; **Kristin Homuth**, Language Center International, Southfield, MI; **Alexander Ingle**, ALPS Language School, Seattle, WA; **Eugenio Jimenez**, Lingua Language Center at Broward College, Miami, FL; **Mahalia Joeseph**, Lingua Language Center at Broward College, Miami, FL; **Melissa Kaufman**, ELS Educational Services, Manhattan, NY; **Kristin Kradolfer Espinar**, MILA, Miami, FL; **Larissa Long**, TALK International, Fort Lauderdale, FL; **Mercedes Martinez**, Global Language Institute, Minneapolis, MN; **Ann McCrory**, San Diego Continuing Education, San Diego, CA; **Simon McDonough**, ASC English, Boston, MA; **Dr. June Ohrnberger**, Suffolk County Community College, Brentwood, NY; **Fernanda Ortiz**, Center for English as a Second Language at the University of Arizona, Tuscon, AZ; **Roberto S. Quintans**, Talk International, Miami, FL; **Terri J. Rapoport**, ELS, Princeton, NJ; **Alex Sanchez Silva**, Talk International, Miami, FL; **Cary B. Sands**, Talk International, Miami, FL; **Joseph Santaella Vidal**, EC English, Boston, MA; **Angel Serrano**, Lingua Language Center at Broward College, Miami, FL; **Timothy Alan Shaw**, New England School of English, Boston, MA; **Devinder Singh**, The University of Tulsa, Tulsa, OK; **Daniel Stein**, Lingua Language Center at Broward College, Miami, FL; **Christine R. Stesau**, Lingua Language Center at Broward College, Miami, FL; **David Stock**, ELS Educational Services, Manhattan, NY; **Joshua Stone**, Approach International Student Center, Allston, MA; **Maria-Virginia Tanash**, EC English, Boston, MA; **Noraina Vazquez Huyke**, Talk International, Miami, FL

Overview

A REAL-WORLD VIEWPOINT

Whatever your goals and aspirations, *Wide Angle* helps you use English to connect with the world around you. It empowers you to join any conversation and say the right thing at the right time, with confidence.

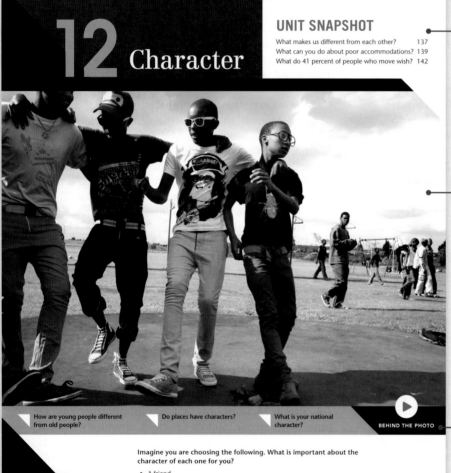

12 Character

UNIT SNAPSHOT

What makes us different from each other? 137
What can you do about poor accommodations? 139
What do 41 percent of people who move wish? 142

How are young people different from old people?

Do places have characters?

What is your national character?

BEHIND THE PHOTO

Imagine you are choosing the following. What is important about the character of each one for you?

- A friend
- A person to work on a project with
- Someone to share accommodations with
- A person to sit next to at work or in class

REAL-WORLD GOAL

Watch a documentary about a famous person you admire

Start thinking about the topic with relevant, interesting **introduction questions**.

blink

Be inspired by the **vibrant unit opener images** from Blink photography. The international, award-winning photographers bring stories from around the world to life on the page.

Watch the **"Behind the Photo"** video from the photographer.

Apply learning to your own needs with **Real-World Goals**, instantly seeing the benefit of the English you are learning.

"I think most people use fashion to show off their character, and especially teenagers. At this age, I think a lot of people want to show off their individuality and their spirit."
Krisanne Johnson

Enjoy learning with the huge variety of **up-to-date, inventive, and engaging audio and video.**

12.4 With All Due Respect...

Understand what to say and how to say it with **English For Real**.

These lessons equip you to choose and adapt appropriate language to communicate effectively in any situation.

1 **ACTIVATE** Discuss the questions with a partner, using the prompts to guide your answers.
   1 When was the last time you criticized someone? Describe who, when, where, why, and how.
   2 When was the last time someone criticized you? Describe who, when, where, why, and how.

2 **ASSESS** Look at the pictures. Discuss the questions with a partner.
   1 What do you think Max, Andy, and Kevin are talking about?
   2 How do you think they might be feeling?
   3 What do you think they could be saying in each situation?

3 ▶ **IDENTIFY** Watch the first scene of the video. Then answer the questions.
   1 What happened to Kevin?
   2 How does Andy feel about this?
   3 Does Max agree with Andy?
   4 Why does Max decide to talk to Sam?

4 ▶ **IDENTIFY** Watch the second part of the video. Discuss the questions with a partner.
   1 What general criticism do Max and Andy have of Kevin?
   2 What specific criticisms do they make?

REAL-WORLD ENGLISH Giving criticism

Criticism can be uncomfortable, but at times, we need to give or receive it. Being polite and considerate of the other person's feelings makes this easier. Follow these tips.

Avoid criticizing the person. Focus on the action instead.
~~You give bad presentations.~~   *The presentation needs some improvement.*

Start with a positive.
~~You are always late.~~   *It's always fun once you arrive, but that's often late.*

Use phrases to introduce criticism.
***With all due respect**, I don't think this is the right approach.*
***Let me put it this way**: you need to do more to help.*

Use phrases to soften the criticism for the listener.
***Don't get me wrong**, I enjoyed it. I'm just not sure I would do it again.*
*He is really noisy, but **to be fair**, he is also a lot of fun.*

5 ▶ **INTEGRATE** Watch the second part of the video again. Evaluate how polite and considerate Max and Andy are of Kevin's feelings.

6 **APPLY** Rewrite Max and Andy's criticisms using the information and phrases in the Real-World English box.
   1 Uh, Kevin? Sorry, buddy, but you're *not* a quiet person.
   2 It's true, mate, you're, erm, kind of noisy.
   3 Well...you're a bit heavy-footed. Your feet *pound* on the floor, like this.
   4 Right. And your voice can be really loud sometimes.

7 **INTEGRATE** Work with a partner. Take turns in the role of Kevin. Practice giving the softer, more polite criticism.

8 **PREPARE** First choose one of the situations in the list (or make up a situation of your own). Then prepare to give criticism appropriately in the situation.
   • Your friend is always late when you meet up.
   • Your teammate hasn't completed the tasks they should have (again!).
   • Your roommate leaves the kitchen a mess after cooking.
   • You are a tutor, and one of your students didn't get a good grade.

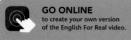
GO ONLINE
to create your own version
of the English For Real video.

Step into the course with **English For Real videos** that mimic real-life interactions. You can record your voice and respond in real time for out-of-class practice that is relevant to your life.

COMPREHENSIVE SYLLABUS

Ensure progress in all skills with a pedagogically consistent and appropriately leveled syllabus.

---

2 IDENTIFY Complete the characteristic definitions with the words in the box. Use a dictionary to help.

jealous	emotional	logical
professional	awkward	humorous

📑+ Oxford 5000™

1 The _____ person is confident and skilled in what they do in their workplace.
2 _____ people feel unhappy and angry because they want something that someone else has.
3 An _____ person feels uncomfortable and shy around other people.
4 _____ people make you laugh and are fun to be with.
5 An _____ person has and expresses strong feelings.
6 _____ people think clearly with good reasoning.

◥ VOCABULARY

The 📑+ Oxford 5000™ is a word list containing the most important words to learn in English. The words are chosen based on frequency in the Oxford English Corpus and relevance to learners of English. Every word is aligned to the CEFR, guiding you on the words you should know at each level.

---

or documents, emails, and academic coursework.

What's more is used in more informal contexts, such as emails, informal letters, and stories.

Even though is considered less formal than *although*.

We can write *and furthermore* and *what's more*, but we do not write *and moreover*.

4 APPLY Complete the sentences with a suitable linking word or phrase from the box.

even though	what's more	moreover
on the other hand	furthermore	

1 I would like you to note that the bed is very uncomfortable, and _____, the sheets are very old.
2 I'm moving out of my student accommodations. _____ I like it, it's just too expensive.
3 As a well-known hotel, I would expect you to deal with the issue immediately. _____, I feel I should be given a partial refund.
4 I'm not sure whether I want to share an apartment with

⊚ GRAMMAR IN CONTEXT Mixed conditionals

We use mixed conditionals to describe an unreal situation, either a past condition with a present result or a present condition with a past result.

In a mixed conditional, the time reference in the *if* clause is different from the time reference in the main clause.

To describe an unreal situation in the past that has a present result, we use *if* + past perfect + *would* + infinitive.
If I hadn't asked for a specific type of room, *I wouldn't be* bothered by this.

To talk about the possible past result of an unreal situation in the present, we use *if* + past tense + *would have* + past participle.
If I were rich and famous, *I would have been given* the exact room I wanted.

We can use other modal verbs in the main clause, especially *could* and *might*.
Huang *could have found* alternative accommodations if he'd known about the room.

See Grammar focus on page 170.

◥ GRAMMAR

The carefully graded grammar syllabus ensures you encounter the most relevant language at the right point in your learning.

 ## To Be or To Learn

Now look at your answers to the quiz. How many times was there a check in both columns?

For most people, there will be quite a few. More than four, and it looks like you're just like your older family members…but is that nature (you take after them) or nurture (you learned from them)? If you've ever wondered whether you were born like them or if you learned to copy them, don't worry, you're not alone—it's a debate that's been going on for decades.

Nature versus nurture: The great debate

We live in an age of genetics. We blame genetics for our bad habits, our height, and our poor grade on last week's math exam. But can we blame them for our personality (the nature theory)? Or did we learn to be who we are (the nurture counterargument)? This is the subject of a very serious debate.

The nature argument is simple; we inherit most of our individual characteristics from our genes—in other words, from our parents and ancestors. If we'd had different parents, we would have developed different personalities. But if the nature argument is true, it presents a troubling philosophical problem. If we are preprogrammed by our genes, do we actually have free will, the thing that many

believe makes us human? Furthermore, if we aren't free, can we be blamed for our actions? On the other hand, there are many who believe the nurture argument; they claim that in spite of the fact that we obviously inherit genes, we are more than just a copy of older family members. We become ourselves through living. It is our early experiences, the cultural attitudes we experience, and what we are taught that make us what we are. In other words, if we had grown up in a different place with different influences, we wouldn't have become who we are now.

To test this, psychologists study identical twins, who have the same genetic makeup. The idea is that if twins were brought up in different places, by different parents, and in different cultures, they would reveal the extent to which nature overcomes nurture. But even though there has been lots of research, the results are inconclusive. The best guess is that we are partly nature and partly nurture.

So, take a look back at the questions you answered before you read this. Can you say for sure whether you learned to be "you" or you inherited "you"?

—adapted from *A Dictionary of Education*, 2ⁿᵈ ed., edited by Susan Wallace

Oxford Reference is a trusted source of over two million authentic academic texts.

Free access to the Oxford Reference site is included with Student Books 4, 5, and 6.

▼ READING AND LISTENING

Explicit reading and listening skills focus on helping you access and assimilate information confidently in this age of rapid information.

12.3 Stay or Go?

1 ACTIVATE Look at the photos of people's homes. If you were moving, which of these would appeal to you the most? Why? Discuss your ideas with a partner.

2 WHAT'S YOUR ANGLE? Discuss the questions in a small group.

1 Have you ever moved?
2 If yes, what were the challenges? Is there anything you wish you'd done differently?
3 If you have never moved, what do you think the challenges would be?

3 INTEGRATE Read the information about the radio call-in show. Then work with a partner to think of three reasons people might have for wishing they hadn't moved.

Wednesday about town

Have you moved?
Sometimes wish you hadn't?
Share your views on our weekly show — we're always interested, whatever you have to say.

Today Radio

142

4 ◀) IDENTIFY Listen to the radio call-in show. What do the callers wish they had or hadn't done? Did you discuss these regrets in Exercise 3?

◀) LISTENING SKILL
Recognizing and understanding vague language

We often use vague language in informal conversation, especially when we can't think of or don't want to spend time thinking of specific words to describe something.
It's kind of interesting, you know, that people think that.
Recognizing this vague language will help you identify the important information in what the person is saying. When describing, the speaker can use vague expressions such as the following:

kind of	sort of	pretty (adv.)	whatever
I don't know	like	you know	I guess

When we use *sort* or *kind of*, we often add *-ish* or *-y* to the following adjective.
It's sort of bluish. It's kind of biggish.
When a speaker is listing or categorizing, you often hear phrases such as the following:

and so on	etcetera	that kind / sort of thing
stuff like that		

5 ◀) IDENTIFY Listen and complete each excerpt from the talk show using vague language.

1 _____, we wanted to make sure that we could visit every day if necessary.
2 There was a cool, _____ relaxed, airy feeling about the place.
3 There's nowhere to walk, no cafés _____.
4 ...the guy was _____ convincing...
5 It's _____...it _____ enabled us to see much more of each other.

6 ◀) APPLY Listen to excerpts from the radio call-in show. Write the main point of each excerpt.

1 It's boring.
2 _____
3 _____
4 _____
5 _____

7 ◀) INTEGRATE Listen to the radio call-in show again. Then discuss and answer the questions with a partner.

1 Why is moving an important event for many people, according to one of the hosts?
2 What changes did Jeremy's move bring about in his life?
3 What was the difference in character between the two places where Jeremy lived?
4 What did Freida like about the character of the new place when she heard the radio ad?
5 How has the way Freida's family lives changed since moving?
6 What does Marie like about her new place?

◀) GRAMMAR IN CONTEXT *I wish...*

We use *wish* to say that we want things to be different from how they are or were.
To talk about the present, we use *wish* + past tense.
I wish I listened to some other radio station!
To express regrets about the past, we use *wish* + past perfect.
I wish we'd chosen somewhere a bit more interesting.
Note: *would* cannot have the same subject and object.
I wish the house was bigger. (NOT I wish the house would be bigger.)
We can use *if only* instead of *wish* in all these situations. *If only* is more emphatic.
If only I hadn't!

See Grammar focus on page 170.

8 IDENTIFY Identify the four sentences with errors and rewrite them to be correct.

1 If only we didn't move when I was younger.
2 I wish I would have a bigger home.
3 I like my home, but I wish it will be in a different place.
4 I wish I had gotten to know my neighbors better before they moved.
5 If only we have more time to consider whether to buy or rent.

9 INTEGRATE Use the prompts to write sentences with *wish* or *if only*.

1 have / a bedroom each / when I was growing up (if only)
2 I / have / a garden when I was a child (wish)
3 I / rent / more modern apartment (wish)
4 I / the neighbors / not make so much noise (wish)
5 we / afford / dream home (if only)

10 WHAT'S YOUR ANGLE? Which sentences do you relate to the least from Exercise 9? Tell a partner.

◀) VOCABULARY DEVELOPMENT
Prefixes *inter-, pre-, trans-, and pro-*

You can form new words by adding a prefix to a root word.

international	prepacked	transport	ensure

Each prefix has a general meaning. This combines with the meaning of the root word to give the definition of the new word.

Prefix	Meaning	Examples
inter-	between	intersection, interchangeable
pre-	before	precaution, predates
trans-	across	transformed, transatlantic
en-	make	ensure, enabled

11 ◀) IDENTIFY Listen to the excerpts and complete each phrase. Add the words to the Vocabulary Development box. Then discuss and check the meaning of all the words in the box with a partner.

1 Her mother's been sick so as a _____ caution, we decided to move nearer to her...
2 You know, we wanted to _____ sure we could visit every day if necessary.
3 ...it's right at an _____ section of two big roads...
4 Whether it's a _____ atlantic move or you're just moving around the corner,...
5 Anyway, it feels like, you know, really modern, even though it actually _____ dates our old place.
6 I feel like my life has been _____ formed for the better.
7 It's funny how a home—four walls—can actually _____ rich your life...
8 I thought homes were kind of _____ changeable.

12 APPLY Complete each sentence with your own ideas.

1 The best way to enrich your life is to _____
2 I think _____ are completely interchangeable.
3 My friendship with _____ predates
4 When I leave the house, I always take the precaution of _____
5 I transformed my home by _____

13 WHAT'S YOUR ANGLE? Compare your sentences from Exercise 12 in a group. How similar are they?

143

Build confidence with the **activation-presentation-practice-production** method, with activities moving from controlled to less controlled, with an increasing level of challenge.

Personalize the lesson topics and see how the language can work for you with **What's Your Angle?** activities.

◀) WRITING SKILL
Using addition and contrast linking words

Writers often use linking words to:
- add information: *moreover, furthermore, what's more.*
- express contrast: *even though, on the other hand, despite, in spite of.*

These can be used at the beginning or middle of a sentence to improve the cohesion of a text and make sentences more complex.

Notes: *furthermore* and *moreover* are more common in formal writing, such as letters of complaint, official letters or documents, emails, and academic coursework.

What's more is used in more informal contexts, such as emails, informal letters, and stories.

Even though is considered less formal than *although*.

We can write *and furthermore* and *what's more*, but we do not write *and moreover*.

4 APPLY Complete the sentences with a suitable linking word or phrase from the box.

6 INTEGRATE Work with a partner. Identify four examples of linking words in the email. What does each show: addition or contrast?

7 WHAT'S YOUR ANGLE? Discuss the questions and share your experiences in a group.

1 Have you ever been in a situation where accommodations (at college, on vacation, or on a business trip) wasn't good enough?
2 What was the situation?
3 How did you handle it?
4 Was it resolved to your satisfaction?

◀) GRAMMAR IN CONTEXT Mixed conditionals

We use mixed conditionals to describe an unreal situation, either a past condition with a present result or a present condition with a past result.

In a mixed conditional, the time reference in the *if* clause is different from the time reference in the main clause.

To describe an unreal situation in the past that has a present result, we use *if* + past perfect + *would* + infinitive.
If I hadn't asked for a specific type of room, *I wouldn't be*

See Grammar focus on page 170.

▼ **WRITING**

The writing syllabus focuses on the writing styles needed for today, using a **process writing approach** of **prepare-plan-draft-review-correct** to produce the best possible writing.

◀) GRAMMAR IN CONTEXT
Second conditional versus third conditional

The second conditional describes an imaginary or unlikely situation in the present or future along with its imagined result.
If I did it again, I would do it differently.
If my children weren't the same as me, I'd be disappointed!
The third conditional describes unreal situations in the past. The condition is imaginary because it didn't actually happen. Consequently, the result is impossible.
I would have been a different person if I had had a different family.
We can replace *would* with other modals in both second and third conditional sentences.
If you heard me speaking, you might think I was my sister since we sound the same.
We can use *unless* in second conditional sentences but never in third conditional sentences.
I wouldn't do it unless there was a very good reason.
I wouldn't have been there unless he had called.

13 INTERACT Compare your sentences in Exercise 12 with a partner. How similar or different are they? Again, for each third conditional sentence say what actually did or didn't happen. For each second conditional, say what the real situation is.

◀) PRONUNCIATION SKILL
Sentence stress in conditional sentences

In conditional sentences, we can change the meaning or add emphasis by stressing certain words.
If I had the time, I'd read more about the theory. (= I wish I could read more about it.)
If I had the time, I'd read more about the theory. (= the person who has the time hasn't done what I would have done)
I'd do it myself if I had the skills. (= I asked someone else, but I wish I could do it)
I'd do it myself if I had the skills. (= I'm commenting that someone else has the skills but isn't doing it themselves)

14 ◀) INTEGRATE Listen and mark the stress in the sentences. Match the sentences with their implied meanings (a–e) according to the stressed words. Then say a sentence and ask a partner to identify which one it is.

▼ **SPEAKING**

Speaking and **pronunciation skills** build the functional language you need outside of class.

xv

A BLENDED LEARNING APPROACH

Make the most of *Wide Angle* with opportunities for relevant, personalized learning outside of class.

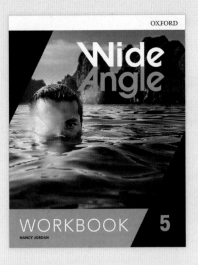

ONLINE PRACTICE

When you see this icon in your Student Book, go online to extend your learning.

With Online Practice you can:

- Review the skills taught in every lesson and get **instant feedback**.
- Practice grammar and vocabulary through **fun games**.
- Access **all audio and video** material. Use the Access Code in the front of this Student Book to log in for the first time at wideangle.oxfordonlinepractice.com.

WORKBOOK

Your Workbook provides additional practice for every unit of the Student Book.

Each unit includes:

- An entirely new reading with skill practice linked to **Oxford Reference**.
- Support for the **Discussion Board**, helping students to master online writing.
- Listening comprehension and skill practice using the **Unit Review Podcast**.
- Real-life English practice linked to the **English For Real** videos.
- **Grammar** and **vocabulary** exercises related to the unit topic.

Use your Workbook for homework or self-study.

FOCUS ON THE TEACHER

The Teacher's Resource Center at wideangle.oxfordonlinepractice.com saves teachers time by integrating and streamlining access to the following support:

- **Teacher's Guide**, including fun **More to Say** pronunciation activities and **professional development** materials.
- **Easy-to-use** learning management system for the student Online Practice, **answer keys**, **audio**, lots of **extra activities**, **videos**, and so much more.

The **Classroom Presentation Tool** brings the Student Book to life for heads-up lessons. Class audio, video, and answer keys, as well as teaching notes, are available online or offline and are updated across your devices.

1 Values

UNIT SNAPSHOT

How do values affect lifestyle choices?   4
Is tourism always good?   8
What makes a "good citizen"?   14

What values are involved in this type of agricultural production?

Are some values more important than others?

What are some ways people can express their values?

BEHIND THE PHOTO

REAL-WORLD GOAL

Express your opinions on a controversial topic

1 What do you value the most in life? Rank each topic on a scale of 1–5 (1 = not important, 5 = extremely important). Then share your answers with the class.

___ family

___ friends

___ nature or the environment

___ health or fitness

___ privacy

___ free time or work–life balance

___ work or money

___ education

2 Take a poll to identify the five things the students in your class value the most from the list in Exercise 1.

1.1 Way of Life

1 ACTIVATE Work with a partner. Read the definition and discuss the questions.

> **values** [pl.] beliefs about what is right and wrong and what is important in life
> - *moral values*
> - *a return to traditional values in education, such as firm discipline*
> - *Young people have a completely different **set of values** and expectations.*

1 What is lifestyle?

2 How are people's lifestyle choices connected to their values? Give an example.

READING SKILL Recognizing scenarios

Writers sometimes use imaginary situations or scenarios in order to draw the reader in, "set the scene," and establish a personal connection between the reader and the topic.

Scenarios are typically written in the second person and often use the simple present, present continuous, or imperative. Sometimes they are introduced with a conditional or present perfect question.

Imagine you're watching the news on TV, and you hear…
You walk out your front door, and suddenly you see…
You're faced with an important decision…
Picture this scene…
What would you do if…?
Have you ever…?

2 APPLY Skim the blog post and identify the imaginary scenario. Then discuss these questions with a partner.

1 How did you recognize the scenario?

2 Which of the elements described in the Reading Skill box did the writer use?

3 What do you think the writer's purpose was for including the scenario?

3 APPLY Read the blog post. What is it about?

Ingels's concept of 8 House

4 EXPAND What values do you think are most important to the blogger? Identify examples from the text to support your ideas. Then share your ideas with the class.

5 IDENTIFY Read the text again. Decide if the sentences are true (T) or false (F).

1 The concept of moral geography is the idea that where people live affects morality. ___

2 The blogger believes that living space is not connected to quality of life. ___

3 The blogger feels that the 8 House project does not deal effectively with social issues. ___

4 The 8 House concept is a good lifestyle choice for people who value having a good balance of work and family life. ___

5 The blog discusses globalization and society's attitudes to other people and cultures. ___

6 The blogger thinks the field of moral geography has broader possibilities. ___

7 The blogger feels pessimistic about the future. ___

 This morning, I'm sitting in a traffic jam, late for work again. I'm listening to a podcast to keep my mind off how angry my boss is going to be. Just by chance, the podcast is talking about the concept of moral geography. It's fascinating—the idea that the features of the geographical location where we live can both affect and be affected by our values and social morals.

An excellent example of this is in the field of urban planning where architects aim to create a more moral society through their designs of living spaces. The aim is to create living environments that provide a higher quality of life, lower stress levels, and increase social interaction, which will in turn lead to kinder, more open, tolerant, and caring communities.

Imagine waking up on an ordinary workday. There's no need to rush; you can take all the time you need. You get the kids ready and head out your front door. You stop by the café for a latte and a friendly chat with a neighbor and a colleague. Then you drop off the dry cleaning, mail a package, and bring the kids to day care, and a minute later you're at the office, all without ever really leaving the comfort of home!

That's the type of living environment architect Bjarke Ingels wanted to create with his 8 House project in Copenhagen. Ingels's project goes beyond ordinary design concepts by addressing issues such as the social class divide, loneliness, and the challenges faced by working parents. The project features a mix of residential homes, offices, and retail businesses, all built around a

We often use the simple present or present continuous to tell stories, anecdotes, and jokes. We use these present tenses to make our stories sound more dramatic and more immediate.

We often use the simple present to talk about the main events in a story or anecdote and to explain the plot of a movie or book.

You bring the kids to day care, and a minute later you're at the office.

I move into my new apartment in 8 House and discover my boss is my next-door neighbor.

My sister accepts a high-paying job at a new company and then realizes she was happier working part time.

We often use the present continuous to describe the background of a story.

We're visiting some friends in the country, we're eating fresh vegetables from their garden every day, and we start thinking maybe city life isn't so great.

Kelly's showing everybody her expensive new car and her Rolex watch, and her husband looks annoyed.

See Grammar focus on page 159.

---

network of attractive pathways and inviting public spaces designed to **foster** social **interaction**, community connections, and a more active lifestyle. That's what I call an advanced **civilization**!

But could this idealistic concept of togetherness be applied beyond single communities to whole cities, countries, and the world? Is there such a thing as "global **citizenship**"? For centuries, long-distance relations among different societies have grown in number and **significance**, and geographical interdependency is an important fact of modern life. But turn on the news, and it's easy to see that there still exist great division and misunderstandings between societies and cultures. We qualify people's viewpoints as "**conservative**" or "liberal" and often find it **unacceptable** when someone's values are very different from our own. These attitudes affect how we as a society react to the plight of other people, for example, after a natural disaster on the other side of the world. In addition, they affect how we view and treat strangers or outsiders who wish to live in our home countries or cities.

Moral geographers have only just begun to explore these issues in detail. I, for one, am hopeful that someday in the future the world can become a better, more peaceful place. But it's going to take all of us working together, one community at a time.

—adapted from *A Dictionary of Human Geography*, by Noel Castree, Rob Kitchin, and Alisdair Rogers

---

6 APPLY Use the dramatic present of the verbs in the box to complete the anecdote. You will use some words more than once and more than one word may fit in some blanks.

be	come	feel	get	happen
have	learn	not speak	realize	speak
start	tell	try	want	

This story ¹ _____ back when I ² _____ in my early thirties. My husband ³ _____ a job for one year as a researcher at a large university in Shanghai, China. I ⁴ _____ very nervous about the move because I've never lived abroad before. I ⁵ _____ the language, and I ⁶ _____ no experience living in a big city.

For the first few weeks after we arrive, I ⁷ _____ to stay calm for my husband, but all I really ⁸ _____ to do is go home! But after a few months, I ⁹ _____ some Chinese, and every day I ¹⁰ _____ more about the culture. I ¹¹ _____ comfortable, and I ¹² _____ to enjoy the international city lifestyle. I ¹³ _____ I may actually be a city person!

Finally, the time ¹⁴ _____ to return to the United States, and my husband ¹⁵ _____ ready to come home, but I ¹⁶ _____ him I wish we could stay another year!

7 EXPAND Use the dramatic present to write a brief anecdote about a lifestyle change you have experienced.

8 VOCABULARY Match the words and phrases from the text to their definitions.

1 citizenship	___		5 interaction	___
2 civilization	___		6 significance	___
3 conservative	___		7 unacceptable	___
4 foster	___			

a a state of human society that is very developed and organized

b the act of communicating with somebody, especially while you work, play, or spend time with them

c the importance of something, especially when this has an effect on what happens in the future

d the legal right to belong to a particular country

e opposed to great or sudden social change; showing that you prefer traditional styles and values

f cannot be accepted, approved, or allowed

g help something to develop

9 **APPLY** Complete the sentences with the words from Exercise 8.

1 The use of electronic devices has resulted in a decrease in face-to-face _____ between humans.
2 Applying for _____ in this country involves taking language classes and learning about the history and culture.
3 In some cultures, it is _____ to disagree with a professor or another person of authority.
4 How can political leaders _____ more friendship and better relationships between countries?
5 In most modern societies, a person's level of education has a lot of _____.
6 In different _____ and throughout time, the concept of physical beauty has changed a lot.
7 Ali grew up in a very _____ family. His parents want him to have a traditional wedding.

10 **WHAT'S YOUR ANGLE?** What's your ideal living environment? Write an imaginary scenario like the one from the blog to describe a living environment that reflects your personal values. Then share it with a partner.

11 **INTEGRATE** Work in a small group. Discuss the questions.

1 Describe your living environment. Does it foster social interaction? Why or why not?
2 Does your current lifestyle match your personal values? Which aspects match, and which do not?
3 Do you feel you have a healthy work–life balance? What are some ways companies and employers can promote that balance?
4 What are some examples of values your friends or family members have that are different from yours?

Ho Chi Minh City, Vietnam

6

1.2 The Great Barrier Reef

1 ACTIVATE In a small group, look at the photos of the Great Barrier Reef. What do you know about the Great Barrier Reef? Where is it located? Why is it important?

2 ▶ IDENTIFY Watch the video. Does it mention any of your ideas from Exercise 1? Were there any facts in the video that surprised you?

3 ▶ APPLY Watch the video again. Answer the questions with a partner.

1 Where is the Great Barrier Reef?
2 What makes it a popular tourist destination?
3 In what ways is tourism causing damage to the reef?
4 What other factors have had an impact on the reef? In what way?
5 Do you think the damage to the reef can be reversed?

4 WHAT'S YOUR ANGLE? What are some places in your country that have been affected by tourism? What have the effects been? What is being done about the issue? Discuss your ideas in a small group.

5 NOTICE Read the essay question. What is the writer expected to do?

> Tourism activity on the Great Barrier Reef should be suspended immediately to protect the marine environment from further damage. To what extent do you agree or disagree?

ᵍ⁺ Oxford 5000™

6 ASSESS Read the essay. Did the writer answer the essay question correctly? Are any of your ideas from Exercises 1 and 4 mentioned?

Located in the Coral Sea off the coast of Queensland, Australia, the Great Barrier Reef is the largest coral reef system in the world. It spans an area of more than 344,400 square kilometers (133,000 square miles) and contains more than 900 islands and 2,900 individual reefs. The reef is home to billions of tiny living organisms called *coral polyps*.

Over the years, tourism has caused considerable damage to the Great Barrier Reef and many of its living creatures. In fact, according to a 2012 study published by the National Academy of Sciences, more than half of the coral on the reef is now dead as a result of tourism and related activities.

Some people feel that reef tourism should be suspended in order to allow the environment to recover. While I agree that the reef must be protected, I disagree with the proposal to suspend tourism.

Firstly, tourism is not the only problem. Climate change is also having a great impact. In fact, the reef has lost more than half its coral since 1985 as the result of extreme weather events.

Secondly, tourism can bring some positive results as well. It generates billions of dollars for the local economy, and many of these funds have been put toward efforts to conserve the reef. If tourism is suspended, the money that could be used for marine conservation would be lost. In addition, many local businesses would be adversely affected. Workers at businesses from hotels and restaurants to tour operators and transportation would be unemployed. If there are no tourists and many of the local people don't have jobs, it will have a devastating effect on the local economy.

Tourism also provides an opportunity to educate visitors and the public and to spread the important message about environmental issues.

In my opinion, businesses in the local tourist industry should take greater responsibility for the way they affect the environment. Business owners should work with local authorities and environmental organizations to monitor the reef situation, raise public awareness, and help visitors learn about the damaging effects of tourism and climate change and what they can do to help.

In conclusion, I agree that quick action is essential to protect the reef from further environmental damage; however, simply suspending tourism is not a viable solution.

Oxford 5000™

7 VOCABULARY Complete the collocations with words from the box. Use the essay to help you.

cause	educate	have	monitor
protect	spread	suspend	take

1 _____ the environment
2 _____ the situation
3 _____ a message
4 _____ an activity
5 _____ the public about an issue
6 _____ responsibility for something
7 _____ damage to something
8 _____ an impact on something

8 **ASSESS** Listen and check. Then listen and repeat.

9 EXPAND Work with a partner. Write a sentence using each collocation in Exercise 7. Share your ideas and sentences with the class.

GRAMMAR IN CONTEXT Present perfect versus present perfect continuous

We use the present perfect and present perfect continuous to connect the past and the present.

We use the present perfect to talk about past experiences that connect to the present.
*Tourism **has become** the main industry in the area.*

We use the present perfect and the present perfect continuous + *for* or *since* when we express how much time an action has lasted.
*They**'ve lived** in Australia **since** the 1990s.*
*She**'s been studying** the effects of climate change **for** more than ten years.*

We use the present perfect continuous when the focus is on an action that is still ongoing
*The reef **has been absorbing** carbon dioxide from the atmosphere.* (It is still happening now.)
*Local officials **have been discussing** what to do.*

We usually use the present perfect, not the present perfect continuous, to talk about states rather than actions with verbs like *be, have, know,* and *seem.*
*We**'ve known** about the problems with the reef for a long time.* (NOT ~~We've been knowing about problems with the reef...~~)
*Officials **have had** years to do something about the problem.* (NOT ~~Officials have been having years...~~)

See Grammar focus on page 159.

10 **IDENTIFY** Choose the correct option to complete each sentence.

1 He's been interested in studying weather and climate *for / since* he was twelve years old.

2 The area *has become / has been becoming* very popular with tourists.

3 We can't quit now, *we've been trying / we tried* to publish this research for years!

4 *I've worked / I've been working* on this project all week, and I'm still not finished.

5 Melanie has been giving talks about the effects of tourism on the reef *for / since* 30 years.

11 **APPLY** Complete the sentences with *for* or *since* and the correct form of the verbs in parentheses.

1 _____ many years, tourism _____ (be) an issue in the local area.

2 The number of tourists visiting the reef _____ (increase) _____ last year.

3 Jamal _____ (go) to Australia every year _____ the past ten years.

4 _____ 1985, about half of the reef's living organisms _____ (die).

5 The government of Australia _____ (try) to find a solution to the problem _____ scientists first learned about it.

> ### WRITING SKILL
> ### Writing paragraphs and topic sentences
>
> Paragraphs have a very formulaic structure that is usually repeated throughout a text. A typical paragraph structure is:
>
> topic sentence → supporting information, reasons, and examples → conclusion
>
> The topic sentence introduces the main idea of a paragraph. It is usually (but not always) the first sentence of the paragraph.
>
> It is important to support your main idea with supporting information, reasons, and examples. This shows that you understand the topic and have researched it well.
>
> In a concluding sentence(s), the writer usually summarizes the main points of the paragraph.
>
> Noticing paragraph structure can help you to improve your writing and make it easier to understand.

12 **APPLY** Work with a partner. What is the topic of each paragraph in the essay in Exercise 6? Identify the topic sentence for each paragraph.

13 **IDENTIFY** Work with a partner. How many supporting sentences are there in each paragraph of the essay in Exercise 6? How do they relate to or support the topic sentence? What kind of information or details do they give?

14 **PREPARE** Think about a problem that is going on in your town, city, or country. Make brief notes on your responses to the following questions.

1 What are some of the reasons or causes for the problem? What is being done about it?

2 Do you agree with these solutions?

3 What other solutions would you propose?

15 **WRITE** Write an essay in response to the questions in Exercise 14. Follow these steps.

1 Write three main topics or points your essay will include. (These will be the topics of your paragraphs.)

2 Write a topic sentence to describe each main topic or point.

3 Write some information, reasons, and examples to support your main ideas.

4 Consider how you will summarize the main arguments in each paragraph in your concluding sentence.

5 Write your essay.

16 **IMPROVE** Read your essay and correct any grammar and spelling mistakes. Check for examples of what you have learned.

Writing checklist

☐ Have you written a topic sentence in each paragraph?

☐ Did you include main ideas as well as supporting information, reasons, and examples?

☐ Did you write a concluding sentence?

☐ Did you use vocabulary related to issues, values, and ethics?

☐ Did you use the present perfect and present perfect continuous to link the present to the past?

17 **SHARE** Read a classmate's essay. Tell them whether you agree or disagree with their opinions. Explain which arguments in their essay you think are strong and what they have done well.

1.3 Opinions

1 ACTIVATE Read the quote. What do you think it means? Do you agree?

"Never, never be afraid to do what's right, especially if the well-being of a person or animal is at stake."
—Martin Luther King Jr.

2 IDENTIFY Work with a partner. The photos illustrate controversial topics. What is happening in the photos? What do you think the topics are? Why are they controversial?

3 🔊 **ASSESS** Listen to the first part of a debate. Decide who is for (F) and who is against (A) testing on animals.

___ Charlotte   ___ Daniel   ___ Senji

4 🔊 **INTEGRATE** Listen to the full debate. Choose the opinions that you hear.

- ☐ 1 Animal testing is cruel.
- ☐ 2 Companies have a responsibility to produce safe products even if they harm animals.
- ☐ 3 Most cosmetics these days aren't properly tested.
- ☐ 4 It is preferable for animals to suffer than humans.
- ☐ 5 Animals don't feel pain the way humans do.
- ☐ 6 Humans should stop using cosmetics.
- ☐ 7 Animal-tested products are more expensive.
- ☐ 8 Refusing to buy animal-tested products will end animal testing.
- ☐ 9 It's up to humans to defend animals.

5 EXPAND Do you agree with the statements in Exercise 4? Why or why not? Discuss in a small group.

LISTENING SKILL
Understanding opinions and speculation

When we communicate with someone about a controversial topic, it's useful to be able to recognize whether the person has a strong opinion so we can respond appropriately.

Opinions are usually expressed with certainty.
In my opinion, animal testing is unethical.
I disagree with that practice.
Companies will never stop animal testing.

A speculation is a guess someone makes about something without having all the facts. The language used reflects less certainty.

Lives must have been saved by modern testing practices.
I wonder what would happen if a product wasn't tested properly.
The government will probably pass stricter laws in the future.
I've heard that…   I'm pretty sure that…

6 🔊 **APPLY** Listen to the debate again. Write whether Charlotte (C), Daniel (D), or Senji (S) gave each statement. Then choose whether the statement expresses an opinion or speculation.

___ 1 The animals probably suffer terribly.
   ☐ opinion   ☐ speculation

___ 2 I definitely don't agree that it should be banned.
   ☐ opinion   ☐ speculation

___ 3 Animal testing may not be pleasant, but I think that's better than risking human suffering.
   ☐ opinion   ☐ speculation

___ 4 I'm pretty sure the majority of medicines are tested on animals, too.
   ☐ opinion   ☐ speculation

___ 5 It won't make a difference if just a few people stop buying the products. We need to encourage people to speak out against this issue.
   ☐ opinion   ☐ speculation

VOCABULARY DEVELOPMENT Verb + preposition collocations with *for*, *on*, and *against*

Verbs are often combined with a preposition. The following are examples of common verb + preposition collocations used when we discuss opinions.

argue stand up	> for	decide insist	> on	argue decide speak out	> against

Noticing and recording these verb + preposition collocations will help you better understand others' opinions as well as express your own.

7 **USE** Complete the excerpts from the debate with the prepositions *for*, *on*, and *against*.

Charlotte: I see your point, Daniel, but I'd have to argue ¹_____ animal testing.

Daniel: Can't people just live without cosmetics? I'd prefer that to buying products that require animals to suffer. Who can argue ²_____ that?

Charlotte: Well, these days there are plenty of companies that have decided ³_____ testing on animals. It usually says so right on the product label. A lot of people insist ⁴_____ buying only those products.

Daniel: We need to encourage people to speak out ⁵_____ this issue. Animals don't have any way to defend themselves. We humans have to stand up ⁶_____ them.

8 🔊 **ASSESS** Listen and check your answers to Exercise 7.

9 **WHAT'S YOUR ANGLE?** Which speaker do you think gives the strongest arguments? Why? Tell the class.

GRAMMAR IN CONTEXT Question types: subject, direct/indirect, with preposition

There are several different types of questions used in English. Each type is formed slightly differently.

Subject questions begin with *who*, *what*, or *which*. We do not use the auxiliary verbs *do*, *does*, or *did*.

What happens if they aren't tested properly?
(NOT ~~What does happen if…?~~)
Who uses these cosmetics? Which costs more?

Indirect questions begin with phrases like *Can you tell me…* and *Do you know if…*. We do not add the auxiliary verb before the subject.

Can you tell me where the animals come from?
(NOT ~~Can you tell me where the animals do come from?~~)

Indirect questions are often used to introduce an opinion in an indirect way.

Don't you think more people should speak out against animal testing?
Wouldn't it be better if the animals were not kept in cages?

In questions where the object needs a **preposition**, the preposition usually goes at the end.

Which test results are the researchers waiting for?
What are the protesters speaking out against?

See Grammar focus on page 159.

---

10 **IDENTIFY** Choose the four incorrect questions.

1 Who is responsible if the testing goes wrong?
2 Who hasn't heard about this issue in the news?
3 For what for the scientists are looking?
4 Which product is tested on animals?
5 Do you know what kinds of animals are usually used?
6 Do you have any idea if that company does test products on animals?
7 What the best solution is to the problem?
8 Whom do you agree with?
9 What does happen when a product is not tested?
10 Can you tell me how to contact the company president?

11 **ASSESS** Rewrite the four incorrect sentences from Exercise 10.

12 **WHAT'S YOUR ANGLE?** What are some controversial issues and topics you sometimes disagree on with friends, colleagues, or family members? How do your opinions differ? Do you think the argument will ever be resolved? Discuss with the class.

Using social media

Eating or not eating meat

Protecting the environment

1.4 Talking Things Through

1 ACTIVATE In what ways do you speak differently to people you are close to and people you are not very close to?

2 ASSESS Talk about the pictures with a partner.

1 Where are the people?
2 Do you think they know each other well?
3 What do you think they're talking about?

3 ▶ IDENTIFY Watch the video and answer the questions.

1 What is Andy planning to do?
2 How will Professor Jackson help Andy with his plans?
3 What does Professor Jackson recommend?
4 Why is Andy worried?

REAL-WORLD ENGLISH Starting a formal conversation

The situation or "setting" we are in determines whether we use formal or informal language. We usually use formal language when we start a formal conversation with people we don't know well.

When we start a formal conversation, we usually use modal verbs such as *could, would, shall,* and *may.*

***May** I suggest something?*
***Shall** I begin the discussion?*
*I**'d** like to…*

A less formal and more neutral way would be to use the modal *can. Can* is appropriate in many settings, so it is common in both formal and informal interactions.

***Can** I suggest something?*
***Can** I begin the discussion?*

Note: In Western cultures, even the person in a higher social position uses polite language in a formal conversation. For example, in the video, Professor Jackson says, *May I make a suggestion?*

ENGLISH FOR REAL

4 ▶ **ANALYZE** Watch the video again and fill in the chart. Then compare your notes with a partner.

1	Where does the conversation take place?	
2	How well do Andy and Professor Jackson know each other? How do you know?	
3	Is the speakers' relationship formal or informal? How do you know?	
4	What is the purpose of their conversation?	
5	Do they use polite formal language or informal language? Give examples.	

5 **ASSESS** Read the conversation openers. Decide if each opener is formal (F) or informal (I).

1 Can I tell you my plans? ___
2 May I start the discussion? ___
3 All right. Let's get started. ___
4 I'd like to start this discussion by saying… ___
5 Can I begin by sharing some of my ideas? ___
6 I'll get the ball rolling. ___

6 **IDENTIFY** Identify the words or phrases in Exercise 5 that helped you decide whether the conversation openers are formal or informal. Then compare your answers with a partner. Discuss which specific words or phrases make the openers sound more formal or informal. Think of one more formal and one more informal way to open a conversation.

7 **INTEGRATE** The following conversation openers are phrased in a neutral way. For each one, write a formal version and an informal version in your own words.

1 Can I speak to you privately?
2 Can I ask you more about the project?
3 Can I tell you how impressed I've been with your work recently?
4 Can I start the discussion by outlining the reasons for this meeting?
5 Can I begin the discussion?

8 **APPLY** Read the scenarios and write an appropriate conversation opener for each one.

1 You are beginning a work meeting with a group of colleagues you've worked closely with for the past year.
2 You are beginning a meeting with a group of your neighbors and friends about starting a community garden in your city.
3 You are beginning a work meeting to start a new project with representatives from a client company whom you have never met before.
4 You are beginning a meeting with a company president to interview them about their policies on animal testing.
5 You are a university professor. You are beginning a meeting with a student to discuss his poor score on a recent test.

9 **INTEGRATE** With a partner, prepare to role-play a short conversation between two people. Choose a scenario from Exercise 8. Use the questions below to help you decide the context.

1 Who are the speakers?
2 What is the relationship between them?
3 How well do they know each other?
4 Where does the conversation take place?
5 Should the language be careful and polite or relaxed and informal?
6 How can you start and end the conversation?

10 **INTERACT** Role-play your conversation for the class. Your classmates can refer to the questions in Exercise 9 to analyze the context.

GO ONLINE
to create your own version
of the English For Real video.

1.5 A Good Citizen

1 ACTIVATE Work with a partner. Look at the photo and answer the questions.

1 What are the people doing?
2 Do you think they are good citizens? Explain.

2 **NOTICE** Listen to Heather telling a colleague about a time when she practiced good citizenship. What did she do? Did she enjoy it?

3 🔊 **IDENTIFY** Choose the correct option according to Heather's story. Listen again if needed.

1 After college, Heather ___.
   a became unemployed
   b wanted to begin her career right away
   c wanted to be a volunteer
2 Heather decided to work for the charity because ___.
   a she had always wanted to do that type of work
   b the pay was good
   c she got along well with the staff
3 Heather helped to create ___.
   a a building
   b a garden
   c some public art
4 Heather believed the project could make the community ___.
   a healthier
   b popular
   c richer

PRONUNCIATION SKILL
Intonation: Showing interest

When we use response phrases to show we are interested in something we hear, our stress and pitch rise and fall more dramatically than when we are just responding neutrally.

Oh, REAlly?   *Is THAT right?*
THAT's INteresting. *THAT sounds GREAT!*

Paying attention to the intonation of these phrases can help your speech sound more natural.

4 🔊 **NOTICE** Listen to the excerpts of Heather telling her story to a colleague. Complete the phrases.

1 What a _____!
2 Oh, wow! That _____.
3 Is that _____?
4 Sounds _____.
5 That's _____.

5 🔊 **BUILD** Listen and repeat the phrases from Exercise 4.

SPEAKING Narrating experiences

When you tell a story about your own experiences, use the following strategies to make it clear and interesting to the listener.

1. Use the dramatic present tense.
2. Give some background. Knowing the place and time of a story sets a mood and helps the audience feel like they're there.
   It's the spring of my last year of college…
   I'm in my forties, and I've just started a new job at an advertising agency.
3. Use a clear structure to help listeners follow the story.
4. Most stories follow a cause-and-effect structure, meaning one event happens and then causes something else to happen.
   cause   effect
   I find a wallet full of money in the street, so I decide to take it to the police station.
5. Choose appropriate details. Details add interest to a story. Using too many details can bore or overwhelm listeners. Using too few will leave them without a feel for the story.
   I'm feeling very nervous.
   There's an elderly man sitting next to me.
6. Consider your listeners' time and attention. Make the story interesting while keeping it as short as possible.

6 PREPARE Plan to tell a story about a time that you practiced good citizenship, such as working on a project to help others. Write the story. Use the information in the Speaking box and Heather's story to help you.

7 IMPROVE Work with a small group. Give each other feedback on language, structure, and pronunciation.

8 SHARE Change groups and tell your revised stories. Use the Pronunciation Skill while talking with others.

9 WHAT'S YOUR ANGLE? Listen to other students' stories. Which stories did you find interesting? Why?

Now go to page 147 for the Unit 1 Review.

2 Memory

UNIT SNAPSHOT

What makes something or someone memorable?   17
How can memory of an event affect us many
years later?   19
What's the best way to remember something?   23

Are childhood memories more powerful than adult memories?

Can we improve our memories?

What are the consequences of a bad memory?

BEHIND THE PHOTO

Think about the questions and make notes. Then discuss your answers with a partner.

1   What are some of your earliest memories? Why do you think you remember them so well?
2   How do you remember important information, for example, when you need to take a test?
3   Do people always remember things in the same way?

REAL-WORLD GOAL

Attend an online or in-person talk

2.1 It's All in the Mind

1 ACTIVATE Work with a partner. Do you find these things easy to remember? Rate them according to which you find easiest to remember, on a scale of 1= *easiest to remember* to 7 = *most difficult to remember*.

___ numbers ___ dates ___ names ___ images
___ words ___ smells ___ sounds

2 INTERACT Work with a partner. Compare your ratings from Exercise 1. How similar are they? What makes some things more memorable than others for you? Do you have any strategies for remembering things?

READING SKILL
Recognizing and understanding chronology

Writers use a range of techniques to help the reader "follow" a narrative. These include using:

Narrative tenses

• Past tenses show the order of events.

• Continuous tenses show events that were in progress when a key event happened. They also emphasize the length of events.

Linking words

• Adverbs such as *consequently*, *subsequently*, or *so* can show the result of an action and indicate the order of and connection between events.

• Adverbs such as *suddenly*, *immediately*, and *gradually* describe the timing of an event and how the details of a story unfolded.

Time expressions

Sometimes a writer suddenly refers back to a time in the past. This is known as flashback. To recognize flashback, look out for expressions such as:

back then   when I was young,
looking back   when I was living in   in the old days

3 IDENTIFY Read the sentences. Identify narrative tenses, linking words, and time expressions that indicate chronology.

1 We had been driving all night. Consequently, I was exhausted.

2 My bike had gotten a flat tire, so I ended up walking home in the rain.

3 Back then, things were different. I didn't use to worry who was looking over my shoulder.

4 I knew we'd met once before, but I couldn't recall the woman's name. Gradually, it came to me.

5 He lost his job and subsequently his home.

6 Suddenly, there was a crashing noise from the backyard!

4 INTEGRATE Read the article from an online magazine. What is it about? Which points did you find interesting or surprising?

5 APPLY Identify one or two examples of how the writer shows chronology in the article. What do they indicate to the reader? Share your ideas with a partner.

6 IDENTIFY Read the text again. Decide if the sentences are true (T) or false (F). Correct the false statements.

1 Personal experiences make up most of our memory. ___

2 Semantic memory is responsible for learning through repetition. ___

3 Muscle memory helps us to become very good at certain movements. ___

4 Déjà vu only happens in new situations. ___

5 With restricted paramnesia, people forget where they are. ___

7 WHAT'S YOUR ANGLE? Have you ever experienced any of the situations mentioned in the text? Share your experiences with a partner or in a small group.

GRAMMAR IN CONTEXT Narrative tenses

We use narrative tenses, including the simple past, past perfect, and past continuous, to describe past events. Narrative tenses give background and show the order of events in a story.

When I reached the square, I knew I was about to see…
While I was driving down that road, I suddenly had the feeling…
As soon as he introduced himself, I knew that we had met before, but I couldn't remember where!

Narrative tenses are often used with time expressions such as *when*, *while*, *before*, *after*, *as soon as*, and *by the time*.

See Grammar focus on page 160.

Do you remember phone numbers but forget someone's name immediately after you're introduced? Do you ever find yourself with a word "on the tip of your tongue"? Has a friend ever talked about an event that you have absolutely no memory of, even though you were there at the time? Memory is a mysterious thing.

It is our episodic memory that enables us to remember personal experiences and events. This gives us a sense of identity and connection with the past, our childhood, and the key events and relationships in our lives. Some events, or details of them, are more memorable for us than they are for others; consequently, people don't always remember the same things, even about very recent events. Although they may hold the most relevance for us, our personal memories make up only a small part of memory. Most of our memory is taken up by information not connected to our personal experiences. Our semantic memory stores facts, figures, and concepts related to the world, such as knowledge of physics, history, and language. Have you ever met someone who seemed to know everything about everything? It all comes down to semantic memory.

Studying for a test? Our procedural memory acts as a personal storage system for knowledge and skills acquired through repetitive learning. It is this mechanism that improves our effectiveness at recalling details and enhances our performance on some types of tests. But what about those people who seem to be able to "do something with their eyes closed"? This is due to muscle memory—the ability to do a particular action, like touch-typing, without conscious thought. Muscle memory is the result of repeating a movement over and over again. This is why basketball players spend many hours practicing the perfect shot. And, talking about doing things with your eyes closed, there's also spatial memory, which controls our ability to move around in a familiar space. You can easily find the light switch in your room, but trying to switch on a light in a dark hotel room is another matter entirely!

But what about when our memories play tricks on us? Does this experience sound familiar? "It happened on my first visit to Paris. I was walking along a street, when I suddenly had this strange feeling that I'd been there before..." This is a typical account of déjà vu—the feeling that you have experienced a new situation before. It is often accompanied by a remembrance of certain imagery and the feeling that you know what is about to happen next—"When I reached the square, I knew I was about to see..." Some people believe déjà vu indicates the power of pre-cognition or a "sixth sense" (being able to "see" something before it has happened). A more likely explanation is that although the overall situation is new, a number of its features have, in fact, been experienced before. It is the combination of these that bring familiarity to this new situation. With déjà vu, the whole of the new experience seems familiar. "I <u>felt</u> that I had lived through it all before but knew that I hadn't."

Then there's restricted paramnesia. A classic example is when you may have a vague awareness of a past connection with a person, but you are unable to identify them when you see them out of context. "I knew that I had met him before, but I couldn't remember where!" Even though our memories might be good, they aren't always what they seem.

—adapted from *The Oxford Companion to the Mind*, 2nd ed., by Richard L. Gregory

8 IDENTIFY Identify and write examples of the narrative tenses and time expressions in the final two paragraphs of the online article. Which tenses are they? How do they show the order of events? Discuss your ideas with a partner.

Simple past: _____

Past perfect: _____

Past continuous: _____

Time expressions: _____

9 APPLY Complete the text with the correct form of each verb in parentheses. Then compare answers with a partner. Why did you choose each tense? How does it show the order of events?

We tend to think of memories as being something we can control, but sometimes they can appear out of nowhere.

I suffer from flashbacks, which means I suddenly remember something from the past—usually something traumatic. The first time it [1] _____ (happen), I [2] _____ (walk) along the corridor at work, and suddenly, I [3] _____ (find) myself reliving a memory.

I [4] _____ (have) completely lost connection with the present. I was really frightened by the experience, so I went to see my doctor. She [5] _____ (tell) me that I [6] _____ (work) too hard and that I needed to take some time off and get more sleep.

VOCABULARY DEVELOPMENT Noun suffixes

Suffixes can be added to a root word (usually a verb or noun) to create a new noun. Common noun suffixes include *-ist*, *-ship*, *-ion*, *-ism*, *-ness*, and *-ry*.

optimist	*relationship*	*suspicion*
journalism	*consciousness*	*machinery*

10 APPLY Change the root words in parentheses to nouns to complete the sentences. Use the suffixes from the Vocabulary Development box.

1 I had an increasing _____ that someone was staring at me. (aware)

2 My childhood friends and I played outdoors for many hours without adult _____. (supervise)

3 One of Elsa's earliest memories was attending a celebration for her father when he finally received his Canadian _____. (citizen)

4 The _____ from that TV show is very disturbing. I couldn't get it out of my head. (image)

5 As a professional _____ , I need to learn and remember song lyrics quickly. (vocal)

6 I know it's hard to hold on to your _____, especially when you've had nothing but bad experiences. (optimal)

11 IDENTIFY Work with a partner. Identify nouns in the online article that are made from root words and the suffixes from the Vocabulary Development box.

12 EXPAND Can you think of any other nouns that are made with the suffixes in the Vocabulary Development box? Make a list with your partner and then compare it with another pair's list.

 PRONUNCIATION SKILL
Word stress in longer words

Paying attention to stress patterns can help your fluency of speech and intonation. When you hear or read a new word, it is useful to record its stress pattern. The stress pattern of a word is shown in its dictionary definition. For example:

connection /kəˈnekʃn/

You can record a stress pattern like this:

connection = oOo comfortable = Ooo

Many online dictionaries and apps have a useful "click to listen" function. Remember to repeat a new word several times to help you remember the stress pattern and improve your fluency.

13 IDENTIFY Listen to these words and mark the syllable that is stressed in each one.

1 scholarship   3 mechanism

2 significance   4 commentary

14 ANALYZE Work with a partner. What is the stress pattern of each word in the box? Say them aloud and work together to put them in the correct column in the chart.

appearance	attentiveness	competition	indecision
optimism	pessimism	racism	relationship
relevance	sponsorship	strategist	transmission
willingness			

1. Ooo	2. oOo	3. oOoo	4. ooOo	5. Oooo
relevance	appearance	relationship	competition	optimism

15 INTEGRATE Listen and check your answers to Exercise 14. Then listen and repeat.

16 INTEGRATE Work with a partner. Can you add any more words to the chart? When you are finished, compare your ideas with another pair.

17 WHAT'S YOUR ANGLE? Books and TV shows use different techniques to show concepts related to time and memory, for example, flashbacks. Can you think of any examples of how flashbacks and similar experiences were used in books you have read or shows you have watched? Share your ideas with a partner or in a small group.

A group of Guarani people in Brazil

2.2 I Remember When

1 ACTIVATE Look at the photos. What are the people doing? How do you think they feel? Share your ideas with a partner.

2 INTEGRATE Read the online journal of a childhood memory. Then work with a partner. What are some of the things the writer remembers? Why do you think these events were so memorable?

Home	About	Articles	Search

By the Ocean

One of my earliest memories is of visiting my grandparents. I remember we had to get up really early because the trip was more than 500 miles long and was going to take us about 14 hours. My brother and I spent time playing in the yard while my father packed the car and my mother made a picnic for the trip. I would always get really excited when we were preparing to depart on a family vacation.

But my mood changed once we were on the road. I hadn't realized then how long it would take to get to my grandparents' house. I don't remember this, but my mother has told me that we had been driving for about 20 minutes when I asked, "Are we almost there?" I remember the car ride wasn't very enjoyable, though. It was summer, and the weather was scorching hot. As we got further south, the traffic got worse and worse, and I could sense my parents' frustration as we slowed to almost a stop. We were in a traffic jam. It was too hot, and we were tired and annoyed, so Mom distracted us by singing songs and playing games like "I Spy."

The rest of the trip is kind of a blur. After an hour or so, boredom started to creep in. We stopped at a couple of gas stations along the way to buy drinks and fill up the gas tank. In fact, the smell of gasoline brings me right back to childhood every time. Eventually, it started to get dark, and I remember looking out the back window watching trees overhead and thinking how pretty they looked with the car headlights shining on them. I had just drifted off to sleep when

suddenly the car stopped and I heard my nana's voice—we had arrived at last.

The vacation was memorable for many reasons. I remember my grandparents' charming house with affection, sitting on the old bench on the deck and falling asleep to the sound of the ocean waves. I had never visited the ocean before. I'd been to the beaches near my home, but this was different. It was a typical beach town with colorful little cottages and painted fishing boats. The fishermen on the pier didn't mind our curiosity as we admired the astonishing number of fish they had caught, and Grandpa bought fresh shrimp to bring home for dinner.

It's funny how I can still remember that vacation as though it was yesterday, but I sometimes forget things I did last week. I guess when you relive a childhood experience, it remains clearer in your memory. Even now, when I have a touch of anxiety or stress, thinking about that trip brings a sense of relief.

⚇+ Oxford 5000™

19

3 WHAT'S YOUR ANGLE? Have you ever been to the ocean? How was your experience similar to the writer's? Did you have a favorite relative or friend when you were young? What was most memorable about your visits? Discuss your experiences with a partner.

4 VOCABULARY Read the words in the box and find them in the online journal. What do they mean? Discuss your ideas with a partner.

anxiety	astonishing	charming	colorful
deck	distracted	enjoyable	

5 IDENTIFY Complete the memories with a suitable word from the box in Exercise 4.

1 I've been feeling so _____ since I got back from my trip. I can't stop thinking about all the fun things I did.

2 Spending time with my brothers and sisters was never very _____. We used to fight all the time.

3 I would always feel a sense of _____ before school started after summer vacation. But as soon as I got back and saw my friends, I was fine.

4 The town I grew up in is very _____. There are a lot of old houses and pretty gardens with lots of _____ flowers.

5 My grandparents' lake house has a large _____. We sit out there and eat when the weather is nice.

6 It's _____ how much my hometown has changed in the past 20 years.

6 INTERACT Work with a partner. Discuss the comments in Exercise 5. Have you had similar experiences in the past? Do the comments remind you of any childhood events?

7 INTEGRATE Choose three or four words from Exercise 4. Think of a memory from your past that relates to each word. Write a true sentence using each word. Share your sentences with a partner or group.

 GRAMMAR IN CONTEXT Past perfect simple versus past perfect continuous

The past perfect simple and the past perfect continuous are both used when narrating a sequence of past events.

The past perfect simple describes an action that was completed before another action or situation in the past.
*I **hadn't realized** then how long it would take to get to my grandparents' house.*
*I **had** never **visited** the ocean before.*

The past perfect continuous describes an action that continued for a period of time before another action or situation happened. It is used to give background to key events in a story.
*We **had been driving** for about 20 minutes when I asked…*
*By the time help arrived, we **had been waiting** by the roadside for two hours.*

Knowing when to use each tense when you are talking about the past will help make your story clear to the listener and will make your English sound more natural.

See Grammar focus on page 160.

8 IDENTIFY Choose the best words to complete each sentence.

1 *I had always wanted / had always been wanting* to take a long car trip, so I was really excited.

2 We *hadn't driven / hadn't been driving* long when the storm hit.

3 *Had your family moved / Had your family been moving* here by the time you graduated from high school?

4 *I hadn't visited / hadn't been visiting* the ocean before, but Amy had.

5 When we got to the beach, our grandfather *had fished / had been fishing* for only a few minutes and he already had a big fish in his bucket.

9 WHAT'S YOUR ANGLE? Think about the photos, stories, and memories discussed in this lesson. Do any of them trigger encouraging childhood memories for you? Discuss with a partner.

10 INTEGRATE Complete the text with the past perfect simple or continuous of the verbs in parentheses. Then compare answers with a partner. Why did you choose the simple or continuous form?

I remember one year when my brother and I were little, my family ¹ _____ (go) to stay with my aunt and uncle and cousins during the holidays. Back then, they lived way out in the country. I can still remember the smell of pine trees when we got out of the car. After dinner, the whole family decided to take a walk together. We ² _____ (walk) along a path beside the forest when my cousins and my brother and I started feeling adventurous. We started playing a game of hide-and-seek among the big trees while our parents continued to walk on the path. We ³ _____ (run) around for a while and going deeper and deeper into the woods. It was cool and dark in the forest and very peaceful and quiet. Suddenly, we looked around and realized we were lost. At first, we stayed calm and searched for the path, but we couldn't find it. Then I looked over and saw that my younger cousin ⁴ _____ (start) to cry. Finally, we started shouting, "Mom! Dad!" as loud as we could. All of a sudden, my uncle's head appeared from around a big tree, and he said calmly, "Yes?" It turned out our parents ⁵ _____ (following) us the whole time! To this day, I can still hear our laughter as we walked back to the house, and I'll never forget the comforting smell of apple pie when we opened the door and walked in.

WRITING SKILL
Discourse markers for time and sequence

Writers use discourse markers to show concepts related to time and the sequence of events in a narrative. When you are writing, help your readers to follow the story by:

- setting the scene: Use words and phrases such as *currently*, *at the moment*, *in the past*, *when I was young*, and *back then*.

- showing sequence (the order of events): Use words such as *first*, *next*, *then*, *before*, and *after*.

- showing how events relate to each other in time: Use words and phrases such as *as soon as*, *when*, *immediately*, *suddenly*, *while*, *meanwhile*, *at the same time*, *at last*, and *finally*.

Noticing how discourse markers are used in texts can help you improve your own writing and make it more cohesive (easy for your reader to understand).

11 IDENTIFY Work with a partner. What is the purpose of a discourse marker? Why is it important to use discourse markers in your writing? Can you give some examples of discourse markers for (a) setting the scene, (b) showing sequence, and (c) showing how events relate to each other?

12 ANALYZE Identify at least six examples of discourse markers in the text in Exercise 10. Compare your answers with a partner. How does each one help the reader understand the story?

13 WHAT'S YOUR ANGLE? In the online journal, the writer describes a lot of memories related to the senses—sight, sound, smell, and taste. Why do you think that is? Can you think of examples of things you remember from the past that relate to the senses? Share your ideas in a small group.

14 PREPARE Plan to write an online journal entry of your own about an early memory. Your classmates will see your entry. Follow these steps.

1 Think of an early memory that is important to you.
2 Write down some ideas about the background, main events, and memorable people, places, and things.
3 What was memorable about the event? Think about how you felt. Consider the senses: sight, sound, smell, and taste.
4 Consider how you will sequence the events and which discourse markers you could use.
5 Write a draft of your online journal entry. It should be at least 250 to 300 words. While you write, refer back to your notes and the information in the Writing Skill box.

15 IMPROVE Read your online journal entry and correct any grammar and spelling mistakes. Check for examples of what you have learned.

Writing checklist

☐ Have you written 250 to 300 words?
☐ Did you use vocabulary words from Exercise 4?
☐ Did you use the past perfect simple and continuous to show the sequence of events?
☐ Did you use discourse markers to show time and sequence?
☐ Did you include sensory references to describe your memory?

16 SHARE Read a classmate's online journal entry. Ask them one or two questions about their memories. Say which events or things in their post you find interesting and what they have done well. If you have had any similar experiences, describe them.

2.3 Repeat after Me

1 ACTIVATE Think of a person you know who is either very good at or very forgetful about remembering facts, information, names, dates, faces, and so on.

2 INTERACT Talk with a partner about the person you chose in Exercise 1. How are you like that person?

**LISTENING SKILL
Understanding a speaker's audience and purpose**

A speaker always has a purpose based on their audience. Before you listen, ask yourself questions such as *Who is in the audience—students, members of the public, experts? What would this audience expect from the speaker— information, clarification, advice, suggestions?*

Ask yourself what the speaker's purpose might be. Is it to teach, report, persuade, suggest, or give advice? This should help you understand the message in more depth.

3 **IDENTIFY** Watch the first part of a lecture. Answer the questions. Then discuss your ideas with a partner.

1 What is the topic?
2 Who is the speaker?
3 What is the speaker's purpose?
4 Who is the audience?

4 **IDENTIFY** Watch the rest of the lecture. Choose the correct letter to answer each question and then compare your answers with a partner.

1 Visual inspection involves using ___ in order to remember something.
   a words
   b numbers
   c imagery
2 Verbal elaboration helps people remember by creating a ___.
   a phrase or sentence
   b song or poem
   c written list
3 Verbal elaboration uses the part of the brain that deals with ___.
   a numbers
   b language
   c color
4 Sleep is a memorization strategy because the brain ___.
   a is in a restful, relaxed state
   b moves information into long term memory
   c shuts down and stops processing information

5 The speaker hopes the information will help her audience to ___.
   a study less
   b remember their childhoods
   c be successful students

5 INTEGRATE In a small group, discuss these words and topics from the lecture. What did the speaker say about them? Who in your group remembers the most? How did they remember the information?

   • Anderson
   • the colors of the rainbow
   • napping
   • short-term and long-term memory

6 ▶ **INTERACT** Watch the video again and check the answers with your group.

7 WHAT'S YOUR ANGLE? Talk with a partner about what kinds of things you have had to memorize for school or work. Why did you need to memorize them? What mechanisms did you use to help you remember them?

GRAMMAR IN CONTEXT Habits and routines

There are a variety of ways we can talk about habits and routines. Common grammatical structures and expressions for present habits and routines include:

1. *be used to, get used to*
*Because I'm so absentminded, I'm trying to **get used to** making lists.*

2. present continuous with *always, continually*, and *constantly* can be used to express annoyance
*I'm **constantly misplacing** my housekeys and **never remember** where I put them.*

3. adverbs of frequency, such as *always* and *never*
*Our parents **always forget** our phone numbers.*

For past habits and routines, we can use:

4. *would*
*In elementary school, **I'd never** raise my hand in class.*

5. *used to*
*I **used to** memorize by repeating things over and over.*

See Grammar focus on page 160.

8 IDENTIFY Read these comments from students who attended the lecture. Identify examples of points 1–3 from the Grammar box.

| 👥 | Find Friends 🔍 | Profile | Account |

Juan Blanco

The memorization techniques from the lecture are really interesting. I would sometimes try to use memorization techniques in high school, but I didn't really get into the habit until I started college. I would often use repetition to memorize math formulas. It worked really well for me, so now I do it all the time. I'm going to try some of the techniques from the lecture over the next week or so and see which works best. I suspect it might be the sleep!

Monica Ellis

I am always worrying about tests. I usually stay up really late trying to memorize things and end up completely exhausted on the day of the exam. I wish I had known about the sleep technique back then!

Yang Lin

I had a teacher in high school who used to always try to get us to use the visual inspection technique to remember information. Unfortunately, we'd be fooling around instead of listening to her advice!

9 INTEGRATE Compare your answers to Exercise 8 with a partner.

10 WHAT'S YOUR ANGLE? Are any of the students' comments similar to your own experiences? Why or why not?

11 INTEGRATE Use the prompts to write sentences about present or past habits. Add *would* or *used to* if possible.

1 When / we / children / my brother / get into / trouble / always.

2 You / study all night / for exams / in college / often.

3 Teachers / teach / students / strategies for studying / but / the / students / not listen / sometimes.

4 When / my family / live / in the country / my mother / work / in the garden.

5 While / Ken / live / Japan / he / write / in his journal / before bed.

12 INTERACT Work with a partner. Compare and check answers to Exercise 11. Then talk about your own memories of past or present habits or routines.

13 WHAT'S YOUR ANGLE? Have you tried any of the memorization techniques from the video? How successful were they? If not, which techniques would you like to try? Why? Share your ideas in a small group.

14 VOCABULARY Read the sentences based on information from the video. Use the context to figure out the meaning of the bold vocabulary words. Match the word in bold in each sentence to its definition.

1 It's easier for the brain to **accurately** recall a smaller volume of information. ___

2 Our brains don't have **adequate** room to store all of that material forever. ___

3 The second successful strategy for **boosting** memorization is called *verbal elaboration*. ___

4 The first **strategy** for remembering what you're studying is called *visual inspection*. ___

5 That's where the brain stores information more **permanently**. ___

6 Thinking of the shape of an image can help **trigger** your memory of the word. ___

📖⁺ Oxford 5000™

a (adv.) in a way that lasts for a long time or for all time in the future; in a way that exists all the time

b (adj.) enough in quantity or good enough in quality for a particular purpose or need

c (v.) to cause a particular reaction or development

d (v.) making something increase or become better or more successful

e (adv.) in a way that is correct and true in every detail

f (n.) a plan that is intended to achieve a particular purpose

24 Pictures from the Past

1 ACTIVATE In what kinds of situations do you participate in a group discussion? Do you feel comfortable participating in discussions when there are more than one or two people involved?

2 ASSESS Look at the pictures. Discuss the questions with a partner.

1 Where are the people?
2 What is the relationship between the speakers? How well do you think they know each other?
3 What do you think they are discussing?
4 Which member of the group is leading the conversation? Why do you think so?

3 ▶ IDENTIFY Watch the video and then answer the questions.

1 What is the topic of the discussion?
2 Do the speakers all agree with each other?
3 What happens when someone doesn't understand something?
4 In what ways do the speakers use body language during the discussion?

4 INTEGRATE Compare your answers to Exercise 3 with a partner and give reasons for them. Then read the information in the box and see if your ideas are mentioned.

REAL-WORLD ENGLISH Listening and participating in a group discussion

During a group discussion, you can ask for clarification if you don't understand what someone said.

Do you mean…?   Are you saying that…?   What do you mean by…?

You can also ask follow-up questions to get more information.

Why is that?   What is the reason for that?   How did that happen?

Others in the group can respond to your questions by acknowledging your ideas, explaining a point, or adding more information.

Yes, that's right.   That's similar to what happened in…   I read a related article that talked about…

The tone of the discussion (formal or informal) usually depends on how well the people in the group know each other.

Often someone takes on the role of the discussion "leader," inviting group members to speak and share their reactions and opinions.

5 **ANALYZE** Read excerpts from the video. What function does each statement serve? Write the correct letter of the matching function from the box.

> a inviting someone's opinion or response
> b asking for clarification
> c asking a follow-up question
> d introducing a new topic
> e giving an example for clarification

1 Don't you all think that's interesting? ___
2 Can you give us an example? ___
3 What do you mean by *re-creation photography*? ___
4 Well, recently, there were four siblings who became famous for recreating photos from their childhood. They wore similar clothing and stood in the same position. Do you know what I mean? ___
5 And the other thing is videos. What are your thoughts on that, Max? ___
6 Can you say more about that? Anyone? ___
7 Emma, you're shaking your head. Do you disagree? ___

6 **INTEGRATE** Work with a partner. Read through the excerpts from Exercise 5 together and compare your answers. Give reasons for your choices.

7 **EXPAND** Work with a partner. Read sentences 1–6 aloud and write the letter of the matching response (a–f). Then discuss which function from Exercise 5 each statement serves.

1 Could you explain the process in more detail, please? ___
2 For instance, the project in California was a problem. ___
3 Let's move on to talk about the project. ___
4 Steve, could you begin? ___
5 How long will it take? ___
6 Are you saying you disagree? ___

a It'll probably take about a year.
b Yes, of course. The way it works is…
c Yes, I agree. It was a disaster.
d Me? Oh, sure, I'll be glad to.
e OK. The project is designed to…
f Not exactly. I'm just not sure I understand.

8 **IMPROVE** Work with a partner. Practice saying the matched questions and responses in Exercise 7 together.

9 **PREPARE** Work with a partner. Choose a topic from the list and write down your ideas and opinions it.

When you were younger, did you have dreams of being famous? Explain.

How do you think social media has changed society since you were younger?

What are the benefits of social media sites for preserving memories?

10 **PREPARE** Work with another pair of students who chose the same topic.

1 Decide who will start the discussion.
2 Practice your discussion together. Remember to ask for clarification or explanations and to ask one or two follow-up questions to get more information. Ask others for their opinions and responses or reactions.

11 SHARE Role-play your discussion.

GO ONLINE
to create your own version
of the English For Real video.

2.5 Repetition, Repetition, Repetition

1 ACTIVATE Work with a partner. What memorization techniques are you familiar with? How well do you learn by memorizing things? Record your thoughts.

2 **IDENTIFY** Listen to the discussion. What is it about? How many students are taking part? Which kinds of memorization techniques do they mention?

3 **IDENTIFY** Listen again and take brief notes to answer the questions.

1 Why does the group want to be able to better memorize information?

2 Which technique is recommended while on the bus or train?

3 What are some of the "tricks" that are mentioned for this technique?

4 What time of day do two students say is a good time to study?

5 Why does one speaker record information?

4 INTEGRATE Compare answers with a partner. Explain the answers in as much detail as you can. Ask your partner for clarification if necessary.

SPEAKING Critiquing and reviewing

Participating in a discussion involves thinking about a topic from all angles and considering both the pros and cons related to it. Before and during a discussion, ask yourself questions such as:

What are the pros and cons of this idea or situation?
How might this affect others?
What arguments could be made for or against it?

You need to recognize whether the points that you or other people make in a discussion are valid. Someone might introduce a point they have not properly considered or is not true. Someone may introduce a concept or idea that others hadn't thought of before. You can review your position and perhaps adjust your views based on new information.

Some example sentences we use to respond to another person's ideas are:

Hmm. I don't know. I think…
Mmm. It sounds really interesting, but I'm not sure…
What do you mean by…?
OK, I can understand that.

5 INTERACT What is your opinion of the techniques that the students mentioned? Can you think of any pros and cons related to them? Would their techniques work for you? Why or why not? Discuss your ideas with a partner or in a small group.

PRONUNCIATION SKILL
Using cadence (speaking speed) and intonation to express certainty or hesitation

We often change our cadence and intonation to express the different feelings behind what we say.

When we are sure about something, our cadence is quick and our intonation is usually somewhat flat and straightforward. Consider these statements from the listening.

I actually agree with that.   No way.

When we are unsure about something or need more time to think, our cadence slows, we add pauses between words, and our intonation may go up and down.

Hmm…   I don't know.
It sounds interesting,…but I'm just not sure…

6 **IDENTIFY** Listen to the excerpts from the discussion. Mark the places where the speakers change their intonation and cadence to express certainty or hesitation.

1 I don't know… I think… that may be taking it a bit too far.

2 No way. Just before bed is the best time to study new information.

3 I actually agree with that. I find reviewing before bed helps me, too.

4 Mmm. It sounds interesting, but I'm just not sure.

5 OK. What do you mean by *visual person*?

6 OK, I can understand that. So, what technique do you use?

7 Hmm. I wonder. It seems like I'd get distracted if I tried to memorize important information while working out.

7 INTERACT Read through your notes from Exercise 1. Choose one technique and discuss the pros and cons with a partner. Check for any language errors.

8 INTEGRATE Form groups of four and continue your discussion. When you are listening to a classmate, think about the technique they are describing. You can ask questions and comment on their technique. Use cadence and intonation to express certainty or hesitation.

9 WHAT'S YOUR ANGLE? How well do you think the group discussion went? What did you do and your classmates do well? Do you feel more confident about having discussions now?

Now go to page 148 for the Unit 2 Review.

3 Discoveries

UNIT SNAPSHOT

What can we learn from ancient civilizations? 29

How have some new discoveries changed
our lives? 31

What have researchers learned about dreams? 34

Is travel necessary for discovery?

Why are people interested in discoveries about the past?

What scientific discoveries have changed your life?

BEHIND THE PHOTO

Answer the questions. Then discuss your answers with a partner.

1 What makes a discovery significant?

2 What kind of things did you enjoy discovering and learning about as a child?

3 What kind of discoveries do the following groups of people make: scientists, explorers, archaeologists, ordinary people?

REAL-WORLD GOAL

Discover a new place in your city or town

3.1 Going Back in Time

1 ACTIVATE Work with a partner. What events do the photos show? Match them to the words in the box.

forest fire	earthquake	tornado
volcanic eruption	flood	

2 VOCABULARY The adjectives and nouns in the chart are often used together to form collocations—common phrases—that relate to the topic of natural disasters. What do the words mean? Write the words in the correct blanks.

Adjectives	Nouns
complete	destruction
total	disorder
utter	panic
widespread	ruin

 Oxford 5000™

1 Three adjective synonyms that mean "100 percent"

_____ _____ _____

2 Two nouns that mean "a state of serious damage"

_____ _____

3 One adjective that means "over a large area or among many people"

_____

4 Two nouns that relate to "a state of confusion"

_____ _____

3 INTEGRATE Use collocations from Exercise 2 to talk about the photos in Exercise 1. Which parts of the world are these disasters most likely to happen in? Why? What are their effects? Share your ideas.

READING SKILL Previewing longer texts

Previewing a longer text with a lot of details and information helps you understand the gist (general meaning) so that you can better comprehend the key information when you read.

There are several strategies to preview a text to get a general idea of what it's about.

1 Look at the title and any pictures with the text and think about what you already know about the topic.

2 Read the bold headings that introduce new sections and topics.

3 Read the first paragraph and the last paragraph.

4 Read the first and last sentence of each paragraph.

5 Use the "5 Ws" technique. Skim the text quickly and look for the answers to these questions: Who is it about? What is it about? Where did it take place? When did it take place? Why did the author write the text? (What is the purpose?)

Using one or more of these previewing strategies will help you better understand the information in longer texts.

4 **APPLY** Choose three of the strategies from the Reading Skill box and use them to preview the online article. Then talk with a partner. What is the article about?

5 **IDENTIFY** Read the online article. Have you heard of any of these lost cities? Tell a partner.

6 **INTEGRATE** Write three or four sentences that summarize the gist of the online article. Use at least two collocations from Exercise 2. Then share your summary with the class.

7 **IDENTIFY** Read the online article again. Identify the answers to the questions.

1 Where were Pompeii and Herculaneum? What were they like?
2 How were the two cities lost?
3 How has finding Pompeii and Herculaneum helped archaeologists with their research?
4 What do archaeologists know about the Indus civilization?
5 What has puzzled archaeologists about Mohenjo Daro?
6 How did scientists locate the lost "White City"?

Finding the World's Lost Cities

For centuries, legends about mysterious "lost cities" have captured the imaginations of explorers, archaeologists, and adventurers worldwide. **Although** many of these lost cities remain undiscovered, those that have been found give us a fascinating insight into the lives of their inhabitants.

Pompeii and Herculaneum

Situated on the Bay of Naples in Italy, these two lost cities are famous for their total destruction in 79 BCE, which was caused by the eruption of the volcano Mount Vesuvius. Pompeii appears to have been a well-known city of economic importance, **while** Herculaneum was a smaller fishing town. Studies suggest that the cities experienced decades of damage caused by earthquakes before Mount Vesuvius erupted in 79 BCE, causing widespread disorder and resulting in utter panic. The cities' unique contribution to archaeology has been the fact that they were so well preserved. The disaster buried the cities under deep layers of volcanic ash. Houses, shops, and businesses have been discovered in good condition, together with artifacts abandoned by people trying to flee the scene of the disaster. Ongoing study of the ruins continues to play an important role in the development of conservation techniques and the use of computerized archaeological methods.

Mohenjo Daro

The city of Mohenjo Daro, by the Indus River in southern Pakistan, was discovered in 1921. Archaeologists believe it formed part of the Indus Valley civilization, which existed almost 4,500 years ago. Research shows that the city benefited from skilled urban planning and a high standard of living. It was built on man-made mounds to keep it safe from floods, and almost every house contained a water supply and bathing area. The valuable artifacts and materials, such as gold and ivory, found in the ruins suggest that the inhabitants must have been wealthy. However, **despite** the fact that archaeologists have found so many artifacts, they have not been able to show exactly who occupied the ancient city as it does not include features such as palaces or monuments that are associated with great civilizations. **In spite of** suggestions that the civilization ended in complete ruin as a result of floods, there is no real evidence to verify this, so research continues.

The "White City" of Honduras

Even though there were rumors of a "White City" lost in the Honduran rainforest since the early twentieth century, scientists were unable to find it until 2012 when a team began searching the area by plane. It found the ruined city with the help of new scanning technology called *LIDAR* (light detection and ranging), which uses lasers to build 3-D images of an area. The images revealed pyramids and other structures, which could be the legendary "White City." In 2015, researchers traveled to the site and discovered artifacts that give clues about the ancient civilization that once inhabited the region. They are planning to use the LIDAR technology to explore the area further to see whether more ruined cities exist.

—adapted from *The Oxford Companion to Western Art*
by Hugh Brigstocke

8 INTERACT Work with a partner. Discuss the answers to the questions in Exercise 7.

9 WHAT'S YOUR ANGLE? Which of the "lost cities" do you find most fascinating? What kinds of ancient civilizations existed where you are from? What do you know about how the people lived? How do you know about their lives?

> **GRAMMAR IN CONTEXT Contrast clauses**
>
> We use a contrast clause to draw attention to information that contrasts in a surprising or unexpected way. A contrast clause comes before or after the clause it contrasts. When the contrast clause comes first in a sentence, we use a comma to separate the contrast clause from the main clause.
>
> **Even though / Although** *many of these lost cities remain undiscovered, new technology is giving archaeologists hope.*
>
> **In spite of / Despite** *the fact that archaeologists have found so many artifacts, they have found no human remains.*
>
> **Whereas / While** *there had been rumors of a "White City" lost in the Honduran rainforest since the early twentieth century, efforts to find it were unsuccessful until 2012.*
>
> *Whereas, despite,* and *in spite of* are considered more formal.
>
> We say *in spite of* but not *despite of.*
>
> We can follow both *in spite of* and *despite* with *either the fact that* or a noun.
>
> We can also follow *despite* with a word with *-ing* form.
>
> **Despite / In spite of** <u>having</u> *been completely destroyed, the site still produced many valuable artifacts.*

See Grammar focus on page 161.

10 IDENTIFY Choose the correct words to complete each sentence.

1 He insisted on searching for the city, *even though / despite* he had no proof that it existed.

2 The team managed to get to the site *in spite of / whereas* the fact that the area was remote.

3 *Despite / While* the buildings were completely buried, they weren't badly damaged.

4 *Despite / In spite of* finding many artifacts at the site, archaeologists don't know who lived there.

5 One team searched the valley on foot *whereas / despite* the other searched by plane.

11 INTEGRATE Complete the news report excerpts with words and phrases from the box. Three items have two possible answers. Compare answers with a partner. Why did you choose each one?

despite	even though	in spite of	whereas	while

1 The houses and their contents, including clothing, tools and cooking pots, were perfectly preserved _____ the fact that they had been buried under the mud of the riverbed.

2 _____ the village was built on the river, archaeologists found no evidence that the people ate fish and shellfish.

3 _____ being ancient artifacts, the tools were very well preserved.

4 It appears that the town was an important trading center _____ its neighbors relied on agriculture.

5 Some experts still doubt the discovery is genuine _____ the evidence.

12 WHAT'S YOUR ANGLE? Think of a past civilization or a type of disaster you have heard about. What kinds of information are known about it? Discuss with a partner.

The Swabian Castle of Augusta in Sicily, Italy

3.2 Living Longer

1 **ACTIVATE** Look at the photos. What do you think these living creatures have in common? What do you know about each one? Discuss your ideas in a small group.

2 **INTEGRATE** Preview the article. What do you know about the topic? Read the article to learn more.

| Home | About | Articles | | Search |

Slow Life, Long Life

A study in 2016 provided evidence that Greenland sharks are the longest-living vertebrates (animals with a backbone) on Earth. A research team used radiocarbon dating technology to figure out the ages of 28 sharks that had been caught in fishing nets in the cold, deep waters of the North Atlantic Sea.

The study data suggested that one of the sharks, a five-meter-long female, was about 400 years old. Marine biologist Julius Nielsen of the University of Copenhagen, who was part of the research team, commented that although they knew the sharks were unusual, they were surprised to find out just how old they actually were.

It is thought that the sharks' slow pace of life contributes to their long lives. According to the research team, 400 is an approximate age because radiocarbon dating is not accurate. However, the shark could have been any age between 272 and 512. This means it was probably born in the seventeenth century.

Does this same principle explain why humans live so much longer than other mammals? The answer is yes, according to an earlier study conducted in 2014.

The study, published in the *Journal of the National Academy of Sciences*, concludes that the slow rate

at which humans and other primates burn calories explains why they grow up so slowly and live so long.

While other mammals with faster metabolisms, such as cats and rabbits, die at relatively young ages, humans and other primates that burn calories more slowly tend to live longer lives.

According to Herman Pontzer, lead author of the study and anthropologist at Hunter College in New York, the results of the study surprised the researchers: "Humans, chimpanzees, baboons, and other primates expend only half the calories we'd expect for a mammal. Someone with a very physically active lifestyle would need to run a marathon each day just to approach the average daily energy expenditure of a mammal their size."

The researchers say studying the relationship between physical activity and energy expenditure may help us better understand metabolic diseases and obesity.

Pontzer says more research is being conducted on the subject, adding: "Humans live longer than other apes and tend to carry more body fat. Understanding how human metabolism compares to our closest relatives will help us understand how our bodies evolved and how to keep them healthy."

3 **WHAT'S YOUR ANGLE?** Are you surprised by the discovery? In what other ways do you think a "slow pace of life" contributes to a longer life? Tell a partner.

4 **IDENTIFY** Number the questions in the order they are answered in the article.

4 Why do scientists think Greenland sharks live so long?

6 How did the researchers feel about the shark discovery?

7 What surprised Herman Pontzer and his team of researchers?

5 What is the principle that explains why humans live so long?

2 What was the discovery regarding Greenland sharks? When did it happen?

3 What are some of the facts related to the study?

1 Who conducted the 2016 study? How did they do it?

8 What will Pontzer's study help us understand better?

5 **INTEGRATE** Work with a partner. Discuss the questions from Exercise 4 in the correct order.

GRAMMAR IN CONTEXT Articles

We use either the article *the* or no article at all with proper nouns that talk about specific locations such as cities, countries, geographical features, or buildings.

We use *the* for the names of rivers, valleys, deserts, mountain ranges, oceans, seas, and groups of islands, as well as plural country names.

*How long is **the** Amazon?*
*We flew over **the** Sahara Desert.*
*Manila is the capital of **the** Philippines.*

We also use *the* before names of theaters, hotels, galleries, and museums.

*Have you been to **the** Guggenheim Museum?*

We use no article (or zero article, Ø) with the names of planets, most countries, continents, states, lakes, and individual mountains.

Scientists discovered [Ø] Neptune with mathematics.
Have you ever been to [Ø] Australia?
The highest mountain in [Ø] Africa is [Ø] Mount Kilimanjaro.

We also use no article with the names of towns or cities, neighborhoods, streets, hospitals, and some universities.

Have you been to [Ø] Paris?

Note: With university names, we use *the* when the title begins with *University of*; we use no article in all other cases.

***the** University of Dublin*
[Ø] Harvard University

See Grammar focus on page 161.

6 **INTEGRATE** Complete the text with *the* or Ø (no article).

| Home | About | Search | 🔍 |

What makes some people live longer than others? Is it geography? We often hear about certain places, such as ¹ Ø Japan or countries near ² the Mediterranean Sea, where people live longer, healthier lives. Scientists have yet to prove whether geographical factors alone lead to a longer life. However, we do know that genetics—our DNA—plays a major role.

In fact, researchers in ³ the United States have found the specific part of our DNA that is responsible for long life. Scientists at ⁴ Ø Harvard University and ⁵ Ø Beth Israel Deaconess Medical Center in ⁶ _____ Boston decided to study families to find out more. They discovered that very elderly people often had siblings who also lived much longer than average. All of them appear to have the same features in part of their DNA. They believe this may be the key to a long, healthy life. The researchers hope to find specific "longevity genes" and eventually use them to develop treatments that would allow people to stay healthier and live longer, no matter where on ⁷ _____ Earth they live.

7 **WHAT'S YOUR ANGLE?** Do you think researchers will find a way to help people live longer? Is this a good idea? Share your ideas with a partner.

8 **INTEGRATE** Work with a partner. Have a race to see who can identify two examples of each type of article with a proper noun (*the* or no article) in the text in Exercise 6.

9 **ASSESS** Work with a partner. Show them the articles you found in the text while completing Exercise 8. Which type is each one? Discuss your ideas.

Being able to summarize an article is a very useful skill for both work and study. A summary shows that you have understood what you have read and provides the reader with a briefer, more accessible source of information than the original article.

When you plan your summary, think about its purpose. What does the reader want or need to know? Use this to decide what information from the article to include. When you're writing, do not copy the writer's words—paraphrase them with your own words. You can do this by:

- changing the grammar (active → passive).
- using synonyms (*show* → *indicate*).
- avoiding direct quotes unless necessary (use reported speech instead).

A summary should be shorter than the original text because it covers only the most important points. A good way to plan your summary is to read the original article and then think of questions that the writer has answered in it. Write these questions and then answer them in your own words.

10 **WHAT'S YOUR ANGLE?** Work with a partner. Have you ever had to write a summary? For what purpose? Why do you think it is important to paraphrase the original text?

11 **INTEGRATE** Read a student's summary of the article "Slow Life, Long Life." How is it different from the original article? Does it mention the same key points? How does it compare in terms of length?

A study of Greenland sharks in 2016 affirmed that they're Earth's longest-living vertebrates. Researchers used radiocarbon dating technology to estimate the ages of 28 sharks that had been caught in fishing nets in the North Atlantic Sea. It appeared that one five-meter-long female was about 400 years old. Julius Nielsen, a marine biologist from the University of Copenhagen, said that the research team was surprised to discover how old the sharks actually were. It is believed that Greenland sharks live for a long time because of their slow pace of life. Because radiocarbon dating is not completely accurate, the female shark could actually have been any age between 272 and 512. However, it is likely that it was born in the seventeenth century.

A similar principle explains why primates, including humans, live longer than other mammals. A previous study conducted by researchers at Hunter College in New York found that animals that burn calories at a slower rate tend to live longer. Lead researcher Herman Pontzer says that more research is being conducted that may help us learn more about human diseases and health.

12 **APPLY** Look back at the Writing Skill box. What techniques (synonyms, grammar changes, paraphrasing) did the student use when writing the summary? Work with a partner, and identify examples in the summary.

13 **PREPARE** Plan to write a summary of your own about a discovery. Follow these steps.

1 Look back at the article "Finding the World's Lost Cities" on page 29.
2 Read the original article and write some questions that it answers.
3 Consider how you can summarize the information.

14 **WRITE** Write a draft of your summary. While you write, refer back to your notes and the information in the Writing Skill box.

15 **IMPROVE** Check your summary for the following and make edits to try to include at least two new skills from this unit. Then swap summaries with a partner and share ideas for how to include any additional new vocabulary or skills.

Writing checklist

☐ Did you use synonyms, grammar changes, and paraphrasing to summarize?
☐ Did you use proper nouns with *the* or no article?
☐ Did you use phrasal verbs?
☐ Did you use discourse markers to show time and sequence?
☐ Did you use contrast clauses with *even though, while, whereas, in spite of,* or *despite*?
☐ Did you use vocabulary related to natural disasters?

16 **SHARE** Swap summaries with a different partner. Read each other's summary and note which skills from Exercise 15 you used and what else you've done well.

3.3 In Your Dreams

1 ACTIVATE Work with a partner. How often do you remember your dreams? What kinds of details do you remember?

2 🔊 **IDENTIFY** Listen to the first part of a podcast. What discovery is the program about? Who is going to give information about it?

3 🔊 **INTEGRATE** Listen to the rest of the podcast. Take notes to answer the questions, and then compare ideas with a partner.

1　Why is Dr. Clark excited about the discovery?
2　Who took part in the study?
3　What did the research involve?
4　Will the technology be available as entertainment in the future?
5　In what other area could the technology be used?

 LISTENING SKILL
Dealing with unknown words while listening

Using strategies for dealing with unknown words while listening allows you to focus on key information. You can usually understand the general meaning without understanding every word.

When you don't understand a word or phrase, relax and stay focused on the context and your background knowledge to help you understand the general meaning.

If the unknown word is important for your general understanding or it is a word you have heard before, write it down to look up later.

4 🔊 **IDENTIFY** Work with a partner. Listen to excerpts from the podcast. Discuss the meaning of each statement. Write any unknown words. How did you figure out the general meaning without knowing them?

 GRAMMAR IN CONTEXT Determiners and quantifiers *each of, every one of, either...or, neither...nor, either of* and *neither of*

We can use *each of* and *every one of* with plural nouns.
*Archaeologists discovered a variety of artifacts in **each of** the lost cities.*
***Every one of** the brain scan images was clear.*

We use *either...or* to contrast or express an option between two items.
*If I could visit an ancient city, I'd choose **either** Cairo **or** Petra.*

We use *neither...nor* to make a negative statement about two items.
***Neither** David **nor** Andrew can ever remember his dreams.*

When we use a plural pronoun or a plural noun with a determiner, such as *the, my,* or *these,* we use *either of* or *neither of*.
*She decided not to participate in **either of** the research projects.*

See Grammar focus on page 161.

5 IDENTIFY Choose the correct determiner or quantifier to complete each sentence.

1　Despite the researchers' efforts, *either of / neither of* the studies ended up with positive results.
2　Even though they were from the same time period, *each of / either of* the archaeological sites was completely different.
3　Whereas none of the volunteers said they remembered their dreams, *either of / every one of* them recognized one or more images.
4　*Neither of / Each of* the volunteers must sign a permission form.
5　In spite of the unusual results, *neither / either* the researchers nor the volunteers were surprised at the discovery.
6　While vehicles are permitted, we prefer that visitors to the archaeological site travel *either / neither* on foot or on horseback.

6 INTERACT Work with a partner. Discuss times and situations in which you might use determiners and quantifiers in your daily life.

VOCABULARY DEVELOPMENT Phrasal verbs

Phrasal verbs (verbs that are used with a preposition or particle) are common in speaking and in more informal situations.

We can recognize phrasal verbs because the verb + preposition combination forms a phrase with a unique meaning.

*They **looked into** the machine to see what was wrong.*
look into = look inside (not a phrasal verb)
*They **looked into** the problem, but it took days to fix it.*
look into = explore, check (phrasal verb)

Phrasal verbs may be:

- separable—an object can come between the verb and the particle.

  *I'm sure we can **work** this issue **out** if we are patient.*

- non-separable.

  *The professor said he would **go over** the instructions for the project.*

Noticing and recording phrasal verbs and how they are used helps you build your vocabulary.

7 IDENTIFY Complete each excerpt from the podcast with a phrasal verb from the box. Change the tense of the verb as needed. Listen again if needed.

arrive at	come up with	end up
go about	go over	go through
hook up	try out	work (something) out

A: So, you've actually ¹ _____ a way to record dreams on video. Is that really possible?

B: It certainly looks that way, and I'm really excited about it. Researchers have ² _____ many different approaches over the years,…and now we've finally ³ _____ a method that works.

A: Yes. I'm sure you and your team ⁴ _____ a lot together before you ⁵ _____ finding success.

B: We sure did. Sometimes there were differences of opinion, but we ⁶ _____ things _____ together. They're very dedicated, professional researchers.

A: Could you ⁷ _____ the basic process for our listeners? How do you ⁸ _____ recording someone's dream?

B: Well, we use technologies like EEG and magnetic resonance imaging, or MRI, to observe the brain as it processes images…. We ⁹ _____ these machines a supercomputer, which can then create a video of whatever a person is dreaming about.

꙳⁺ Oxford 5000™

8 EXPAND Work with a partner. Match each phrasal verb from Exercise 7 to its meaning below. Decide whether each phrasal verb is separable (S) or inseparable (I).

a experience *go through, I*

b explain; review _____

c start working on _____

d decide on, identify _____

e connect; attach _____

f find yourself in a situation _____

g develop; discover _____

h solve a problem _____

i test _____

PRONUNCIATION SKILL Linking

When speaking, we often link the consonant sound at the end of a word with the vowel sound at the beginning of the next word.

that's a   an interesting   surprised at   form of

1. What kinds of things are you interested in?

2. This is an interesting study about an ancient civilization.

3. This is a great article

4. These images are quite a bit clearer.

5. This is one of the most important discoveries of our time.

9 IDENTIFY Listen to the sentences. Draw a line to show the linked consonant and vowel sounds. Then listen again and repeat.

1 Humans are naturally inclined to be curious and to work out problems together.

2 The invention of the Internet is the most important discovery of all time.

3 It's unfortunate that all of the greatest explorers have already passed away.

4 There aren't any more original discoveries; everything has already been found.

5 What's an invention that has made our world a better place?

6 All of the greatest inventions eventually end up being copied by someone else.

10 APPLY Work with a partner. Compare and discuss your answers to Exercise 9.

11 WHAT'S YOUR ANGLE? Think about discoveries. What do you think is the most important discovery ever made? Or that may be made in the future? Share your ideas with the class.

3.4 That's a Good Point, But...

1 ACTIVATE Think of a current topic that people have different opinions about. How comfortable are you expressing your opinion or disagreeing with others' opinions? How do you express disagreement when you know the person well versus when you don't the person well?

2 PREPARE Look at the pictures. Discuss the questions with a partner.

1 Where are the people?
2 Do you think their interaction is more casual and social or more formal and professional?
3 What do you think Andy's role is?

3 ▶ IDENTIFY Watch the video and then answer the questions.

1 What is the topic of the discussion?
2 Is it formal or informal?
3 Do all the speakers agree with each other?
4 How do they show each other they agree or disagree?
5 How do the speakers use body language to show their opinions?
6 What happens when two people speak at once?

REAL-WORLD ENGLISH Agreeing and disagreeing

When you are discussing a topic, you may agree with someone's views, or you may disagree. There are different ways to respond to the opinions of others.

We usually express agreement quickly and directly with short phrases. For example:

Right.   *Exactly.*   *I completely agree.*   *I think so too.*

Disagreement is usually expressed indirectly. For example, the speaker may pause before expressing disagreement and may begin the statement with:

Hmm,...   *Well,...*   *Actually,...*

The speaker may also start with a positive statement + *but*.

Yes, but...   *I see your point, but...*   *That's interesting, but...*

In formal settings, speakers who do not know each other well usually avoid directly saying *No*, *That's wrong*, or *I disagree* unless they want to strongly argue their point.

Note how people use body language in discussions, for example, nodding their head in agreement or shaking their head when they disagree. They may gesture with their hands to emphasize a point.

4 IDENTIFY Read the excerpts from the discussion. What is the purpose of each bold word or phrase? Discuss with a partner.

expressing an opinion	agreeing
asking for someone's opinion	disagreeing

1   No. **I don't think** the driver was speeding. The LIDAR from the farmer's corn field interfered with the police's speed readings.

_____

2   **I'm not sure about that.** I don't think the farmer's LIDAR interfered. Sam, **what's your opinion?**

_____

3   **Well, you could argue that, but on the other hand,** the lack of a law doesn't prove that. The police can request that the LIDAR be shut down because it can interfere with an investigation.

_____

4   **That's interesting, but...**

Yes, but...oh, sorry. **What are your thoughts**, Sam?

_____

5   **That's a good point. So, Phil, explain** how the LIDAR can affect a reading.

_____

6   **Sure.** LIDAR is used by farmers to identify crop production areas. LIDAR can also be used to measure velocity. So, if the officer's system was LIDAR, not RADAR, it could have been read by mistake.

_____

5 ANALYZE Discuss the phrases for agreeing and disagreeing in Exercise 4. What is the level of directness of each one? Rate each one on a scale of 1–4 (1 = most indirect, 4 = most direct). Then share your ideas with the class.

6 🔊 **APPLY** Listen and repeat the opinion phrases.

7 EXPAND Work with a partner. Discuss the following statement. Express your opinions and ask your partner's opinion. Use some of the phrases from the video, the Real-World English box, and Exercise 6.

Computer technology has been the most important discovery of all time.

8 PREPARE Work in a small group. Prepare a short group discussion.

1   Choose one of the topics.
   • There should be no speed limits on interstate highways.
   • Fines for speeding should be a percentage of a driver's yearly income.
2   Take a few minutes to note any opinions that you would like to contribute to the discussion.
3   Consider any opinion phrases you might use.
4   Practice your discussions together. Remember to respond to others' opinions by agreeing or disagreeing and using body language appropriately.

9 IMPROVE Work with another group and watch their discussion. Afterward, talk about how effective the speakers were at giving their opinions and responding to the opinions of others.

GO ONLINE
to create your own version
of the English For Real video.

3.5 Mysteries of the Past

1 ACTIVATE The photo shows an example of Nazca Lines in Peru. Have you heard about the Nazca Lines? If so, what do you know about them? Discuss with the class.

2 IDENTIFY Listen to the discussion. What is it about? How many people are taking part?

3 WHAT'S YOUR ANGLE? Are there any famous past mysteries from your area or country? Is there any place or thing in the world that has always fascinated or puzzled you? Discuss with a partner.

SPEAKING
Supporting opinions with evidence and examples

Opinions are stronger and more meaningful when you can support them with reasons, examples, and evidence. Supporting your opinions will help you to feel confident about contributing your ideas during a discussion and ensure that people listen to your views and take them seriously.

We can use the phrases like these to introduce supporting evidence:

According to a number of sources…
…supports the theory that…
There's evidence to suggest that…
There are several theories about…
Some scholars say…
Researchers have theorized that…

---

4 IDENTIFY Listen again and take brief notes to answer the questions.

1 What are the Nazca Lines?
2 How is it possible to see the lines?
3 What are some of the theories about why the Nazca Lines were made?
4 What have archaeologists found at the end of some Nazca Lines?
5 How do some people think the lines were made?

5 INTERACT Compare answers with a partner. Explain your answers to Exercise 4 using phrases for supporting options with evidence and examples.

6 PREPARE Prepare to have a group discussion in response to the question. Make notes and consider how you will support your opinions with evidence, reasons, and examples.

Which do you think is more important: discovering things about the past or making new discoveries?

7 IMPROVE Read through your notes with a partner. Do you have enough evidence, reasons, and examples to support your opinions? Check for any language errors.

8 INTEGRATE When you are ready, form groups of three or four and have your discussion. When you are giving your opinions, remember to support them with evidence, reasons, and examples.

9 SHARE Discuss in your group. How well do you think you justified your opinions? Which points do you think your classmates made and supported well?

Now go to page 149 for the Unit 3 Review.

4 Privacy

UNIT SNAPSHOT

What are the pros and cons of using the Internet?   41
What are some ways people are dishonest online?   43
Is it possible to lead a truly private life?   46

Can you have privacy in a public place?

Why do people value privacy?

Is privacy a right or a privilege?

BEHIND THE PHOTO

Answer the questions. Then discuss your answers with a partner.

1   How does viewing events through a screen or camera lens affect our experiences?
2   What kinds of things do you do online? What type of sites or apps do you use most often? Why?
3   What impact does the use of smartphones and cameras have on our lives when we are out in public?

REAL-WORLD GOAL

Talk about something you regret

4.1 You Are Not Alone

1 ACTIVATE Look at the infographic. What does it show? Did you know about these ways that others can get information about you?

2 IDENTIFY Work with a partner. Look at the infographic again. List words and phrases from the infographic text that are related to computers and using the Internet. What do they mean?

WHAT HAPPENS WITH

JUST ONE CLICK?

1 Every time you log on to a website, companies can collect personal data about you.

2 Small pieces of information called *cookies*, which keep a record of your Internet searches and online activity, are stored in your web browser.

5 Your social media profile can reveal personal details about you, which others can use.

3 Your personal data is sold to advertising companies.

4 Advertising companies use your browsing history to build a profile of your likes and dislikes.

READING SKILL
Understanding an argument and counterargument

Writers often try to present a balanced view of an issue by examining the arguments for and against it. This shows that they have considered the issue from a variety of perspectives rather than just focusing on expressing their own opinions.

When you are reading, try to identify any arguments and counterarguments in the text. Look for opinion words and phrases (*in contrast*, *don't think*, *disagree*) as well as contrast conjunctions (*but*, *however*) and clauses containing words such as *although*, *despite*, *however*, and *in spite of*. Being able to identify and follow the arguments throughout the text helps you to understand the writer's perspective and their purpose for writing.

3 IDENTIFY Identify words or phrases in the sentences that introduce arguments or counterarguments. Then compare your answers with a partner.

1 I don't think people should use social media in public even though many people would disagree.
2 Of course there are benefits to technology; however, we also need to consider the impact it will have.
3 Despite the popularity of that social media site, I have concerns over its security.
4 In my opinion, the way people use the Internet is not controlled well enough.
5 On the one hand, shopping online is very convenient, but on the other hand, there are definite risks.

4 APPLY Look at the picture and read the title. Read the first and last sentence of each paragraph. Then talk with a partner. What do you think are the main points of the article?

Use It and Lose It

The Internet has become a powerful force that has had an impact on societies at all levels. In developed countries, it seems to be everywhere, with high-speed access from desktop computers and handheld devices at ever-decreasing costs. In some ways, it makes life simpler, but it also presents serious risks. On the one hand, it can be used to build social or professional networks, **accomplish** a wide variety of tasks, or access valuable information and **expertise**. On the other hand, it can be used to spy on our activities, denying us our human right to privacy. So, let's consider the pros and cons of online activity in more detail.

Technologies such as the Internet contribute to loss of privacy because they can be controlled and **exploited**. The benefits of being online include the convenience of being able to browse greater shopping choices, control personal finances, access news and information, share ideas and opinions, **clarify** arguments and questions, and participate in a wider social network, all from the privacy of your own home or personal space. But we are never alone on the Internet. As soon as we click on our Internet **icon**, our privacy is under threat. Law enforcement and national security agencies can easily monitor and analyze email and Internet traffic. And we **don't have to** actively give our personal details for a company to get information about us. Advertising companies can collect data for marketing purposes, without our permission, in a variety of ways. Collecting website access details, placing small pieces of information, or "cookies," on users' devices to track their activities, and asking users to enter personal information before allowing access to certain web pages are all **invasions** of privacy. Although we have the right to protection of privacy, we shouldn't necessarily expect it because the many ways that companies, organizations, and individuals exploit the Internet are still so difficult to monitor.

Workplace use of the Internet is an area in which issues related to privacy can arise. In general, employers can monitor what workers do at the workplace, and **consequently**, the monitoring of emails is permitted in certain circumstances. Of course, employers **need to** ensure that their employees aren't spending time on social media during working hours. But simply informing employees that their online activities are being monitored is not enough since circumstances may arise where they need to send or receive mail that is personal and private. As a result, some employers allow emails but make it clear that employees **must not** access certain websites at work. However, employer–employee privacy issues go further than that. There have been cases reported in the media where employees have been fired for things that they posted on social media in their free time, even though their actions were not related to the company they work for. In such a situation, employees may feel concerned about their privacy, but it's difficult to argue that when you post your personal activities in a public **forum**.

So, as a relatively new technology, the Internet can be both convenient and invasive. It creates new opportunities and offers greater freedom of expression, but it also brings many legal and moral questions related to privacy. Although greater regulation of privacy abuses is needed, ultimately, it is the responsibility of the Internet user to ensure that they do their best to maintain their own privacy to protect themselves from being exploited by others.

🎓+ Oxford 5000™

—adapted from *Encyclopedia of Human Rights*, edited by David P. Forsythe

5 **IDENTIFY** Read the article. What are some of the arguments and counterarguments the writer presents? Take notes in the chart and share your ideas with a partner.

Arguments	Counterarguments
In some ways, it makes life simpler,	but it also presents serious risks.

6 **INTERACT** Do you agree with the writer's arguments? Why or why not? Discuss with a partner.

7 **WHAT'S YOUR ANGLE?** How important is online privacy to you? Have you (or anyone you know) had any negative experiences? Tell a partner.

8 VOCABULARY Read the words in the box. Identify them in the article and use context to figure out the meanings. Then use the words to complete the sentences.

accomplish	exploited	clarify	forum
consequently	icon	expertise	invasion(s)

1 Social media sites are often a _____ for people to discuss current events and issues.
   (place where people exchange opinions)

2 I asked her to _____ her explanation; I didn't understand it the first time.
   (make clearer)

3 Elderly people are frequently _____ by criminals.
   (treated in order for personal gain)

4 The company's management team found that average employees spent at least an hour per day on social media sites; _____, they banned the use of social media altogether.
   (as a result)

5 Do you think it's an _____ of your privacy if someone looks over your shoulder when you're reading a newspaper on the bus or train?
   (an unwelcome act)

6 I prefer to work alone; I can _____ much more that way.
   (succeed in completing)

7 The technician explained that I was clicking on the wrong _____.
   (small symbol on a computer screen)

8 We are looking for someone with _____ in computer programming.
   (expert knowledge or skill)

GRAMMAR IN CONTEXT
Modals of necessity, obligation, and prohibition

We use certain modals and verbs when we want to express:

• obligation and necessity: *must, have to, need to, shouldn't.*
   Employers **need to** *ensure that their employees aren't spending time on social media.*
   Employees **must** *use only their company email accounts while at the office.*

• lack of obligation and necessity: *don't have to, don't need to.*
   We **don't have to** *actively give our personal details for a company to get information about us.*
   You **don't need to** *enter the password every time you log in, just the first time.*

• permission and prohibition: *can, can't.*
   Even though some employers allow emails, employees **cannot** *access certain websites at work.*
   In general, employers **can** *monitor what workers do in the workplace.*

See Grammar focus on page 162.

9 IDENTIFY Choose the best option in each sentence.

1 You *don't need to / can't* access the shared database without the correct password.

2 You *don't have to / shouldn't* post personal photos or videos on the company website.

3 We *can / have to* receive personal emails at work.

4 It's OK; you *don't need to / shouldn't* explain. I understand the situation.

5 You *can / have to* sign a permission form before you take photos.

10 INTEGRATE Complete the company memo with modals from the box. Three of the items have two possible answers. Then discuss the policies with a partner. Do you agree with the rules? What do you think are reasonable company policies for computer or Internet use?

can	cannot	don't have to
may	must	need to

✉

Memo

To: All employees

Re: New (strict) computer policy

The following points are updates to the company computer policy. These policies ¹ _____ be strictly followed by all employees.

Company computers and Internet are for company business only. They ² _____ be used by employees for personal reasons during work hours.

If employees ³ _____ send emails or use the Internet for personal reasons, they ⁴ _____ do so only during their lunch breaks.

In emergency situations, employees ⁵ _____ request permission to use company computers or Internet for personal reasons.

Finally, office computers ⁶ _____ be shut down at the end of the workday. Section managers will check each employee's browser history at the end of the shift.

Thank you for your cooperation.

11 WHAT'S YOUR ANGLE? Can you imagine life without the Internet? Would it be a good thing or a disaster? Why? Share your ideas with a partner or small group.

1 ACTIVATE Look at the poster. What message is it designed to give? Why is this issue so important? Discuss your ideas with a partner or in a small group.

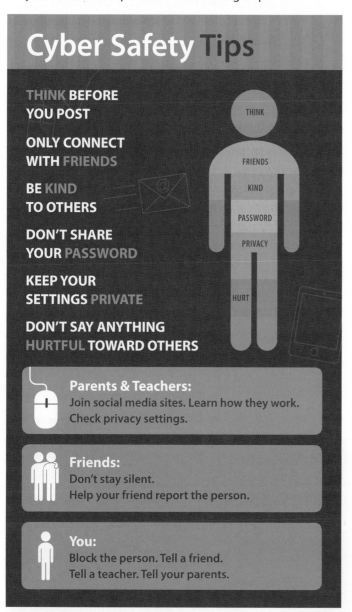

2 INTEGRATE Discuss the questions with a small group.

1 What are some of the pros and cons of using social media?

2 What do you think about the advice in the three boxes at the bottom of the poster?

3 At what age is it OK for children to start using social media? Why?

4 Should parents monitor their children's social media accounts?

3 INTEGRATE Read the essay. What issue does the writer present? What is the writer's opinion about it?

Keeping Kids Safe Online

The question of whether parents should have access to their children's online activity is one that any family with Internet access no doubt discusses frequently. In my opinion, when it comes to online activity, personal safety and security are the most important factors, and, therefore, parents should be able to monitor their children's online activities.

Teenagers are beginning to feel the need for more independence and, therefore, may have strong feelings about their personal privacy. They may not want their parents to know about certain friends or relationships or other details about their social lives since their parents may disapprove. Additionally, teens may conclude that they are mature and responsible enough to recognize and avoid the potential dangers that may be found online. However, since teenagers are not yet adults, I believe it is ultimately parents' responsibility to ensure that their child is being safe and responsible while online. Teens are not always aware of the dangers of sharing personal information online, and as a result, they are more likely to be exploited. Some teens who share personal details, such as their address or where they go to school, with online strangers may be putting themselves in danger.

In addition to protecting kids from "stranger danger," parents might detect issues such as cyberbullying, which could have a negative impact on their child's mental well-being. Consequently, if problems arise, parents can help their child deal with them in an appropriate manner. It could be argued that parents' monitoring of their children's online activity suggests a lack of trust. A few years ago when I was a high school student, I was offended when my parents asked for the passwords to my social media accounts. I felt like they just wanted to control my life. At first, I refused to share my log-in information. However, looking back, I should have understood that it wasn't me that my parents mistrusted; it was the people "out there" on the Internet. I shouldn't have argued. I understand now that due to the many potential dangers, parents need to know if their children are doing something dangerous online.

In conclusion, despite the fact that everyone has a right to privacy, parents' main priority should always be to ensure that their children are safe. For this reason, I believe parents should monitor their children's online activities and social media accounts until their children are mature and responsible enough to fully understand all the risks and how to avoid them.

4 ASSESS Read the statements about the essay. Decide if the sentences are true (T) or false (F).

The writer thinks that…

1 many families deal with this issue. ___
2 problems can arise due to children's need for independence. ___
3 most teens know how to avoid the dangers of online activity. ___
4 parents can help their children deal with problems. ___
5 her parents were wrong to ask for her social media passwords. ___
6 parents should monitor their children's online activities. ___

WRITING SKILL
Using reason and result linking words

We use linking words and phrases to express reason and result. These are especially useful when we are writing about important issues and presenting arguments. Common examples include:

- reason: *because, on account of, since, as, due to, in case*

  Since *teenagers are not yet adults,…*

- result: *as a result (of), therefore, consequently, as a consequence*

  …***as a result**, they are more likely to be exploited.*

Being able to express reason strengthens your arguments, and explaining the results or consequences of an action shows that you have considered an issue from more than one perspective.

5 IDENTIFY Identify these examples of reason and result linking expressions in the essay. Write the missing linking word or phrase.

1 Teenagers are beginning to feel the need for more independence and, _____, may have strong feelings about their personal privacy.
2 They may not want their parents to know about certain friends or relationships or other details about their social lives _____ parents may disapprove.
3 Teens are not always aware of the dangers of sharing personal information online, and _____, they are more likely to be exploited.
4 Parents might be able to detect issues such as cyberbullying, which could have a negative impact on their child's mental well-being. _____, if any problems arise, parents can help their child deal with them in an appropriate manner.
5 I understand now that _____ the many potential dangers, parents need to know if their children are doing something dangerous online.

A young tourist in Lecce, Italy

6 APPLY Complete the sentences with a suitable reason-result linking word or phrase from the box. Sometimes more than one answer is possible.

on account of	since	due to
consequently	therefore	as a result

1 The company started using targeted marketing and _____, sales have increased.

2 My brother doesn't do online banking anymore _____ his account was hacked.

3 The amount of junk email I get has decreased _____ of my new privacy settings.

4 We can't access certain websites through our work computers _____ employees spending too much time on social media.

5 Sales of the product have decreased _____ the problems that people have reported online.

6 _____ of the news report that showed video cameras being used to spy on ordinary citizens in their homes, many people started covering the camera lenses on their personal computers.

7 INTERACT Identify the sentences in Exercise 6 with a partner. Which part of each sentence or sentences expresses the reason? Which part expresses the result?

> **GRAMMAR IN CONTEXT Modals of regret**
>
> We use *should have* or *shouldn't have* + past participle to express regret or disapproval about something we or others did or didn't do in the past.
>
> *Karen lost all her work when her computer was stolen. She really* **should have** *stored her files online.*
> *You* **shouldn't have** *opened that email. It looks like it contained a computer virus.*
>
> When we speak or write informally, we use the contraction *should've*.

See Grammar focus on page 162.

8 IDENTIFY Find the two examples of modals of regret in the essay in Exercise 3. What does the writer express regret about?

1 _____

2 _____

9 WHAT'S YOUR ANGLE? Do you have any personal "rules" for your own or your family members' use of the Internet? What do you or your family members do to protect yourselves from different dangers online?

10 IDENTIFY Read the essay again. Make notes to answer the questions. Then compare ideas with a partner.

1 How many paragraphs are there?

2 What is the main idea of each paragraph?

3 Look at the arguments and counterarguments in the essay. How are they organized? Can you see a pattern?

4 How does the writer conclude the essay? Are there any new arguments introduced in the concluding paragraph?

11 PREPARE Plan to write an essay of your own on one of the following topics.

- Parents should be able to track their children's location using their smartphones.
- Parents should be able to control which social media sites their children use.
- People shouldn't expect privacy if they want to use social media.

Follow these steps.

1 Write down two arguments and think of counterarguments for each.

2 Plan the four paragraphs of your essay: introduction, argument 1 + counterargument, argument 2 + counterargument, and conclusion.

3 Consider what reasons or examples you will include to support each argument and counterargument.

12 WRITE Write a draft of your essay. While you write, refer back to your notes and to the information in the Writing Skill box.

13 IMPROVE Read your essay and correct any grammar and spelling mistakes. Check for examples of what you have learned.

Writing Checklist

☐ Have you written a total of four paragraphs?

☐ Did you include both arguments and counterarguments?

☐ Did you use linking words showing reason and result?

☐ Did you use modals of regret, necessity, obligation, or prohibition?

☐ Did you include a conclusion that summarizes your overall opinion?

14 SHARE Read a classmate's essay. Say which arguments in their essay you agree with and what they have done well.

4.3 Privacy Matters

1 ACTIVATE Look at the photos. In what ways is our privacy invaded? Do you feel that these ways of watching the public are acceptable? Share your ideas in a small group.

LISTENING SKILL Listening for gist

When we listen, we often don't need to focus on every detail. When we listen to longer pieces of information, such as news stories or lectures, it's usually enough to listen for the gist. This means focusing on just the general topic and the main ideas. As you listen, ask yourself questions such as:

- What is the genre (e.g., radio show, debate, news report, etc.)?
- What is the topic?
- How many speakers are there?
- What are some of the main points?

Listening for gist is a useful strategy to help you understand the most important points of a longer listening.

2 ASSESS Listen to the first part of a radio show. What kind of show is it? What is it about? Who is going to take part in the discussion?

3 IDENTIFY Listen to the rest of the radio show and focus on getting the gist. What are the main points each caller makes? Take notes as you listen.

1 Barry: _____

_____

2 Maya: _____

_____

3 Sandra: _____

_____

4 INTERACT Compare your ideas about the gist of the radio show with a partner. What are some other things you listen to in English where listening for gist would be useful?

5 IDENTIFY Listen to the radio show again. Decide whether Barry (B), Maya (M), or Sandra (S) expressed each opinion. More than one answer may be possible.

1 "I never connect on social media with someone I don't know." ___

2 "Probably no one's going to watch me on video." ___

3 "The online privacy problem is the fault of social media companies." ___

4 "People need to live their lives without feeling like they're being watched." ___

5 "Ordinary people don't have to worry about being watched by video cameras." ___

6 "The police can take video of anyone at any time." ___

VOCABULARY DEVELOPMENT
Phrases for clarification

When we are speaking, we often use phrases for clarification to help the listener understand what we mean. Some common phrases are *that is*, *that is to say*, *to clarify*, *to put it another way*, and *in other words*. These phrases are particularly useful when we are trying to justify our opinions or convince others that we are right.

After these phrases, the speaker clarifies what was said previously by providing examples or more details, or by repeating the information in different words.

6 IDENTIFY Listen to the excerpts from the radio show. Complete each excerpt with a clarification phrase. Compare your answers with a partner.

1 I don't see cameras as an invasion of privacy. _____, if I haven't done anything wrong, why do I have to hide?

2 _____, there are plenty of people out there committing crimes, and the police have to catch them somehow.

3 _____, we must have the freedom to live our lives without feeling like we're being monitored.

4 _____, I want my privacy, and surely, I have a right to it, don't I?

5 _____, I have a rule that I never connect with someone unless I know something about them. That's my right, isn't it?

7 WHAT'S YOUR ANGLE? Look again at the statements in Exercise 6. Do you agree with them? Tell a partner.

GRAMMAR IN CONTEXT
Past modals of deduction

When we make a deduction, we use information or clues that we have in order to make a conclusion or a guess about something.

We use *must have* (or *must not have*) + past participle when we feel we are certain about something.

*She **must have** forgotten her credit card at the gas station. That was the last place she used it.*
*The thief **must not have** noticed the camera in the store.*

Tip: In speaking and informal writing, we generally use *'ve* instead of the full form *have*.
*He **must've** been mistaken.*

We use *can't* or *couldn't have* + past participle when we feel certain something didn't happen or wasn't true.

*John **couldn't have** posted that picture. He hates using social media.*

We use *might*, *could*, or *may have* + past participle when we think something possibly happened or was possibly true.

*I **might have given** him my email password a long time ago. I can't remember.*
*She wasn't certain, but she said it **could have been** John in the video.*

See Grammar focus on page 162.

8 APPLY Complete the sentences with a past modal of deduction + the past participle of the verb in parentheses. More than one modal may be possible for some items.

1 Police found the criminal's car at the station. He _____ the area by train. (leave)

2 Philip left his job at the computer security company. He _____ that type of work. (enjoy)

3 The investigators weren't sure what caused the computer problem. They think it _____ an employee error. (be)

4 You _____ me on the video. I didn't leave home yesterday. (see)

5 Liza didn't report her wallet missing for several hours. She _____ (notice) it was missing.

6 Alex missed the company meeting about Internet security. He _____ about it. (know)

PRONUNCIATION SKILL
Reduced form of *have* in past modals

When speaking, we often contract *have* to *'ve* or ə (known as the schwa sound). This helps to make our speech sound more natural in English.

must've / mustə   might've / mightə   could've / couldə
must not've / must nottə   might not've / might nottə
couldn't have / couldn'ə

Note that in the negative reductions the *t* is also reduced or silent.

9 ◀)) **IDENTIFY** Listen to the sentences. Cross out the past modal and write the reduction you hear.

1 They might have been on vacation when the robbery happened.

2 He couldn't have known where I was unless he had followed me.

3 Tom must not have gotten the company memo about the new policy.

4 She must have been really upset when she saw your comment online.

5 You could have called the police when you learned your account had been hacked.

6 If I had known about the privacy issue, I might not have sent that email.

10 APPLY Work with a partner. Take turns reading the sentences from Exercise 9 aloud. Use the reduced forms of the past modals.

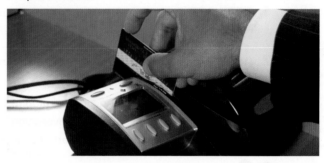

11 INTEGRATE Complete the sentences with your own ideas. Use modals of deduction.

1 There's money missing from my bank account! Someone _____.

2 Oh, no! I lost my credit card! Do you think _____?

3 How did that company know my address? My personal details _____.

4 I've looked everywhere for my keys. I guess _____.

5 I keep getting pop-up ads on my computer screens. I _____.

12 INTERACT Read your completed comments from Exercise 11. Have you had any similar experiences? Share them with a partner.

13 WHAT'S YOUR ANGLE? Think of a time when you felt your privacy was invaded. Prepare to tell a partner about it by writing a few notes to answer the questions. Then share your story with a partner or small group.

1 What was the situation?

2 Who invaded your privacy? How did they do it?

3 How did you feel?

4 How could you prevent it from happening again?

4.4 If Only I Hadn't

1 ACTIVATE Work with a partner. What are some things that people often have regrets about? Have you ever hurt someone's feelings without meaning to? What happened? How was the situation resolved?

2 ASSESS Look at the pictures. Discuss the questions with a partner.

Picture 1: Where are Kevin and Andy?

Do you think they are having a formal or informal conversation? Why?

Picture 2: Who is involved in this conversation? How well do they all know each other? Do you think they are having a serious or lighthearted conversation? Why?

3 ▶ IDENTIFY Watch the video and find out what happened. Answer the questions.

What regrets does each person have?

Sarah: _____   Max: _____

_____   _____

Andy: _____   Kevin: _____

_____

REAL-WORLD ENGLISH Expressing regret

Most phrases for expressing regret can be used to express both minor and more serious types of regrets.

I shouldn't have had a second cup of coffee.   I wish I'd never quit school.

In addition to the words you use, the context of the conversation, tone (sighing, speaking in a sad- or thoughtful-sounding voice), and body language (looking downward, making a sad or worried facial expression) indicate the level of seriousness.

The listener also needs to be able to recognize and respond appropriately when someone expresses regret. You can do this by using phrases that show agreement, sympathy, or support.

I'm sorry.   I know what you mean.   That's too bad.   Well, at least you ordered a small coffee.

You can also use body language to react to someone's expression of regret, for example, nodding or shaking your head or—if you know someone well—touching the person's arm or patting them on the back or shoulder to show support.

ENGLISH FOR REAL

4 EXPAND How serious do you think the person's regret is in each case? Rate each one on a scale of 1–4 (1 = least serious, 4 = most serious) and explain your choices.

	Regret 1	Regret 2
Sarah		
Andy		
Max		
Kevin		

5 NOTICE What are some of the ways the others respond to each of the regrets (e.g., with sympathy, with advice)?

6 EXPAND How do the speakers use body language to show their feelings?

7 🔊 **IDENTIFY** Listen to excerpts from the video. Complete the sentences.

1 Well, I _____ started drinking it. Now I can't wake up without at least two cups!

2 I knew I _____.

3 It was a joke! I really _____ done that.

4 Yeah, _____ sent it to Phil.

5 I _____ to be someone I'm not by wearing ridiculous clothes.

6 _____. Everyone will forget about it eventually.

7 I _____ a year off to travel before going to college.

8 Max _____. Go talk to him.

8 ANALYZE Work with a partner. Read through Exercise 7 together and compare your answers. Do the sentences express regret or respond to others' regrets? Write the numbers of the sentences in the correct columns.

Expressing regrets	Responding to regrets

9 INTERACT Do you feel the people in the video responded appropriately to each other's regrets? How did they use words and body language?

10 WHAT'S YOUR ANGLE? Which of the regrets expressed in the video do you feel was the most serious? Why? Have you or has anyone you know had similar regrets about things they've done or haven't done? What were they? How did the situations work out in the end?

11 PREPARE Choose a regret from the list (or use an example of your own). Write down a few phrases you will use to express your regret.

- You arrived at your favorite restaurant to find out that the wait for a table is two hours.
- You bought something that was too expensive.
- You wore something inappropriate for a particular situation.
- You didn't ask for something you want or need (for example, a higher salary, better working conditions).
- You don't spend enough time with someone.

12 INTERACT Now work with a small group to share your regrets. Practice responding to others' regrets. Afterward, talk about how effectively everyone expressed regret and responded appropriately considering the level of seriousness.

GO ONLINE
to create your own version
of the English For Real video.

4.5 Reply All

1 **ACTIVATE** Work with a partner. Look at the title of the lesson. When and where do you see the phrase *reply all*? Do you use the *reply all* option regularly? Why or why not?

2 **IDENTIFY** Look at the illustrations. What do you think has happened? What might the people be thinking? How do you think they feel?

3 ◀))) **IDENTIFY** Listen to someone telling a colleague about an experience they once had at work. How do the images in Exercise 2 relate to this experience?

🎯 SPEAKING Describing experiences

When we describe experiences, our narrative often follows a cause-and-effect format. We describe one action—either our own or another person's—and then we explain the reaction or consequence of that action. Being able to do this effectively will help you "paint a picture" of your experiences to the listener.

To describe your actions and the reasons for them, use phrases such as *due to*, *as*, *since*, *because*, and *on account of*.

To describe the consequences of your actions, use phrases such as *as a result*, *because of this*, *so*, and *consequently*.

---

4 ◀))) **IDENTIFY** Listen again and take brief notes to answer the questions.

1. How does Ian feel about telling his story now?
2. What did he think about his new boss at first?
3. What was the content of the boss's email?
4. Why does Ian think he got the email?
5. How did Ian react?
6. What were the consequences of Ian's actions?

5 **INTEGRATE** Compare answers with a partner. Describe Ian's experience in as much detail as you can. Do you know anyone who has had a similar experience?

6 **IDENTIFY** Look at the excerpts from the conversation. Identify words and phrases that outline actions and consequences.

1. I was completely surprised since he had never spoken to me or given me any clue that there was a problem.
2. He clicked "reply all" by accident, and as a result, the message ended up in my inbox, too.
3. On account of my anger when I saw the email and realized what it was, I did something I probably shouldn't have.
4. I said that I didn't want to work for him anyway because he was such a rude person, and I thought he was the one who shouldn't have been hired.
5. The president said the company needed people who could work well together and whom he could trust to use email appropriately; consequently, he fired both of us.

7 **PREPARE** Prepare to describe a time when you said (or wrote) something to someone that you shouldn't have.

1. Take a few minutes to write down the main actions you (or they) took and their consequences.
2. Consider any words and phrases you can use to outline actions and their consequences.
3. Remember to say how you felt and explain any regrets you have about the incident.

8 **INTEGRATE** When you are ready, work in a group to give your descriptions.

9 **WHAT'S YOUR ANGLE?** Work with another group and listen to their descriptions. Afterward, give them feedback.

Now go to page 150 for the Unit 4 Review.

5 Alternatives

UNIT SNAPSHOT

Are robots replacing humans? 52

What does it mean to live "off the grid"? 58

Will alternative medicine take over
mainstream treatments? 62

▼ What alternatives does
this photo illustrate?

▼ Why do some people choose
"alternative" lifestyles?

▼ Is it good to be different?

BEHIND THE PHOTO

REAL-WORLD GOAL

Consider an alternative
way of doing something

Answer the questions. Then discuss your answers with a partner.

1 Look at the topics in the box. What are some examples of each topic that might
be described as "alternative"? Why?

| living spaces | transportation | fashion or style |
| health or medicine | education | art |

2 What is your opinion of any of the alternative things you mentioned in question 1?

3 Do you think society is generally accepting of "alternatives"? Why or why not?

4 Can you think of alternatives that might offer solutions to any of the problems affecting
the modern world?

5.1 The Human–Robot Connection

1 ACTIVATE Look at the photos. How are the people interacting with robots? Do you ever communicate with robots? How and why?

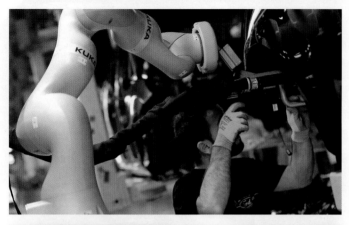

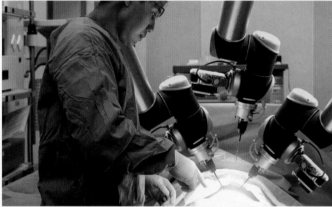

2 INTERACT Work with a partner. Answer the questions and discuss your ideas about the photos in Exercise 1.

1 What are other ways that humans interact with robots or robotics?

2 How has the use of computers and robots changed society?

3 How might society continue to change as a result of

3 ASSESS Read the online article. Does it mention any of your ideas from Exercises 1 and 2?

 ## Social Robots

In the past, designers of electronics amazed the public with complicated robots that displayed lifelike physical features and behaviors. Science fiction authors further excited readers' imaginations with androids with superhuman qualities that had the ability to do great harm to human society. Later, the commercial and research fields began to focus more on practical applications on the factory floor, where robotics provided automatic operations for repetitive tasks, such as welding and painting. More recently, modern robotics has begun to return to its roots since advances in science and engineering are enabling the creation of "intelligent" machines that can interact directly with people. What was once science fiction is now a reality, and the future will probably bring robots and humans closer together.

The field of social robotics combines several fields outside engineering and computer science—namely, design, psychology, and sociology—with the aim of making interactions between robots and humans more natural. Creating robots with humanlike physical and emotional attributes opens possibilities for a social structure of human–computer interaction. Design helps to realize the physical, emotional, and expressive qualities of a social robot. Principles of cognitive psychology lend models for human learning and communication. Sociology provides an understanding of the social structure of human societies. Together the robot design team must attempt to present these intelligent and expressive behaviors on the part of the robot. With increasingly sophisticated technology, robotics engineers hope that the robots of the future will "feel" and express the full range of human emotions. Indeed, it is not unrealistic to predict that humans and robots will someday form true interpersonal relationships, that is, human–robot friendships.

Communication and dialogue

Natural interaction between robots and humans requires all modalities of human–human interaction to apply to robots as well. Basic abilities that are being developed for robots include gestures, facial expressions, and speech recognition. At the more advanced level, robots must be able to reason about human behavior and must learn to respond appropriately. However, given the time required for robots to process and react to information, some people believe that robotics researchers are never going to recreate the natural speed and spontaneity of human communication.

Social learning

Through a programming process called *online learning*, social robots are provided with a rich model of human social behavior and massive input concerning social interactions. Through this process, robots develop an internal database of responses for use in future interactions with humans. Various companies and universities are currently developing social robots, and the next several decades are going to bring a considerable number of social applications for robots. This includes teaching children with learning difficulties, and serving as companions for the elderly or for those who are confined to their homes due to illness.

Emotional intelligence

There is significant debate over the role of emotion in robotic systems. Some social roboticists argue that the path to effective interaction with humans is for robots to model internal human emotions as accurately as possible, in effect producing a human replica. Researchers continue to conduct experiments with the goal of developing social robots that model human feelings, such as frustration, happiness, and loneliness. Despite their best efforts, however, it is unlikely that robots will ever be able to reach the full level of complexity of human emotion.

—adapted from *Science, Technology, and Society*, edited by Sal Restivo

When you read, you will sometimes come across words that are spelled the same way but that have completely different meanings. These are called *homographs*.

field
(n.) subject or activity that somebody works in or is interested in
The **field** of social robotics combines several **fields** outside of engineering and computer science.
(n.) area of land used for growing crops or keeping animals in
The farmer brought the horses from the **field** and put them in the barn for the night.

Homographs may be the same part of speech, as in *field*, or they may be different parts of speech.

process
(n.) series of things done in order to achieve a result
(v.) treat something in a particular way to achieve a desirable change

The homographs for *process* have the same stress and pronunciation; however, some homographs have different stress patterns.

record (re' cord) [short e sound, stress on the first syllable]
(n.) written account of something
record (re cord') [long e sound, stress on the second syllable]
(v.) put down in writing or some other permanent form for later reference

Homographs can interfere with comprehension. If a word doesn't make sense in context, check the part of speech first, then use a dictionary to find out if there are other meanings.

4 IDENTIFY Match the words to their definitions. Then identify the words in the article. Which definition, A or B, is being used?

| ☐ express | ☐ conduct | ☐ rich |
| 1 commercial | ☐ models | ☐ present |

	Definition A	**Definition B**
1	noun: a television or radio advertisement	adjective: concerned with or engaged in commerce
2	noun: the manner in which a person behaves	verb: to organize and carry out
3	verb: to convey (a thought or feeling) in words or by gestures and conduct	adjective: operating at high speed
4	noun: examples to follow or imitate	noun: people employed to display clothes by wearing them
5	adjective: existing or occurring now	verb: to show or offer (something) for others to scrutinize or consider
6	adjective: having a great deal of money or assets	adjective: existing in plentiful quantities

5 **INTEGRATE** Read the article. Decide if the sentences are true (T) or false (F), or not given (NG).

1   Social robots that can interact at natural speed with humans already exist. ___

2   Social robots learn about social interactions through exposure to a huge amount of data about human social behaviour. ___

3   Researchers model human interactions which the social robots use to build up a database of responses they can use for future interactions. ___

4   Potential uses for social robots include being companions for people who are old or too ill to leave their homes. ___

5   Creating robots with emotions is incredibly challenging, but given time, it's probable that robots will eventually be able to express all human emotions. ___

6 **WHAT'S YOUR ANGLE?** How could a social robot improve your life now?

GRAMMAR IN CONTEXT Future forms

In English, there is no future tense. We use a number of different forms to talk about the future.

We use both *will* and *be going to* to make predictions. *Will* indicates a guess or a prediction that isn't certain.

*Robots **will** probably take over most manufacturing jobs in the future.*

We use *be going to* when we are more certain of an outcome and when we specify a time in the future.

*In the next five years, researchers **are going to** develop a fully automated car that needs no human input at all.*

We use the simple present to talk about an event on a schedule or timetable.

*The robotics lecture **starts** at 10.30.*

We use the present continuous to talk about arrangements and fixed plans.

*A robotics expert **is visiting** the university next month.*

See Grammar focus on page 163.

7 **ASSESS** Identify all the predictions in the article. What future forms do they use? Are they based on personal opinion or actual evidence?

8 **APPLY** Complete the sentences with the verb in parentheses using the correct future form. Sometimes more than one answer is possible.

1   By the year 2010, I predict that robot professors

_____

all classes at the university. (teach)

2   The Robotics Department

_____

an open house on their latest research next week. (hold)

3   Humans' overreliance on technology

_____

major problems for future generations. (cause)

4   My appointment with the robot doctor

_____

at 3.15. (be)

5   Someday, we

_____

robots were never invented. (wish)

**VOCABULARY DEVELOPMENT
Adverbs of probability**

We use adverbs of probability to express how certain we are about our predictions.

Not certain: *maybe, perhaps, possibly*

Somewhat certain: *probably, (it is) likely (that), (it is) unlikely (that)*

Very certain: *surely, definitely, doubtless*

***Maybe** in the future robots will feel sadness and happiness. The future will **probably** bring robots and humans closer together.*

*Many companies will **doubtless** invest in social robots to reduce their staff and pension costs.*

Pay attention to sentence structure: some adverbs of probability are used at the beginning of a sentence, and some before the main verb or after *be*.

9 **BUILD** Read the statements. How certain are the predictions? Rate them 1–3 (1 = very certain).

1   Surely robot drivers will be safer than human drivers.

2   Some people are probably going to lose their jobs to social robots.

3   My children will likely work with social robots, but I won't.

4   Perhaps a robot will be a more trustworthy friend than a human!

5   The global economy is doubtless going to be affected by robots in the workplace.

10 **EXPAND** Write predictions using the prompts and your own opinion. Use adverbs of probability to show how certain you are.

1   robot doctor / cure cancer
    A robot doctor will probably cure cancer.

2   social robots / create new jobs

3   children / love having robot friends

4   people / find robots frightening

5   there / be / war with robots

11 **WHAT'S YOUR ANGLE?** Do you think human-like social robots will exist in your lifetime? How comfortable would you feel if your doctor, teacher or taxi driver was a robot? Would you like a robot as a friend? Why or why not?

5.2 Alternative Solutions

1 ACTIVATE Look at the images. Answer the questions.

1 What chore is the person doing in each picture? How do they feel about the task?

2 Rate your feelings about the chores in the pictures on a scale of 1–4 (1 = I enjoy doing it, 4 = I hate doing it).

3 Are there any everyday chores you wish you didn't have to do? What are they?

2 ▶ IDENTIFY Watch the video. What is the purpose of the TaskRabbit website?

3 ▶ INTERACT Answer the questions with a partner. Then watch the video again and check.

1 Why does Tony think people hire "task rabbits"?

2 How does the website work?

3 Why might being a "task rabbit" be a good alternative to other jobs?

4 What types of tasks are common?

5 Which types of skills pay best?

6 What are the benefits of being a "task rabbit," according to Tony?

7 What plans does Tony have for his future?

4 WHAT'S YOUR ANGLE? Have you heard of any sites like TaskRabbit? Would you be interested in hiring or becoming a "task rabbit"? What types of tasks would you hire someone to do? What tasks might you be able to do for others?

5 ASSESS Read the student essay. What was the student's problem, and how did she solve it?

My advisor has asked me to write about my experiences in order to help new students. Universities and colleges are aware of the challenges students face in financing their education and paying their living expenses, and they know that many of their students work part time. In some cases, this has an adverse effect on their studies. I was in the same predicament when I started my degree two years ago, but I found a solution which others might like to consider. By the time I graduate, I will have been working for three years, and I will have increased my job prospects. In other words, working part time as a student can be a good thing if you choose the right work.

I am a mature student in graphic design, and I have extensive experience working in business administration. Although I had saved enough money to pay for my tuition, I didn't have enough for essentials such as rent and food. I realized I would need to have an income to support myself while I was in school. However, most of the jobs available required long hours or hours that clashed with my class schedule. Then I found what looked like the perfect position: a local graphic design company needed someone to do their accounts and general business administration tasks. There was one problem: they were looking for an unpaid intern, not an employee. However, when I looked at their list of requirements, including experience using particular accountancy programs, I thought it was unlikely that they would find an intern. So, I contacted them and offered them an alternative: I would work for them at an hourly rate, and they could contract me for particular tasks. When they failed to find an intern, they generously agreed to my proposal.

That was two years ago. This time next year, I will have graduated, and I'll be looking for a permanent position. My part-time job means I will have completed my studies without running up huge debts. I've made valuable contributions at a company I respect. If they are unable to promote me to a full-time position, I'll still have gained three years of valuable work experience that I can include on my resume. But the benefits aren't all mine. Specifically, my employers have had the convenience of a professional business administrator without the expense of a permanent staff member that their small business couldn't afford.

ℙ⁺ Oxford 5000™

6 EXPAND Read the essay again. Choose the correct phrase to make each statement complete and true.

1 Many students work part time because they need to *get work experience / earn money*.

2 The student is an experienced *business administrator / graphic designer*.

3 The company initially wanted a(n) *professional / intern* to do their admin tasks.

4 The student gets paid *a regular salary / depending on the work she does*.

5 The company has *the convenience of a business administrator / a permanent business administrator*.

GRAMMAR IN CONTEXT
Future perfect

We use the future perfect to talk about an action that will be completed before a certain time in the future or will be still in progress up to a certain time in the future. We form the future perfect using *will + have +* past participle. We often use *by* or *before +* a time expression to say when the action will be finished.

*The student says she **will have graduated** by this time next year.*

We use the future perfect continuous to talk about a present action that will continue up to a particular time in the future. Time expressions are normally used.

*I'll **have been working** for this company for five years in December.*

See Grammar focus on page 163.

---

7 IDENTIFY Identify all the instances of future perfect in the essay in Exercise 5. How many are there? What time expressions are used?

8 ASSESS Choose the correct form—future perfect or future perfect continuous—to complete each statement.

1 The government will have *spent / been spending* $100 million on the project by the end of the current fiscal year.

2 Marcella hopes she'll have *passed / been passing* her driving test before April.

3 The professor talks too much! He'll have *talked / been talking* nonstop by the end of the lesson!

4 I'll have *studied / been studying* for five years by the time I am fully qualified.

5 We're late! The lecture will *have finished / been finishing* before we get there!

9 APPLY Complete the text using the correct form of the future perfect or future perfect continuous and the verbs in parentheses.

Lots of people think that being a student is easy because you don't have any real responsibilities,

---

but that's not true. My older sister is studying chemical engineering at university, and I know how hard she works. By the end of this year, she [1]_____ (work) and studying simultaneously for two years. What's more, she [2]_____ (have) only two weeks' vacation. She motivates herself by setting goals. By the end of the semester, she hopes she [3]_____ (complete) her course work and [4]_____ (give) all her presentations. Then, she [5]_____ (do) all the hard work before the exams the following year.

WRITING SKILL Introducing examples and explanations

We use particular words and phrases to introduce examples and explanations. These are useful "signposts" in our writing, which help our readers follow our ideas.

Common signposts for examples and explanations include: *to illustrate / demonstrate, as an illustration, specifically, that is, in the case of, such as,* and *in other words.*

Try to notice how writers use these words and phrases in texts and use them in your own writing. Being able to give examples and explain them in more detail shows that you have considered or researched an issue thoroughly and understand it.

10 IDENTIFY Identify three examples and explanation expressions in the student essay.

11 INTEGRATE Complete each sentence with an expression for introducing examples or explanations.

1 Specialized skills, _____, skills that require specialized training, earn more money than less skilled tasks.

2 To _____ the problem, imagine a student attending lectures all day and working all evening. When will they have time to study?

3 In my free time, I do volunteer work. _____ I work at a home for the elderly.

4 You need a variety of skills, _____, carpentry, plumbing, and electrical skills, to do this job.

5 In the _____ elderly people, they often appreciate help with their grocery shopping.

12 VOCABULARY Complete the job ad with the words in the box. Change the form as needed.

contract (vb)	income (n)	extensive (adj)
contribution (n)	finance (vb)	generously (adv)
prospect (n)	promote (vb)	

Administrator wanted

Small business requires part-time administrator. The perfect candidate will have [1]_____ experience of office management and accountancy. You will be [2]_____ at an hourly rate, with an estimated [3]_____ of $15,000 per year. No pension [4]_____ or vacation pay, but there is the [5]_____ of being [6]_____ to a full-time position for the right candidate. The company would be willing to [7]_____ further study in business administration and would reward [8]_____ an ambitious, hard-working employee.

13 EXPAND Write definitions for the words from the essay in Exercise 8 and from Exercise 12. Use context to help you. Check with a dictionary.

14 PREPARE Plan to write an essay of your own. First, choose one of the following topics to write about:

- When have you found a good solution to a problem? What was the problem and how did you solve it? What benefits did your solution have?

- Imagine you want to change jobs. What alternative career would you choose? What skills does it require? What benefits (income, prospects, opportunities) would the alternative career bring?

Next, follow these steps:

1 Take notes on the information and details you want to include.

2 Write examples and explanation for your ideas. Consider what words and phrases you can use to introduce them.

3 Write an outline for each paragraph of your essay, including the introduction and conclusion.

15 WRITE Write a draft of your essay. It should be about 400 words. While you write, refer back to your notes and the information in the Writing Skill box.

16 IMPROVE Read your essay and correct any grammar and spelling mistakes. Check for examples of what you have learned.

- [ ] Have you written about 400 words?
- [ ] Did you include examples and explanations?
- [ ] Did you use new vocabulary from the unit?
- [ ] Did you use tenses such as the future perfect appropriately?

17 SHARE Exchange essays with a partner. Tell each other which ideas you found interesting and why.

A cowboy performer uses his lassoing skills in New York, the United States

5.3 Living Off the Grid

1 ACTIVATE Look at the photos. What examples of alternative energy sources and building materials do they show? Why are some people choosing these instead of traditional ones? What are the pros and cons of these lifestyles?

2 **IDENTIFY** Listen to the first part of a podcast interview. What is it about? Why do you think Jeff was chosen to be interviewed?

3 🔊 **IDENTIFY** Read the Listening Skill box, then listen to the excerpts from the podcast interview. What can you infer? Answer the questions.

1 How does the announcer feel about the number of households living off the grid?

2 a How does Jeff feel about the idea of living off the grid?

   b Does he think the trend will continue in the future?

   c What does he think about "what's going on in the world"?

3 How does the interviewer feel about the idea of living off the grid?

4 What type of lifestyle does Jeff prefer?

4 🔊 **APPLY** Listen to the excerpts from Exercise 3 again. What gave you the clues to make your inferences? Take notes as you listen.

> ### 🅠 LISTENING SKILL Making inferences
>
> People don't always express their ideas directly. Sometimes the listener must infer what the speaker means, thinks, or feels.
>
> Making inferences involves using various types of clues and evidence that the speaker gives (often in combination with your own knowledge) to deduce information that is not stated directly. You can use a combination of the following to make inferences.
>
> • Specific words or phrases
>
> *What we're finally seeing right now in society is the beginning of this movement toward independence.*
>
> Inference: From the use of the word *finally*, we can infer that the speaker feels that it has taken a long time for the movement to get started.
>
> • The speaker's tone
>
> The speaker may hesitate or add stress on certain words or syllables in order to express different emotions when speaking. These aspects of tone can often tell you the speaker's attitude about the topic.
>
> *Hmm, I guess these really aren't new ideas.*
>
> Inference: The hesitation expression *Hmm* at the beginning combined with the stress on the word *guess* tells you that the speaker is uncertain whether the ideas are new.
>
> Thinking about what you can infer, in addition to what the speaker states directly, will help you to gain a deeper, more complete understanding when you are listening.

5 🔊 **ASSESS** Listen to the rest of the podcast interview. Decide if the sentences are true (T) or false (F) based on what you can infer from the interview.

1 Jeff approves of the way people get food nowadays.

2 Being off the grid is better for us than living a modern lifestyle.

3 Off-the-grid homes can't be luxurious.

4 The interviewer thinks living off the grid could also be enjoyable.

5 Jeff works hard to promote the off-the-grid lifestyle.

6 **WHAT'S YOUR ANGLE?** Could you live off-grid? What things would you find it hard to live without? What benefits would off-grid life have for you?

PRONUNCIATION SKILL Compound nouns

🔊 Compound nouns in English are common. Compound nouns are words made up of:

noun + noun: water heater, rooftop

adjective + noun: greenhouse

In a noun + noun combination, we usually put the stress on the first word.

water supply

In an adjective + noun combination, we usually put the stress on the noun.

natural world   organic farm

7 🔊 **NOTICE** Work with a partner. Listen to each sentence and identify the compound noun. Mark the stressed part of the compound noun. Some sentences may have more than one. Then listen again and repeat.

1 Off-grid communities often use solar energy.
2 The alternative therapies lecture was held at the conference center.
3 Being off the grid means not using the state system.
4 Collecting and using rainwater can help prevent excess water usage.
5 Alternative therapies can improve people's mental health.

8 🔊 **INTEGRATE** Work with a partner. Take turns saying the compound nouns. Decide whether each is a noun+noun or adjective+noun. Then listen and repeat.

carbon footprint	lifestyle
log cabin	power system
rainwater	water source
wind power	electrical grid
natural gas	solar panels

9 **INTEGRATE** In a small group, discuss ways you can change your lifestyle to decrease your carbon footprint. Think of three good ideas to share with the class.

GRAMMAR IN CONTEXT
Future perfect versus future continuous

We use the future perfect to talk about an action or event that will be completed before a certain time in the future or will still be in progress up to a certain time in the future.

We'll have increased our membership to more than 20,000 by the end of the year.

We use the future continuous with a future time phrase to talk about an action that will be in progress at a certain time, or over a period of time in the future.

In fact, I'll be helping to build one of those this weekend.

We can use both the future perfect and *will* to predict events in the future.

Do you think you will have achieved your energy goals by 2025?

Do you think you will achieve your energy goals by 2025?

See Grammar focus on page 163.

10 **IDENTIFY** Choose all phrases that can be used to correctly complete each sentence.

1 I *won't have finished / won't be finishing / won't finish* the project by Friday.
2 The government *will have updated / will be updating / will update* its energy policy this spring.
3 This time tomorrow, *I'll have met / I'll be meeting / I'll meet* Jeff from the Green Lifestyle Collective.
4 Will the people *have decreased / be decreasing / decrease* their energy consumption by 2025?
5 Before lunchtime, the committee *will have voted / will be voting / will vote* on its next leader.

11 **APPLY** Complete the conversation with the correct tense of the verbs in parentheses. More than one answer is possible for some items.

A: So, Jeff, how's the new project going?

B: Really well. The solar panels _____ (work) by tomorrow, and we _____ (fix) the water source before the weekend.

A: How many people do you think _____ (change) to a greener lifestyle before the next decade?

B: I'd say hundreds of thousands, if not millions. People _____ (realize) the danger of not changing. The planet _____ (not be able to) cope if we don't change our habits.

12 **WHAT'S YOUR ANGLE?** Do you like to do things in a more traditional way or in a more innovative way? How might you live differently in the future?

5.4 Taken by Surprise

1 ACTIVATE Think of a time when you told someone a surprising or shocking piece of news. What was the news? How did you feel about telling the person? Discuss these questions with a partner.

2 INTERACT Look at the pictures. Discuss the questions with a partner.

1 Where are Andy, Cathy, and Jenna?
2 What is the relationship between them?
3 Do you think the conversation is formal or informal? Why?

3 ▶ IDENTIFY Watch the video and answer the questions.

1 What news does Andy have for Cathy and Jenna?
2 What is the change in plans?
3 How do Cathy and Jenna respond to Andy's news?
4 How does Andy feel about the plans? Why?
5 What solution does Cathy suggest?

REAL-WORLD ENGLISH Delivering bad news

In some situations, we need to deliver a piece of bad news to someone. These conversations can be awkward because we may feel bad about upsetting or inconveniencing the other person. However, the following four-step conversation structure can help you deliver bad news in a sensitive way.

Use an opener:
I have something to tell you.
There's something I need to discuss with you.

Add (or begin with) a positive lead-in:
I really enjoy working with you.
You know you're my dearest friend in the world, right?

Give some background:
Remember how I applied for that job in Paris?
You know how I borrowed your favorite sweater?

Deliver the problem statement:
Well, I got the job. There's only one problem. They want me to start next week.
Well, I washed it in hot water, and it shrank.

Note that the first two steps can be reversed, but be sure to set a positive tone and give background before presenting the problem.

ENGLISH FOR REAL

4 ▶ **IDENTIFY** Watch the video again and complete the excerpts.

1 Andy: You both know _____, right?
 Cathy: And we've been very happy with your work.
 Jenna: Uh-huh. Absolutely.

2 Andy: Well, Jenna, Cathy…I have _____.
 Cathy: Mm-hmm. What is it?

3 Andy: Well, _____ for that summer internship in London?
 Jenna: Mm-hmm. Yes, right.

4 Andy: Well…I _____!
 Cathy: Wow! That's fantastic, Andy!
 Jenna: No way!

5 Andy: _____. They want me to start at their office here next week for training. For two months to be exact.
 Jenna: Two months?
 Cathy: So, when are you leaving for London?

5 **ANALYZE** Work with a partner. Review the phrases in Exercise 4. Write the statements Andy uses for each purpose.

Opener:

_____

Positive lead-in:

_____

Background statement:

_____

Problem statement:

_____

6 ◀ **INTEGRATE** Listen and check your ideas. Then listen and repeat.

7 **PREPARE** Work with a partner. You are going to take turns delivering bad news.

1 Choose two of the following situations each.
2 On your own, read the situations and think of extra details.
3 Note some phrases you can use as the opener, positive lead-in, background statement, and problem statement.

Situation 1: You're going to study abroad. You'll have to leave your apartment in six weeks', and your roommate will need to find someone else to move in. Tell him/her the news.

Situation 2: Your boss asked you to attend an urgent meeting. You had promised to help a co-worker with a report, but now you don't have time. Tell him/her you can't help them.

Situation 3: Your best friend is having a party and is really excited about it. You've already booked a vacation for that date. Tell him/her you can't come to the party.

Situation 4: Your parents' house was burgled while they were on vacation. Lots of things have been stolen. Tell them what happened.

Situation 5: Your brother/sister lent you an expensive camera, and you accidentally deleted all their unsaved photos. Tell him/her what you did.

8 **INTERACT** Work with your partner. Take turns telling each other your scenarios. Follow the four-step conversation structure for delivering bad news. Ask follow-up questions to keep the conversation going.

9 **EXPAND** As a class, talk about how it felt to deliver bad news in English. Discuss how people in your culture usually deliver a piece of bad news.

GO ONLINE
to create your own version
of the English For Real video.

5.5 The Next Big Thing

1 ACTIVATE Look at the photo. What are the people doing? What benefits do you think such an activity has? Why?

2 **IDENTIFY** Listen to two students, Gita and Jack, discussing a prediction about the future. What is the prediction?

SPEAKING Making speculations

We often make speculations (guesses) or predictions about the future based on our opinions, experience, and background knowledge.

When we make speculations, we use phrases or modals that indicate uncertainty.

I guess it's possible that some types of medicines will be unnecessary someday.
I suppose doctors in the future *might* prescribe social activity.
I imagine it *could* be a long time before alternative medicine truly catches on.

We use adverbs of possibility to indicate how likely we feel our predictions are to happen.

A lot of people will **definitely** be resistant to the idea of social activity as an alternative to medicine.
Perhaps by the next century, people's attitudes toward alternative medicines will have changed.

---

3 **IDENTIFY** Listen to the conversation again and take brief notes to answer the questions.

1. Why does Gita think that more people are suffering from health problems these days?
2. What do experts predict will happen to health services in the near future?
3. What does Gita think she'll be doing for her patients in the next three or four years?
4. Does Jack think that social prescribing will be beneficial to patients?
5. What reaction does Gita predict her future patients will have to social prescribing?

4 **APPLY** Listen again. Complete the excerpts with the ways the speakers express likelihood.

1. In the next three or four years, _____ sending patients out of my office with recommendations to do social activities as treatment for their illnesses.
2. Mm-hmm…_____. There are a lot of benefits to having a good social life—I know that from my psychology course.
3. People _definitely_ _____ conventional medicine for many illnesses, but some will just need that extra boost of confidence you get from being part of something bigger.
4. So, _I guess will be doing_ _____ social prescribing in the future.
5. It makes sense to me, too, but __I imagine many__ _____ conventional medicine.
6. Well, it might sound unlikely, but more than 55 percent of the people who were interviewed in a recent survey said they would like their doctor to offer social prescribing. So, I think _they will probably be_ _____ open to the idea.

5 INTERACT Work in a small group. Talk about the predictions in the example sentences in the Speaking box and in the excerpts from Exercise 4. Do you agree with them? Make your own speculations and predictions about social prescribing and other types of alternative medicine.

6 PREPARE Prepare to answer the following question.

Twenty-five years from now, what kinds of new alternatives to common things like food, transportation, medicine, or lifestyle do you think there will be?

1. Take a few minutes to write down your predictions and the reasons and evidence to support them.
2. Consider any words and phrases you might use to express likelihood or make predictions.
3. Practice making your predictions. Remember to support any predictions you make with reasons, examples, and evidence.

7 IMPROVE Work with a partner. Read through your notes together and check for any language errors.

8 SHARE When you are ready, work with a new partner to give your predictions.

9 WHAT'S YOUR ANGLE? Have you ever heard of social prescribing or similar approaches? What do you think of the idea? What sort of people would it be most likely to benefit? Would it appeal to you? Why or why not?

Now go to page 151 for the Unit 5 Review.

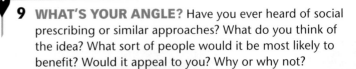

6 Fun

UNIT SNAPSHOT

What do our brains do when we have fun?   65
What would make a sports facility better?   68
Is competition always a good thing?   71

Is fun only for young people?

Why is fun important?

What things make life fun?

BEHIND THE PHOTO

Answer the questions. Then discuss your answers with a partner.

1   What local activities or attractions are available to you? Think of five and rank them from most to least appealing to you.

2   If you could start a business in the sports or entertainment industry in your area, what would it be? Why? What people would it appeal to?

3   What are the benefits of having fun? Consider yourself, family and friends, colleagues, and communities in your area.

REAL-WORLD GOAL

Try a new activity or hobby that you think would be fun.

6.1 It's Good to Have Fun

1 ACTIVATE Work with a partner. Look at the photos. What are the people doing? How much fun do you think they are having?

2 INTEGRATE Work with a partner. Compare ideas about the photos in Exercise 1. Rank the activities 1–4 in order of the most to least fun.

3 IDENTIFY Read the article and make a list of the writer's suggestions for fun activities.

4 INTERACT Compare your list with a partner and discuss the questions.

1 Which of the fun activities from the post do you do already?
2 Which activities do you think would be or are the most fun?

5 IDENTIFY According to the writer, what should we do more, and why? Discuss the question with a partner.

Worth Playing For

Growing up, I never thought about fun at all. I was a kid! I remember being **totally** absorbed in whatever I was doing. Everything was new and exciting. Fun was just a by-product of life, and life was just, well, simpler. But then I grew up, and life got busy, **extremely** busy—with college, friends, relationships—and then I found myself on the path to my dream career, moving to the city, networking, and work, work, work. I had achieved my goals, yet something seemed to be missing. It was a few years before I realized what it was: somewhere along the way I had stopped having fun.

You know where this is going, don't you? I'm going to tell you to have more fun, and I bet you're wondering how you're going to fit fun into your already busy life, right? Wait! Hello? Before you decide to click on another site, just bear with me a moment… I **really** regret not having fun for all those "lost" years. But I've learned to do it again, and you can, too. There is an easy way to bring fun back into your life. Your fun self is still in there just waiting to come out! So, here's how to do it: *Play!*

But play is just for kids, right? *Wrong!* Play is really important for people of all ages. It allows us to "switch off," to lose ourselves in the moment, and to engage with the people around us. Play doesn't need to be scheduled in or written on your to-do list (put that cell phone back in your pocket right now!). Play is not a "free time" thing. (Free time? What is that anyway?) It should be part of your everyday life. It could simply be hanging out with friends, sharing a joke with the person in the line at the grocery

store, kicking a soccer ball around in the parking lot with your colleagues at break time, or doing magic tricks to amuse your friends' kids. Why not try doing a completely new activity, one that you've never thought of doing before?

Sounds easy, right? Absolutely! And there's more. Play has health benefits, too. When we have fun, our brains release chemicals called *endorphins*, which make us feel good. Having a fun, playful attitude to life helps us feel more relaxed in stressful situations, and it enables us to build and improve relationships. Doing activities such as socializing, playing board games or chess, completing puzzles, and solving memory challenges improves brain function and keeps us young, active, and energetic, which in turn boosts our immune system and helps to prevent illness.

So, get out there and do the things you like doing! Try to arrange regular nights out with friends and colleagues doing fun activities like karaoke, bowling, or mini golf. And having fun doesn't have to be expensive either. The best things in life are free, right? Why not organize a regular game night with friends or family? Or invite people over to share a meal and a few laughs or stories. You're guaranteed a *fun*-tastic time! Schedule time to hang out in a park or go to the beach. And don't forget to bring a ball and a kite or, if you're feeling really adventurous, a pail and shovel!

ℙ+ Oxford 5000™

6 IDENTIFY Match the sentences to the features in the Reading Skill box.

1 It's absolutely *fun*-tastic! _____

2 If you're feeling really brave, why not join us for a game of chess? _____

3 Why do some couples avoid going to the gym? They're worried their relationship won't work out.
   _____

4 You know what I mean, right? And I'm sure you agree.
   _____

7 INTERACT Discuss the sentences from Exercise 6 with a partner. Which words and phrases communicate the informal or humorous tone?

8 INTEGRATE Read the article again. Identify examples of where the writer does the following.

1 Tries to build rapport with the reader

2 Uses a rhetorical question

3 Uses a pun

4 Uses exaggeration or sarcasm

9 WHAT'S YOUR ANGLE? What do you like to do for fun? Share your ideas with a partner.

GRAMMAR IN CONTEXT Verb + *-ing* or *to* infinitive (same or different meaning)

Some verbs use the *-ing* form or the *to* + infinitive with little or no change of meaning.

*I love **playing** games. I love **to play** games.*

Other verbs that have little or no change in meaning include *like, hate, prefer, begin, continue,* and *start.*

However, some verbs have different meanings depending on whether they are followed by *-ing* or *to* + infinitive.

*Somewhere along the way I had **stopped having** fun.*
*Sorry we're late. We **stopped to get** some coffee.*

Other verbs that also change meaning include *try* and *remember.*

See Grammar focus on page 164.

10 IDENTIFY Are the meanings of these sentence pairs the same or different? Mark each pair as same (S) or different (D).

___ 1 A: I love playing board games with friends.
     B: I love to play board games with friends.

___ 2 A I remembered to post on Jamie's timeline on his birthday.
     B: I remembered posting on Jamie's timeline on his birthday.

___ 3 A: We stopped buying candy to take to the movies.
     B: We stopped to buy candy to take to the movies.

___ 4 A: I prefer being outdoors!
     B: I prefer to be outdoors!

___ 5 A: Can you remember booking the bowling alley?
     B: Can you remember to book the bowling alley?

___ 6 A: I tried to "play" for 30 minutes every evening.
     B: I tried "playing" for 30 minutes every evening.

11 WHAT'S YOUR ANGLE? Complete the prompts on the topic of fun so they are true for you. Then compare your sentences with a partner.

1 I try to _____ every weekend.
2 I have never tried _____ing…
3 My friends and I have stopped _____ing…
4 I think it's important to stop to…
5 I never forget to…
6 I remember _____ing when I was young.

VOCABULARY DEVELOPMENT Intensifying adverbs

We use intensifying adverbs to modify adjectives to show how strongly we feel about something. The choice of adverb depends on the type of adjective.

Gradable adjectives, such as *tired*, describe a quality that has a range of intensities.

a little tired   **very** tired   **really** tired   **extremely** tired

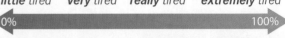

Non-gradable adjectives, such as *exhausted* (= *extremely tired*), describe a quality that is absolute or extreme.

absolutely exhausted = **completely** exhausted = **totally** exhausted

12 INTEGRATE Which adverb completes the example from the article? Review the article to check your answers.

1 *totally / a little* absorbed
2 *absolutely / extremely* busy
3 *totally / really* important
4 *a little / a completely* new activity
5 *really / absolutely* adventurous

13 INTEGRATE Work with a partner. Write questions using the adverb-adjective combinations in Exercise 12. Add three more questions with adverb-adjective combinations of your own.

Which activity have you been totally absorbed with recently?

14 WHAT'S YOUR ANGLE? Interview a new partner using your questions from Exercise 13. How much do you have in common?

6.2 Getting Out and About

1 ACTIVATE Look at the photos. What activities do they show? Are activities like this available in your area? Have you ever tried them, or would you like to? Share your ideas with a partner.

2 IDENTIFY Read the survey. What is it about? What is the aim of the survey?

Sports and Recreation Survey

Name: _____

Age group (please circle):

16–20   21–25   26–35   36–50
51–65   66–70   71+

1   Do you feel that the number and type of local sports and recreation facilities are satisfactory? If not, what other facilities would you like to see in the area?

_____

_____

_____

2   How often do you use local sports and recreation facilities? If you don't use them, please give reasons.
    never   once a month
    2–3 times a month   4–6 times a month
    Reasons: _____

3   Rate the following facilities according to how satisfying your experience of using them is (1 = the lowest and 8 = the highest).
    ___ community pools
    ___ recreation centers
    ___ local parks
    ___ hiking and bike trails
    ___ outdoor sports facilities
    ___ arts and crafts classes
    ___ cultural and historical sites
    ___ climbing center

4   Which four local facilities do you most enjoy? Rank them (1 = the best).
    ___ community pools
    ___ climbing center
    ___ recreation centers
    ___ cycle tracks

3 INTEGRATE Complete the survey with your views. Then interview a partner to find out their views.

4 IDENTIFY Read the student report based on the results of a survey conducted at her college. Is the information similar to or different from your opinions about your local facilities?

Recently, we conducted a survey into the availability and popularity of local sports and recreation facilities. In the survey, we interviewed a number of young people and asked a range of questions that were designed to determine whether the provision of local sports and recreation opportunities was considered satisfactory as well as how often people used the facilities.

In an attempt to find out which facilities were the most popular, the participants were also asked to rate their experiences using the facilities.

According to the survey, 81 percent of the participants felt that local sports and recreation facilities were satisfactory, although some felt that more opportunities could be made available for teenagers, such as skate parks, youth clubs, and gaming centers.

The majority of participants (78 percent) responded that they use local facilities at least two to three times a month, with 15 percent using them more frequently, particularly in the case of sports and swimming facilities where they attend weekly classes or events. However, 7 percent replied that they do not regularly use any local facilities. Reasons given included lack of knowledge about the facilities and scheduled classes, not having enough time due to work or study commitments, and facilities being too expensive.

In terms of satisfaction, the most popular facility is the local park, followed by the recreation center, with popular activities including soccer, baseball, badminton, and martial arts. Many participants have started using the recently opened climbing center, although not all had tried it. Those who had tried it rated it highly for satisfaction.

Community pools were also ranked highly by 21 percent of the participants, and similarly, 19 percent enjoy the experience of using local hiking and bike trails. In contrast, the lowest-ranking facility was the walking paths, the difference being that although the cycle paths are well-maintained, walking paths are not. Of all the facilities, the recreation center was the most popular. The climbing center and bike trails both came in second in terms of popularity. The fourth most popular facility was the community pool.

Overall, the evidence suggests that local sports and recreation facilities are considered satisfactory and are used by the majority of participants, and these participants enjoy using them. Conversely, however, some participants seem to think the town would benefit from more facilities, especially for younger people. Other recommendations include better advertising of available facilities to make people aware of them and more affordable prices for some activities. These changes would encourage people to participate.

WRITING SKILL
Phrases that signal similarity and difference

We use a range of phrases to indicate similarities and differences. These are especially useful when we are writing about facts or data that we want to compare. Common examples include the following.

- Similarity
  similar (to), similarity between…and…, the same (as), equal, equally, likewise, similarly (to)
- Difference
  different from, differently than, difference between… and…, in contrast, in comparison, conversely, however, although

Try to notice how these phrases are used in texts. This will help you understand and make comparisons between subjects and data.

5 IDENTIFY Use one word to complete each sentence. Use the phrases in the Writing Skill box to help you.

1 The new schedule starts next week, and you'll have the _____ instructor _____ before.

2 People say they can see a _____ between me and my cousin, but I can't.

3 Well, that's my opinion. I know you feel _____ than I do.

4 Some people think soccer and American football are the same sport, but they're wrong—they're completely _____.

5 Most of the participants responded positively, which we expected. _____, we got some negative responses, which were a surprise.

6 Climbing is much safer in _____ to snowboarding.

6 INTEGRATE Identify examples of similarity and difference phrases in the report. What does each phrase compare or contrast?

7 WHAT'S YOUR ANGLE? Work with a partner. Take turns describing your local facilities. Then share your ideas with another pair.

8 ASSESS Read the survey and the report again. Identify the answer(s) to each survey question in the report. What do you notice about how the report is organized?

When one verb follows another verb, the second verb is either the *-ing* form or the infinitive, with or without *to*. The form you choose will depend on the first verb.

- Verb + *-ing*

  can't help, imagine, stand, don't mind, enjoy, feel like, hate, involve, like, love, miss
  Jenny **likes doing** outside activities the most.

- Verb + infinitive with *to*

  agree, aim, appear, arrange, expect, hope, refuse, seem, tend, want
  People **expect to see** better facilities in the future.

- Verb + object + infinitive with *to*

  advise, allow, authorize, encourage, need, remind, teach (how), tell, want
  The facilities **allow me to exercise** before work.

See Grammar focus on page 164.

9 IDENTIFY Review the conclusion of the report and identify an example of each type of verb structure from the Grammar box.

10 INTEGRATE Complete each sentence with the correct form of the verb in parenthesis. Add the object if necessary.

1 Many people love _____ dangerous sports, but others dislike them. (play)

2 The trainer reminded _____ their safety helmets. (put on; the climbers)

3 Learning to ride a bicycle involves _____ confident enough to take a risk. (be)

4 We arranged _____ on a camping trip during summer break. (go)

5 My daughter doesn't like _____ any of her piano classes. (miss)

11 IDENTIFY You are going to conduct a survey. In a small group, choose one of the following topics or think of your own.

- Attitudes toward extreme sports
- The popularity of cell phone games
- Attitudes toward video games

12 PREPARE In your group, follow the steps to design, conduct, and analyze your survey.

1 Write four to six questions related to your survey topic. Use different types of questions such as *yes/no*, ranking, and rating questions.

2 Work with a partner from another group and ask them your survey questions.

3 Work with your group again. Then share all your data and analyze it.

4 Plan your report using the model and the Writing Skill box as references.

13 CREATE As a group, write a draft of your report. While you write, refer back to your notes and the information in the Writing Skill box.

14 IMPROVE Read your report and correct any grammar and spelling mistakes. Check for examples of what you have learned.

☐ Phrases for organizing a report
☐ Phrases for showing similarity and difference
☐ Vocabulary related to sports or activities
☐ Verb patterns with *-ing* and *to* infinitive

15 EVALUATE Read a report from a different group. Do any of the findings surprise you?

Soccer players at Amahoro Stadium in Kigali, Rwanda

6.3 In It to Win It

1 ACTIVATE Look at the photos. What is happening? How do you think the people are feeling? Why? Share your ideas with a partner.

2 INTEGRATE Discuss the questions in a small group.

1 Why is winning fun?
2 What are positive aspects of taking part in competition?
3 What are negative ones?

3 IDENTIFY Working with a partner, match each word in the box to a definition. Use a dictionary to help.

acquire	challenge	concentration
determination	opponent	stick to
under pressure		

♟+ Oxford 5000™

1 Learn or develop something, such as a skill or habit _____

2 The quality of being determined; firmness of purpose _____

3 Someone who competes with or opposes another in a contest, game, or argument _____

4 Invite someone to take part in a contest or to do something very difficult _____

5 Continue or confine oneself to doing or using (a particular thing) _____

6 The action or power of focusing all one's attention on something _____

7 In a state of stress caused by having too many demands on one's time or resources _____

4 INTEGRATE Complete the definition of *competition* with the words from Exercise 3. Which of your ideas from Exercise 2 does the definition include?

Competition

A competition can be a formal contest in which a winner emerges. In sports, the matching of opponents is essential for a fair competition. In a competition, an individual or group seeks to show that they are better at a particular activity than their [1] _____. Although sports depend on cooperation, there are positive but also negative aspects to playing a sport, particularly for children. On the one hand, children can become angry at losing or be put [2] _____ by competitive parents. On the positive side, children can [3] _____ new skills while enjoying a healthy activity and developing [4] _____. Participants can also develop [5] _____, try to do their best, [6] _____ themselves, and learn to [7] _____ something for an extended period.

—adapted from *A Dictionary of Sports Studies* by Alan Tomlinson

GRAMMAR IN CONTEXT Other uses of -ing form

We can use the *-ing* form of a verb in a number of ways:

1 as the subject or object of a sentence.
   *In my opinion, **winning** is absolutely everything.*
   *I like **being** the best at whatever I do.*

2 in adjective or noun + preposition + *-ing*.
   *You get so **tired of losing** because it gets harder to motivate yourself.*
   *I won't compete if there is a **chance of losing**.*

3 with time conjunctions, such as *before, after, since,* and *while.*
   *My social life's gotten much better **since joining** the team.*
   *Just ask yourself whether you feel happy **while playing**.*

See Grammar focus on page 164.

5 🔊 **IDENTIFY** Correct the sentences by adding an *-ing* form. Then listen and check. Identify the form of *-ing* word from the Grammar box.

1 For me, go to tournaments is fun because it brings us together as a team. _____ ___

2 You get so tired of lose because it makes it harder to motivate yourself to stick to the training. _____ ___

3 That's really important in build team spirit because when we have fun together, our relationships on and off the netball court get stronger. _____ ___

4 My social life's gotten much better since join the team. _____ ___

5 To be honest, I'm not so sure the focus on win is the best idea. _____ ___

6 I love challenge myself to stay ahead. _____ ___

7 I'm not interested in run if I know I won't win! _____ ___

8 Just ask yourself whether you feel happy while play. _____ ___

6 **APPLY** Identify six examples of the *-ing* form in the text for Exercise 4. Match each example to one of the three points in the Grammar box.

7 **INTERACT** In Exercise 8, you will listen to four people speak in a college talk about playing sports. What do you think each person might say about playing sports? Discuss your ideas with a partner.

1 A student who plays sports for the college:

_____

2 An elementary school teacher:

_____

3 An international athlete:

_____

4 A sports psychologist:

_____

8 🔊 **IDENTIFY** Listen to the radio talk show. Then number the speakers in the order you hear them. Do they mention any of your ideas from Exercise 7?

___ Vicky

___ Petra

___ Landon

___ Alexander

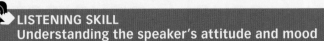

People often give clues about their attitude and mood when they are speaking. Pay attention to both verbal and nonverbal clues.

Verbal clues

• Opinion phrases that indicate a positive or negative attitude

• Words and phrases that indicate certainty (*definitely, absolutely*) or uncertainty (*seem, appear, perhaps, maybe*)

• Words with positive (*beneficial, fortunately, luckily*) or negative (*serious, unfortunate*) connotations

• Clauses that indicate contrast: *but, while, despite, in spite of*

Nonverbal clues

• Tone of voice: A positive attitude can be indicated by a happy voice and enthusiastic fillers such as *uh-huh* and *yeah*. A negative attitude sounds hesitant and unenthusiastic, with negative-sounding fillers like *erm, um,* or *huh* and sighs.

• Volume: A louder volume often indicates the speaker is confident about what they are saying.

• Pitch: A frequent or constant rising pitch can show the speaker is uncertain.

• Speed: When a speaker slows down, this can show the speaker thinks the information is important.

9 **INTERACT** Which speaker's attitude is closest to yours? Why? Do you disagree with any of the speakers' points? Share your ideas in a small group.

10 🔊 **IDENTIFY** Listen to the talk again. Decide if each description matches Vicky (V), Alexander (A), Petra (P), or Landon (L). As you listen, note features of the speakers' language that indicate their attitude. Then compare notes with a partner.

1 Doesn't feel winning is important ___

2 Thinks winning is the most important thing in sports ___

3 Is critical of another group of people ___

4 Feels sports have improved their social life ___

5 Gives a warning about winning ___

6 Is negative about the idea of losing ___

11 **WHAT'S YOUR ANGLE?** Think of a time when you or someone you know well won or lost something. Make brief notes about what happened, who was involved, and how they felt. Did the person learn anything from the experience? When you are ready, share your stories.

6.4 Casual Conversations

1 ACTIVATE Discuss the questions with a partner.

1 How do you think Kevin is feeling in the first photo?

2 When did you last feel like that?

3 Who do you talk to when you feel like that?

2 ▶ IDENTIFY Watch the video and answer the questions.

1 What's wrong with Kevin?

2 How do the others respond to his news?

3 What do Andy and Max do to help Kevin feel better?

4 How do they use body language to show their feelings?

REAL-WORLD ENGLISH Expressing sympathy

When other people share bad news with us, we need to react appropriately to show support. We do this by using reactive words and expressions that show a range of emotions, including sympathy. It is appropriate to express sympathy in both informal and more formal situations.

More formal

I'm very sorry to hear that.   That's terribly bad luck.

Informal

Oh, that's too bad.   That's rough.

Expressing sympathy helps the person you are with feel valued and listened to. We often use body language (for example, nodding or shaking our heads or patting someone on the shoulder if we know them well) when we express sympathy.

3 ▶ **INTEGRATE** Watch the video again and complete the phrases Max and Andy use.

1 Max: You _____ you haven't slept for days.
2 Max: That's _____, Kevin.
3 Max: What's _____?
4 Max: Oh, no way! _____.
5 Max: Your great-grandfather? _____.
6 Andy: Oh, no! _____?
7 Andy: Sorry! That's _____.
8 Andy: I remember him! Aw, _____.
9 Andy: I disagree! You're _____.
10 Andy: I'm sure _____ of you, Kevin, whatever you decide to do.

4 **IDENTIFY** Which phrases from Exercise 3 do the following?

- Express sympathy directly _____
- Give positive feedback _____
- Show concern or interest _____

5 **IDENTIFY** Work with a partner to choose the most appropriate response to each statement.

1 I've got a really bad headache.
  a How terribly unfortunate.
  b Oh, that's rough.
2 Thank you for changing the meeting venue. The fire caused a lot of damage in the office.
  a Aw, that sucks!
  b I'm very sorry to hear that.
3 I'm really nervous about giving the presentation.
  a Don't worry. You'll be great.
  b Too bad. There's nothing you can do about it.
4 A tree fell on my car and wrecked it.
  a How awful.
  b I wish to offer my deepest condolences.
5 I'm not at all sure about this project and the team I'm on.
  a You're wrong to feel that way.
  b They are all really nice people. I am sure everything will work out fine.

6 **INTEGRATE** Practice the statements and responses from Exercise 5 with a partner. Use body language to help.

7 **APPLY** Work with a partner. Write a response to each statement. Make sure it has an appropriate level of formality.

1 Excuse me, could you help? I just tripped and fell, and I think I might have sprained my ankle.
2 Hi Sam, it's me. I just found out my great aunt got taken to hospital last night.
3 Owww! I've got the most terrible toothache.
4 Have you gotten your grade yet? I have. I failed!
5 I'm afraid I have to finish the presentation early because I don't feel well.

8 **INTEGRATE** Practice the statements and responses from Exercise 7 with your partner. Ask another pair to listen and identify whether the response is formal or informal.

9 **PREPARE** Prepare to express sympathy directly, give positive feedback, and show concern and interest. First, write three or four statements related to the following topics to which someone else would express sympathy.

- you or someone else being hurt or feeling sick
- some bad news about school or work
- a problem in a friendship

10 **INTERACT** Work in a small group. Take turns sharing your statements. Your group members should respond with appropriate phrases to express sympathy directly, give positive feedback, and show concern and interest.

11 **SHARE** Share your feedback on how your group members responded to your statements.

GO ONLINE
to create your own version
of the English For Real video.

6.5 Off the Beaten Path

1 ACTIVATE Work with a partner. Look at the photo. What do you think *going off the beaten path* means? Tell your ideas to the class. Did anyone guess correctly?

2 🔊 INTEGRATE Listen to a man named Danny begin a presentation about his favorite hobby. Then answer the questions with a partner.

1 What is Danny's hobby?
2 How many sections does his presentation have?
3 What information is he going to give in each section?

3 🔊 IDENTIFY Listen to the next part of the presentation. Take brief notes to answer the questions and then compare answers with a partner.

1 Why did Danny start mountain biking?
2 What other hobby did he start, and why?
3 What do his hobbies involve?
4 What are some of the challenges and dangers of his hobbies?

4 WHAT'S YOUR ANGLE? Have you tried either mountain biking or making amateur video recordings? From what Danny says, would you like to try them?

🔊 SPEAKING Structuring a presentation

When we give a presentation, we usually divide it into sections. This helps us stay on track and deliver our presentation in a way that is organized and easy for the audience to follow. We can use signposting language, which involves words or phrases that let the reader know when we are going to:

1 introduce the different sections of the presentation.
2 indicate a change of topic.
3 move on to a new point or section.
4 refer back to a topic or signpost from earlier in a presentation.

Try to notice how others use signposting phrases in their presentations. This will help you feel more confident that your presentation is clear and well structured.

5 🔊 IDENTIFY Work with a partner. Listen again to Danny's entire presentation. Identify examples of signposting language. Then identify which function from the Speaking box the phrase serves.

🔊 PRONUNCIATION SKILL Stress and rhythm

🔊 In English, we usually use stress and rhythm to make our speech sound more fluent. To do this you can:

- Make the vowel sounds longer and slower in the stressed syllables of verbs, nouns, adjectives, and adverbs.
- Reduce and shorten articles, prepositions, pronouns, conjunctions, and auxiliary verbs.

THEN on the WEEkend we go out to the MOUNtains with our BIKES.
We did a CYcling TREK in the MOUNtains and it was TOtally amAZING!

6 🔊 ASSESS Listen to the following phrases. Mark which syllables are stressed. Then listen again and repeat, being sure to make the vowel sounds clear and long.

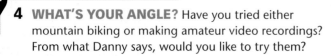

1 Moving on to the next topic now…
2 As I explained at the beginning of the talk…
3 So, let's look at the first reason for this.
4 Coming to my final point…
5 To sum up, the solution is very simple.

7 PREPARE Prepare a two- to three-minute presentation about a hobby or activity that you enjoy or are interested in.

1 Make brief notes on the number of sections you will have and what you will say in each one.
2 Consider which signposting phrases you can use in your presentation. Use the information in the Speaking box to help you.
3 Also think about how you can use stress and rhythm when giving the presentation.

8 SHARE Work in a small group. Give your presentations to each other. Discuss the following questions.

1 Was the presentation easy to follow?
2 What signposting phrases worked well?
3 What can anyone do to improve their presentation?

Now go to page 152 for the Unit 6 Review.

7 Solutions

UNIT SNAPSHOT

What problem does a placebo solve?   77
How might spending money make you happier?   79
How does being in another country affect your
creativity or ability to solve problems?   82

▼ What everyday solutions do people take for granted?

▼ What makes a good problem-solver?

▼ Does every problem have a solution?

▶ **BEHIND THE PHOTO**

Answer the questions. Then discuss your answers with a partner.

1 What are some of the problems the world faces today? Consider current and future issues.
2 Who is responsible for finding solutions to the world's problems? Why?
3 When you have a problem, who do you turn to? Why?

REAL-WORLD GOAL

Search online for a list of "life hacks"

7.1 Heal Yourself

1 ACTIVATE Look at the photos. What are advantages and disadvantages of some ways people deal with health problems?

2 VOCABULARY Read the sentences. Choose the best meaning for the words in orange.

1 An infection **activates** your body's defenses. That's why you get a fever. ___

2 I hurt my back. I need some **assistance**. ___

3 I can't exercise for a while. I've injured my foot and need time to **heal**. ___

4 The exercises that the doctor suggested are really helping my **recovery** from my illness. ___

5 Sometimes a **conventional** treatment doesn't work and you have to try something new. ___

6 One **innovative** approach to obesity and other diet-related health problems is controlling the bacteria in your digestive system. ___

7 People around the world have used willow bark to **relieve** pain. That's how aspirin was invented. ___

8 There's often a **perception** that we need medicine to deal with a cold or other mild illness. ___

9 When you get sick, your **immune** system helps you deal with the sickness. ___

🔊+ Oxford 5000™

a help

b to become well again

c to make active

d traditional, usual

e the way in which something is understood

f a return to the normal state of health

g to cause pain or difficulty to become less severe

h advanced, original, new

i protected from the effects of something; resistant to infection

3 BUILD Complete the sentences with the correct orange words from Exercise 2.

> People often depend on ¹ _____ medicine when they are sick or injured. There's a ² _____ that medicine cures most problems. For example, people take aspirin to ³ _____ the pain of a headache. Or they take medication to help them ⁴ _____ from an infection or illness. Some medicines fight bacteria that cause infections like pneumonia. It's true that these methods often help. However, people can also get other kinds of ⁵ _____ in their ⁶ _____. A healthy diet, meditation, and the right kind of exercise can help you get better, too. And your body's ⁷ _____ system also helps you get better or stay healthy.

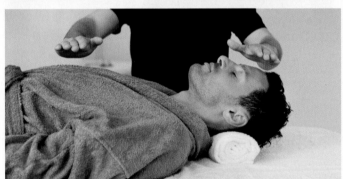

4 IDENTIFY Read the article on the placebo effect. Choose the best expression of the main idea.

a Medical professionals use the placebo effect to treat diseases such as stomach ulcers and depression.

b The placebo effect uses the mind to help the body recover by making us think we will get better.

c The placebo effect uses special chemicals in the brain to promote the body's healing.

1 Modern medicine provides many solutions to health problems, including medication, surgery, and physical therapy, along with other innovative approaches. However, some treatments, especially medications, come with harmful side effects. How can we get better with fewer problems? One powerful solution <u>that is a safer alternative</u> takes a different approach: using the patient's mind to speed recovery. This solution is known as the placebo effect. People <u>who are unwell</u> often begin to heal as soon as they receive medical assistance but before the treatment takes effect or even when the treatment is a fake. The mere perception of treatment can help the patient's recovery.

2 According to recent research, the placebo effect is strongest and most reliable in the treatment of pain, <u>where placebos such as sugar pills, cold creams, and even words have been found to bring significant relief.</u> But placebos can also be effective in the treatment of other diseases, including stomach ulcers, heart disease, depression, and Parkinson's disease. One of the most important advantages of placebos is that they have no serious side effects, and they will not put a patient at risk for overdose. However, if a patient needs medication, taking only a placebo may be dangerous.

3 There is still a lot to learn about how placebos actually work. Cross-cultural studies show people respond differently to placebos. For example, placebo medicine works for 60 percent of patients with stomach ulcers in Germany but hardly at all in Brazil (7 percent). Placebo treatments tend to have results specific to the particular ailment (e.g., placebo pain-relieving cream applied to the left hand does not relieve pain on the right). So, the effects are not entirely due to changes in the patient's general mood.

4 How does the mind "talk" to the body's healing systems in such specific ways? One theory involves certain chemicals in the brain. These chemicals, <u>which are called *endogenous opiates*,</u> are produced in the brain and act like opiate drugs. These chemicals activate the body's healing response.

5 If people can get better through their own efforts, why does the mind first put a brake on healing? Why doesn't it begin to repair itself immediately and without outside help?

6 Let's look at what happens when the body is under attack, whether from illness or injury. It organizes defenses such as pain and fever to counterattack infections. The body also uses weapons such as the antibodies in the immune system to defeat invading bacteria and pain to tell your hand to pull away from danger. However, all of these defending measures have a cost (e.g., pain is exhausting), so the body may not want to use them every time. Sometimes, a speedy recovery is best, but other times, it might be better to remain unwell for a while, simply resting, and save your resources for a different battle.

7 In the past, environmental information contributed to our decisions about when and how best to heal ourselves. For example, you might notice that other people recover in a few days, so you can just wait the illness out. But with modern medicine, people have learned that the best way to predict a good outcome when they are sick is the existence of doctors, conventional medicines, and so on, nearby. The idea of medical attention activates our bodies' responses, which helps us solve our own health problems.

—adapted from *The Oxford Companion to the Mind*, 2nd ed., by Richard L. Gregory

5 ASSESS Read the article again. Decide if the sentences are true (T) or false (F).

1 Placebos cause harmful side effects. ___

2 Placebos like sugar pills can help relieve pain. ___

3 People in different cultures respond the same way to placebos. ___

4 Some chemicals in the brain act like strong drugs. ___

5 Sometimes it may be better for the body to stay sick for a while. ___

6 The simple presence of doctors or other medical assistance may be enough to help us get well. ___

 READING SKILL
Recognizing and understanding metaphors

A metaphor is a way of describing or explaining something by comparing it indirectly to something else. A writer might use verbs, nouns, or adjectives to create the metaphor. Recognizing and understanding metaphors can help you understand unfamiliar ideas by relating them to something more familiar.

*How does the mind **talk** to the body in such specific ways?*

(The use of the verb *talk* suggests that the way the mind sends signals to the body is similar to the way one person talks to another.)

*If people can get better through their own efforts, why does the mind first **put a brake on** healing?*

(The way the mind can act to prevent healing is compared to slowing or stopping a car with the brake pedal through the use of the phrase *put a brake on*.)

6 **IDENTIFY** Review the Reading Skill box. Read paragraph 6 in the article again. What is the body's response to illness and injury compared to? What words are used to make the comparison?

7 **INTEGRATE** Complete the chart with specific words from paragraph 6 in the article that help create the metaphor of war. Use a dictionary to look up any unfamiliar words.

Verbs (2)	Nouns (4)	Adjectives (2)

8 **WHAT'S YOUR ANGLE?** Have you ever experienced the placebo effect or seen it work on someone else? Discuss your ideas with a partner.

GRAMMAR IN CONTEXT
Defining and nondefining relative clauses

We use relative clauses to connect a sentence to a noun phrase. There are two types of relative clauses.

- A **defining relative clause** defines a noun. It identifies who or what we are talking about.

  *People **who are unwell** often begin to heal as soon as they receive medical assistance but before the treatment takes effect or even when the treatment is a fake.*

- A **nondefining relative clause** gives us extra information about something already identified.

  *These chemicals, **which are called** endogenous opiates, are produced in the brain and act like opiate drugs.*

A relative clause usually begins with a relative pronoun. We use *who* for people, *which* or *that* for things, and *whose* for possession. We can also use *where* for places and *when* for times. We can leave out the relative pronoun when it is the object of the relative clause. We use *that* instead of *which* in defining clauses.

*According to recent research, the placebo effect is strongest and most reliable in the treatment of pain, **where placebos such as sugar pills, cold creams, and even words have been found to bring significant relief**.*
*One powerful solution **that is a safer alternative** takes a different approach: using the patient's mind to speed recovery.*

See Grammar focus on page 165.

9 **IDENTIFY** Choose the correct option in each sentence.

1 People *who / which* have high blood pressure and other stress-related health problems should try meditation.

2 General anesthesia, *who / which* is used for major surgeries, poses certain risks for the patient.

3 Even cold medication can have side effects *who / that* are harmful if it is taken too long.

4 Acupuncture is a popular method of relieving pain in China, *when / where* it has been practiced for thousands of years.

5 Patients *who / whose* cold symptoms are uncomfortable may buy over-the-counter medication.

6 In an article *where I read / I read about* meditation, it said that even a few minutes a day can help.

7 The first 24 hours after a major operation is a period *which / when* the patient is often at the greatest risk.

8 This is a practice *uses / that uses* very small needles inserted into the skin.

10 **EXPAND** Read the completed sentences in Exercise 9 again. Decide which relative clauses are defining and which are nondefining.

11 **EXPAND** Choose two of the approaches in Exercise 1 to compare and contrast. Use as many of the vocabulary words in Exercise 2 as you can. Share your ideas with a partner.

12 **WHAT'S YOUR ANGLE?** In a small group answer the questions.

1 What health problems have you or someone you know well had?

2 What solutions did you or they try? How well did the solutions work?

3 How did the perception of the treatment affect the recovery?

7.2 Ask the Experts

1 ACTIVATE Read the list of items and services. Which have you spent money on in the past?

- ☐ a new car ___
- ☐ an expensive vacation ___
- ☐ an adventure / extreme sport ___
- ☐ a housecleaning service ___
- ☐ a grocery shopping or meal preparation service ___
- ☐ an organization that helps people (charity) ___
- ☐ an expensive watch ___

2 WHAT'S YOUR ANGLE? Rank the items in Exercise 1 according to their importance to you (1 = most important). Compare ideas with a partner.

3 IDENTIFY Read the letter. What is the topic? Discuss with a partner.

Sunnyvale College
1879 Main Street
Santa Cruz, CA

Dear Dr. Santiago,

I am writing to request your help with a personal financial matter. Recently, I received an unexpected amount of money as an inheritance from my uncle who died. It's not a huge amount of money, but it is much more than I usually have. Having written several books on the wise use of money, you are in a great position to give me advice on what to do. I would very much appreciate any guidance.

Not having been in this position before, I don't have any personal experience in this area, so I've been reading a lot about the best way to spend this money. Usually considered an exciting gift, money coming from an unexpected source often causes problems. People spend it foolishly, get into debt, and sometimes become poorer and less happy than they were before. I want to avoid those problems. While a fancy new car might be nice, research shows that I'll get used to it quickly and soon it won't bring me joy.

Having researched the relationship between money and happiness, I've come up with several possible plans. I have a small amount of debt, so I will pay that off immediately. With the rest of the money, I could do one or more of these options:

1. Give the money to a good cause. Studies show that when people give money away to a charity with which they have a connection or to help people they know, it makes them happier.

2. Spend some money on a trip. Researchers have found that people remember the experiences they spent money on with greater happiness than the objects they spent money on. I'm thinking about traveling with my brother to Tibet.

3. Buy some time. Having read a study by the Harvard Business School and the University of British Columbia, I know that I will probably be happier if I use the money to give myself more time. For example, I could get a housecleaning service for a year or maybe use a laundry or grocery service. I guess I should figure out how much time I will gain and if the expense is worth it.

Any feedback you could give me on these ideas would be very much appreciated. If you think they all have value, I would be grateful for suggestions on how to distribute the money.

Thank you in advance for your assistance.

Best regards,

Simon Lloyd

Student at Sunnyvale College

4 **ASSESS** Locate these features in the letter.

1 Return address
2 Salutation, greeting
3 Reason for writing to recipient
4 Explanation or description of topic
5 What the writer wants the recipient to do
6 Expression of appreciation
7 Closing

 WRITING SKILL
Checking your work: Audience and purpose

It is important to check your work before, during, and after writing to make sure you have stayed "on track" and achieved your aims. To do this, ask yourself:

- What type of text am I writing? Is it a letter, a review, an essay, a blog post?

- What are the key features of this kind of text?

- What is my purpose for writing (to request or give information, explain facts, describe an experience, give opinions, persuade the reader)?

- Who is my audience? Is it a teacher, other students, the general public, or someone with specific knowledge about the topic?

- What would my audience expect (to be informed, entertained, challenged)?

Considering your audience and purpose will help you focus your writing and use the appropriate tone. Try to notice how other writers take audience and purpose into account in their writing.

---

5 **INTEGRATE** Imagine you wrote the letter in Exercise 3. Read it again and note answers to the questions in the Writing Skill box.

6 **INTERACT** Discuss your answers to Exercise 5 with a partner. Refer to the letter to support your ideas.

7 **WHAT'S YOUR ANGLE?** Answer the questions. Then compare answers with a partner.

1 Did any information in the letter surprise you?
2 Which of the solutions did you like best? Why?
3 How would you spend the money?

 GRAMMAR IN CONTEXT Participle clauses

We use a participle clause when we want to include information more concisely in a sentence. Participle clauses can replace a clause with subject + verb. They are common in more formal contexts.

Participle clauses begin with either a present participle (e.g., *being*, *considering*) or a past participle (e.g., *given*, *considered*).

*Money is **usually** considered an exciting gift*

We can sometimes use a participle clause instead of a relative clause.

Money (that is) coming from an unexpected source often causes problems.

We use *having* + past participle to talk about the past.

***Having written** several books on the wise use of money, you are in a great position to give me advice on what to do.*

We put *not* in front of the participle to express a negative.

***Not having been** in this position before, I don't have any personal experience in this area, so I've been reading a lot about the best way to spend this money.*

See Grammar focus on page 165.

8 **IDENTIFY** Complete the clauses with the correct form of a participle from the box.

concern	find	know	read	receive

1 _____ some unexpected money, I've decided to pay off my student loan immediately.
2 Not _____ the letter thoroughly, I'm not sure why money doesn't always make people happy.
3 _____ as an expert on financial matters, he is often asked for his advice.
4 We didn't understand all of the issues _____ the budget.
5 _____ his address online, I decided to write for more information.

9 INTEGRATE Rewrite the sentences to include participle clauses. Then compare answers with a partner.

1 Have you asked the person who is overseeing the project?

2 Because she was an expert, Jan was able to explain the problem to us.

3 Because I work in an office, I like to get outdoors as much as possible.

4 Because he didn't heal right away, he went to a medical specialist.

5 Because I have considered all the options, I think the first solution is the best.

10 PREPARE Plan to write a formal letter of your own. Follow these steps.

1 Think of a problem or issue. (It can be personal, local, national, or global.)

2 Plan to write to an expert requesting advice about it.

3 Consider your audience and purpose.

4 Think about how you could use one or two participle clauses.

11 WRITE Write a draft of your letter. While you write, check your work by referring back to your notes and the information in the Writing Skill box.

12 IMPROVE Read your letter and correct any grammar and spelling mistakes. Check for examples of what you have learned.

Writing Checklist

☐ Have you included all of the parts the letter should contain?

☐ Did you include evidence that you have considered audience and purpose?

☐ Did you use relative or participle clauses?

☐ Did you use vocabulary related to problems and solutions?

13 SHARE Read a classmate's letter. Imagine you are the person they are writing to. Offer them some advice and say what they have done well in their letter.

A health expert gives advice to a woman in Swaziland

7.3 Overcoming Creative Block

1 ACTIVATE Work with a partner. Look at the photos. What are the people doing? What type of skills do these jobs involve?

2 INTERACT Work with a partner. Compare ideas about the photos in Exercise 1. How easy do you think it is to do these jobs on a daily basis? What kinds of challenges might these people face in their jobs? Make a list of the challenges and suggest one or two solutions for each challenge.

3 🔊 **IDENTIFY** Listen to the podcast. What is the topic?

> ## LISTENING SKILL Listening and note-taking
>
> You may want to take notes while you are listening to longer or more complex information. To write cohesive, relevant notes, consider these techniques:
>
> - Organize your notes using headings or bullet points to indicate key information.
>   *Strategies*
>   *1. Step away from proj.*
>
> - Note down important numbers, dates, facts, and statistics.
>   *Walking boosts creat. 60%*
>
> - Leave out unnecessary words (e.g., articles, auxiliary verbs).
>   *~~One thing I do when I get stuck is~~ step away from ~~the~~ work*
>
> - Use abbreviations (shorter versions of long words) and symbols.
> | | |
> |---|---|
> | *project = proj.* | *creative, creativity = creat.* |
> | *different, difference = diff.* | *activity = act.* |
> | *increase, boost = ↗* | |
> | *decrease, reduce = ↘* | |
> | *cause, lead to = →* | |

4 🔊 **ASSESS** Listen to the podcast again. Complete the notes. Then compare notes with a partner and revise as necessary.

> Topic: _____
> A creative block is _____.
> Strategies
> 1 Step away from proj.
> 2 Walking _____
> 3 New surroundings
>   a Travel _____
>   b Info from senses _____
> 4 Go back to _____
> 5 Look at _____
> 6 Make creat. act. _____
> 7 Think about it _____

5 EXPAND Answer the questions about the podcast. Use the information from your notes.

1 What did the Stanford study show about the effects of walking?

2 Do people get benefits from walking inside?

3 How does living abroad affect your creativity?

4 What did the writers Kafka, Darwin, and Chekhov have in common?

5 What is one tip to help you to see a creative project in a different way?

 GRAMMAR IN CONTEXT *would rather*

We use *would rather* + infinitive without *to* to talk about preferences. If we want to mention the alternative to our preference, we use *than*.

Note: In speech or informal writing, we usually use the contraction *'d* for *would*.

I'd much **rather leave** the project for a while than stay with it and get frustrated.

To make the negative form, we use *rather not*.

I'd **rather not make** something that's only adequate if I can make something extraordinary.

In questions, we often use *would rather* to ask about preferences or give options.

Would you **rather** work with other people or alone?

See Grammar focus on page 165.

6 IDENTIFY Complete the statements with *would rather* and the verbs in the box.

stay	sit	meet	do	pay	work

1 The first time we test a product, we _____ it outside for safety reasons.

2 I'_____ on the weekends, but I have to finish this project. (not)

3 If you'_____ someone to solve the problem than spend time on it yourself, it might be quicker.

4 We _____ at our desks. We get more ideas when we're moving. (not)

5 I _____ here just waiting for a good idea. I'm going out! (not)

6 _____ you _____ right now? We could get together tomorrow. (not)

7 WHAT'S YOUR ANGLE? Complete the questions with *would* (or *'d*) *rather* + *you* + bare infinitive. Then answer the questions about yourself. Share your ideas with a partner.

1 _____ (work) at home or in a busy coffee shop?

2 _____ (study) abroad or in your own country?

3 _____ (walk) indoors or outside?

4 _____ (push) through your creative block or step away for a while?

 VOCABULARY DEVELOPMENT Opposites

We often use opposites when we are making or emphasizing a contrast. Emphasizing the differences between two things makes your ideas more interesting and memorable. You can use opposite pairs that are adjectives, nouns, or verbs.

Common opposite verb pairs include *leave–stay*, *increase–reduce*, *borrow–lend*, and *learn–teach*.

Note: Some opposites are often confused with each other, such as *lend–borrow*. To avoid confusion, it helps to write down these words in context as part of a sentence.

⟡+ Oxford 5000™

8 IDENTIFY Choose the correct option in each sentence.

1 Do you have a book about web design? If so, can I *borrow / lend* it? I'm looking for ideas.

2 I want to take a painting class. I'd rather *teach / learn* how to present my ideas in a visual way than write about them all the time.

3 Many people would rather *stay / leave* at their computers until they finish a project, but I often step away.

4 My classmate *borrowed / lent* me her camera, but I can't figure out how to use it.

5 I'm worried that our marketing plan is not innovative enough. What can we do to *increase / decrease* sales?

9 INTEGRATE Look at your notes from the podcast. What are four pairs of contrasting ideas mentioned in the podcast?

 10 WHAT'S YOUR ANGLE? Work with a partner or in a small group. Look back at the photos in Exercise 1. Which of these creative professions would you rather or rather not do? Explain your reasons.

7.4 Spring Break

1 ACTIVATE Imagine you're trying to plan a trip with a friend. Which of the following would you use to persuade your friend to go someplace? Why?

"I've heard it's absolutely amazing. The beaches are wonderful."

"This is a great price. It won't last forever."

"We'll be so relaxed that it will be easy to come back and work hard."

2 IDENTIFY Look at the pictures. Discuss the questions with a partner.

Picture 1: What do you think Max and Andy are doing? How do you think they are feeling?

Picture 2: Where are Andy and Max? What do you think they are doing? How do you think they are feeling? Why?

3 ▶ ASSESS Watch the video, and decide if each statement is true (T) or false (F). Compare your answers with a partner.

1 Andy doesn't agree with Max's plan to fix the plumbing. ___
2 Andy and Max have a similar attitude toward time and trip planning. ___
3 Max calls Stavros. ___
4 Their tickets are for a later train. ___
5 Max and Andy end up going to New York. ___

4 ▶ IDENTIFY Watch the video again and answer the questions.

1 What does Andy persuade Max to do? Why?
2 What does Max persuade Andy to do? Why?
3 How do they try to persuade each other?

When we persuade people, we both disagree and make suggestions for a different course of action.

Express disagreement with expressions like:

Hmm, I don't know…
Really? I'm not so sure.
OK. Why do you think that's the case?
I really don't think that's a good idea / valid point.
I'm sorry, but I disagree with that.

Give a counter opinion or make an alternative proposal.

I actually think…   *Why don't we…*
I think we should…   *But don't you think…*
Most people in this situation would…
Another option would be to…

5 ▶ **ANALYZE** Watch the video again. What language do Andy and Max use to do the following?

1   Andy expresses disagreement:
_____

2   Andy makes an alternative proposal:
_____

3   Max expresses disagreement:
_____

4   Max makes an alternative proposal:
_____

6 **EXPAND** Work with a partner to answer the question.

Was Max easier to persuade regarding the plumbing or was Andy easier to persuade at the train station? Why do you think this would be the case?

7 **APPLY** Complete the conversation below with appropriate expressions and ideas. Then practice with a partner.

A: I got a terrible grade on the last test. I think I should drop the class.

B: _____ talk to the teacher.

A: I don't think that will do any good. I just don't understand the material.

B: _____.

8 **INTEGRATE** Work with a partner. Choose one of the situations and discuss how you would persuade someone to your point of view.

- Persuade someone in your family to try an alternative approach to treat terrible back pain or headaches (meditation, acupuncture, diet) rather than traditional medicine or surgery.
- Persuade your employer to spend $25,000 on a creative marketing idea or project you're interested in.
- Persuade a friend who doesn't have a lot of money to take an expensive trip to another country with you.
- Persuade your teacher to take the class on a field trip to an art museum.

9 **BUILD** With a partner, prepare a role play for one of the situations in Exercise 8.

10 **SHARE** Role-play your conversation for the class. Afterward, discuss the strategies and arguments you found most persuasive. Give reasons for your opinions.

GO ONLINE
to create your own version
of the English For Real video.

85

7.5 Hack Your Life

1 ACTIVATE Work with a partner. What do you think *hack* means? Tell your ideas to the class. Did anyone guess right?

2 🔊 **IDENTIFY** You are going to hear three students discussing a task. What object are they talking about? What solutions do they come up with?

◀ SPEAKING Evaluating and synthesizing

When you evaluate ideas, you weigh strengths and weaknesses. You will often use expressions of agreement, disagreement, and conceding (when you agree with part of the idea but disagree with the rest). When you synthesize ideas, you put them together.

Evaluating ideas

Agreeing	Disagreeing	Conceding
That's a great idea.	I'm not sure that will work.	It's interesting, but…
It might just work.	I'm not really convinced.	That's a valid point, but…
Brilliant!	It needs a lot more work.	The idea has potential, but…

Synthesizing ideas

If we take…and combine it with…
Let's put those ideas together.
What if we use…and add it to…
Taking…in combination with…, we could…

3 🔊 **IDENTIFY** Listen again and complete the phrases the speakers use to evaluate and synthesize ideas. Compare answers with a partner.

1 That's a neat trick, _____ is it stable? I mean, it _____ _____ _____ to type if it was moving around. ___
2 I _____ _____ _____, but I tried it, and it actually worked. ___
3 That's _____ _____ _____, but I'm _____ _____ _____ it _____ work. ___
4 I mean, _____ _____ _____ you try to unclip the peas? ___
5 What _____ _____ _____ my photo display idea with Jen's cell phone holder? ___

4 APPLY For each sentence in Exercise 3, decide if the speaker is agreeing (A), disagreeing (D), conceding (C), or synthesizing (S).

◀ PRONUNCIATION SKILL Focus words in chunks

🔊 When we speak, we divide the stream of speech into "chunks," or smaller pieces that usually contain a related idea. In each chunk, one word is always said more clearly and with a pitch change. This focus word is usually the last word in the chunk.

*With a little **imagination***
*and **innovation**,*
*we can use it to **solve***
*a lot of frustrating **problems***
*we deal with **every day**.*

When we use chunking, it's easier for listeners to understand our ideas.

5 🔊 **IDENTIFY** Listen to the sentence read in two different ways. Which one sounds better and is easier to understand? Listen again and mark the pauses with a slash (/).

With a little imagination and innovation, we can use it to solve a lot of frustrating problems we deal with every day.

6 🔊 **INTEGRATE** Read the sentence. Mark where you think the pauses will be with a slash (/). Then listen and check your answers.

The assignment was to come up with solutions to everyday problems, or hacks, using this—an ordinary binder clip.

7 PREPARE Prepare to contribute to a group discussion about how everyday items can be used to solve everyday problems. Choose an item from the list or use an idea of your own.

piece of paper	duct tape	pen	keys
sealable plastic bag	paper clip	rubber band	

1 Take a few minutes to choose your item
2 Think of two or three ways you can use it to solve everyday problems.
3 Review the Speaking box for ways to synthesize and evaluate (you will need to do this in the discussion).

8 INTEGRATE Practice explaining your problems and solutions with a partner. When you are ready, work in a small group and share your ideas. Make sure you evaluate ideas during your discussion. Where possible, synthesize ideas to come up with more or improved solutions.

Now go to page 153 for the Unit 7 Review.

8 Words

UNIT SNAPSHOT

What is a neologism?   89
What did Malala say about education?   93
What is a trick to make speeches more interesting?   94

BEHIND THE PHOTO

Are words or actions more important in friendship?

Do you pay attention to the words of public figures like politicians? Why?

In what ways do words lead to misunderstandings?

REAL-WORLD GOAL

Identify new words added to the Oxford English Dictionary in the past year.

Work with a partner to guess answers to the questions in the quiz. Then compare answers with another pair before you read the answer key.

1   Which language has the most words?
   Spanish   English   Chinese

2   How many words are currently in use in the English language?
   <100,000   >170,000   >300,000

3   In which country do people speak the language with the fewest words?
   Vietnam   Bhutan   Suriname

4   How long is the longest word in English?
   22 letters   30 letters   45 letters

8.1 More than Words

1 ACTIVATE Work with a partner. Look at the words that are "new" to the English language. Do you know what they mean? If you do, tell your partner the meaning. If not, think about the sound or "look" of the words and invent a meaning.

> figital

> hangry

> staycation

2 INTERACT Get together with another pair to share your ideas from Exercise 1.

3 VOCABULARY Match the neologisms (new words) to their meanings.

crowdsource	brunch	chillax
datahead	selfie	binge-watch

1 to relax and stop feeling angry or nervous about something: _____
2 a photo of yourself taken with a smartphone or a webcam to put on social media: _____
3 obtain information or help from a number of people over the Internet: _____
4 a person who has good general knowledge _____
5 viewing multiple episodes of a TV show one after the other: _____
6 a meal between breakfast and lunch: _____

4 BUILD Complete each sentence with a neologism from Exercise 3.

1 When I need a recommendation for a new restaurant or ideas for a vacation, I _____ them.
2 I don't plan to go out all weekend. I want to stay in and _____ some shows.
3 You look kind of tense. You need to _____ a little.

4 "Do you know the answer?" "No! Ask Dave, he's the _____!"
5 Wow! What a view. Come on, let's take a _____!
6 I know you're busy, but do you have time to meet for _____ on Thursday?

5 IDENTIFY Work with a partner. Read the text on the next page. Check your answers to Exercise 4.

6 INTEGRATE After reading the text, match each word or neologism with the correct information.

1 assentatour ___
2 brunch, smog ___
3 cell phone ___
4 education ___
5 google ___
6 ASAP, posh? ___
7 tablet ___
8 binge-watch ___

a compounding
b blending
c clipping
d conversion
e successful borrowing from Latin
f unsuccessful borrowing
g old word in a new context
h acronym

7 ASSESS Look at the words in the box. How do you think these words entered the English language? Refer to the categories in Exercise 6 if appropriate. Discuss your ideas with a partner.

karaoke	to microwave	sitcom	scuba

I like words! I won't apologize for saying it. I am a blogger, after all. I've come across so many words recently that have both fascinated and distracted me that I have decided to dedicate this blog post to them.

The English language has benefited from diverse sources. This diversity mostly comes from the English Renaissance when writers complained that there was a lack of useful vocabulary in English. Consequently, they borrowed freely from foreign languages—mostly having an eye for Latin, French, and Greek words. We can thank a couple of people in particular for adding new vocabulary. William Caxton, who introduced printing into England in 1477, is credited in the *OED* with the first use of now common words such as *admiration*, *capacity*, *desperate*, *factor*, and *ingenious*, among many others. It might be hard for modern readers to imagine a time when those words seemed foreign or absurd. Another early word-borrower, Thomas Elyot, wrote in the early sixteenth century. Like Caxton, Elyot had successes including *attraction*, *education*, *irritate*, and *persist*. But between them, they also had many failures—words such as *applicate* and *assentatour*—that never really made it into the English language.

The result of all this word-borrowing, though, is that we now have a rich and fascinating language that has been built over many centuries. The majority of English words originate from Greek, Latin, and Anglo-Saxon.

Popular notions of etymology, or the study of word origins, are often quite colorful—and quite wrong. To cite but one example, many well-educated people claim that *posh* comes from an acronym, or set of initials, that means "port outward, starboard home," and that the word refers to the most desirable positions in an ocean liner. In actual fact, though, professional etymologists haven't been able to support that—indeed, they've pretty much rejected it. So, under *posh*, most dictionaries say "origin unknown." Although the popular notion would make it a colorful term, the facts unfortunately get in the way of a good story.

Now more than ever, we're seeing neologisms—new words or expressions or new meanings that arise from existing words over time—enter our dictionaries. These serve as a fascinating reminder that language is constantly changing with the times, being edited and added to. For example, words such as *selfie* and *chillax*, which we take for granted now, were unheard of until relatively recently.

You can make neologisms in a variety of ways. It's a piece of cake. You can put two words together to form a new compound word, such as *datahead*, *binge-watch*, or *crowdsource*. This is called *compounding*. Technology has brought the winds of change to language, too. You can use an old word in a new context to describe new tools, such as *tablet*. My favorite is to simply blend two words to create a new one, such as *smog* (*smoke* + *fog*) or *brunch* (*breakfast* + *lunch*). *Conversion* is what occurs when you use a word as a different part of speech, such as changing the noun *Google* to the verb *to google*. And shortening a word like *telephone* to *phone* is called *clipping*. Like them or not, we need to acknowledge that neologisms fill gaps in our language as new unnamed ideas, concepts, and innovations emerge. What's next? We'll just have to wait and see—but probably not for long.

—adapted from *Garner's Modern English Usage*, 4th ed., edited by Bryan A. Garner

---

READING SKILL
Recognizing and understanding idioms

An idiom is a group of words whose meaning (when they are used together) is different from the meanings of the individual words. Writers often use idioms to make texts more fun and engaging.

get in the way (of)
change with the times

When you come across an idiom, try to work out the meaning by considering the overall context and reading the sentences around it carefully. You could keep a section in your vocabulary notebook for recording idioms.

8 IDENTIFY Look at the idioms in the box. Do you know what they mean? Identify these idioms in the blog post. Look at the context to figure out their meaning. Then share your ideas with a partner.

winds of change	piece of cake	take for granted

 9 WHAT'S YOUR ANGLE? Answer the questions. Then discuss your ideas in a small group.

1 Is anything about language learning "a piece of cake" for you? What aspects of language learning are easiest?

2 Do you agree that technology has brought the "winds of change" to our lives, including the way we use language and words? In what ways?

3 What do native speakers of a language take for granted? How does that affect communication with nonnative speakers?

We can use a variety of verbs to report what was said. Reporting verbs can be followed by a number of different structures:

- verb + *to* + infinitive (*agree, ask, demand, offer, promise, refuse, threaten*)
  *Last week, a friend **offered to take** me out to brunch.*

- verb + person + *to* + infinitive (*advise, ask, convince, encourage, invite, order, persuade, remind, tell, warn*)
  *My tutor **encouraged me to apply** for the grant.*

- verb + (preposition) + *-ing* verb (*admit, apologize for, deny, insist on, suggest*)
  *He **suggested arriving** early to get a seat.*
  *I won't **apologize for saying** it.*

- verb + person + preposition + *-ing* verb (*accuse… of, blame…for, congratulate…on* or *for, praise…for, thank…for, warn…against*)
  *We **can thank a few people** in particular **for adding** new vocabulary.*

- verb + (*that*) + clause (*add, admit, argue, claim, complain, deny, explain, mention, predict, promise, suggest, think, warn*)
  *This diversity mostly comes from the English Renaissance when writers **complained that** there was a lack of useful vocabulary in English.*

See Grammar focus on page 166.

10 IDENTIFY Choose the correct term to complete each example of reporting language.

1 "Don't use the neologism in the report!" → He warned me *not to use / don't use* the neologism in the report.

2 "I didn't crowdsource the data." → He denied *to crowdsource / crowdsourcing* the data.

3 "I'm sorry I posted that selfie." → She apologized *for posting / that she posted* the selfie.

4 "I wrote the article myself." → He claimed that *he'd written / for writing* the article himself.

5 "Well done, guys!" → He congratulated us *of / on* giving a good presentation.

11 EXPAND Write sentences using the prompts in parentheses.

1 "I'll come to brunch on Thursday." (Jess / promise)

2 "New words are added to the dictionary all the time." (Jack / explain)

3 "Some new words are confusing." (she / warn)

4 "*Binge-watch* is now in the dictionary." (we / confirm)

5 "I'll look up the definitions." (Matt / insist on)

6 "The dictionary will have sample sentences." (the teacher / reassure her)

12 WHAT'S YOUR ANGLE? Work in a small group. Discuss the following questions.

1 Can you think of examples of "borrowed" words, idioms, or neologisms in your first language?

2 If so, how are they formed? Do you have any favorites? Give some examples and explain why.

8.2 Mark My Words

1 ACTIVATE Work with a partner. What do the quotations mean? How do they all say something similar about words? Which do you agree with?

1 *"A word after a word after a word is power."* ___

2 *"Good words do not last long unless they amount to something."* ___

3 *"And once sent out a word takes wing beyond recall."* ___

2 IDENTIFY Who do you think said each quote in Exercise 1? Match the letter to the quote. Read the blog post to check your guesses.

a Margaret Atwood, 1939–, Canadian novelist: "Spelling" (1981)

b Horace, 65–8 BCE, Roman poet: *Epistles* Bk. 1, no. 18, l. 71

c Hin-mah-too-yah-lat-kekt, aka Chief Joseph, c.1840–1904, Nez Perce chief: on a visit to Washington in 1879

3 NOTICE Read the blog post at right. What is the "single word" referred to in the title?

4 ASSESS Match the paragraphs in the blog post to the descriptions. Write the paragraph numbers.

___ Engaging directly with the reader

___ Comparing words to birds to show that they are alive

___ Explaining that words need to mean something, not be simply empty words

___ Telling a story to introduce the topic

___ Using quotes to discuss the power of words

5 EXPAND Answer the questions about the blog post.

1 Where did the writer go in the first paragraph?

2 Did the writer enjoy the trip? Why or why not?

3 What did the writer decide to do to improve her life?

4 How does she use the word?

5 Has it improved her life?

6 WHAT'S YOUR ANGLE? Do you think a single word could help you improve your life in some way? If so, which word(s) in the box are the most powerful for you? What other words could you use?

love	hope	justice	kindness	peace
pleasure	anger	commitment	determination	

| Home | About | Articles | Search | 🔍 |

The Power of a Single Word

1 Last month, I went with a friend to a lake in the mountains. The weather was perfect, the setting beautiful. But I had a lot on my mind—deadlines at work, an argument with a family member, bills I had to pay. I can't remember many details about the day at all. I returned home just as stressed and distracted as when I set out in the morning. I wondered why I hadn't enjoyed myself. I decided I needed to pay more attention to what was going on around me to find as much joy as I could in my everyday life.

2 According to Margaret Atwood, the Canadian novelist, "a word after a word after a word is power." By this I think she means that connected ideas or sentences, whether in speech or in writing, give us power over those ideas—and maybe power over our own lives. The British politician Benjamin Disraeli might have been saying something similar when he remarked that "with words we govern men" (and women too, I'm sure). However, I think even a single word, well chosen, can do a lot. When used correctly, it can remind us of what is important in our daily lives.

3 What word might be powerful enough to improve my life? I decided on *joy* because it is so positive and might help me remember what is important. I set a reminder on my phone, so periodically throughout the day, I would remember to find joy in the world around me. In 1879, Nez Perce Chief Joseph said that "good words do not last long unless they amount to something." I think this is still true. As beautiful as the word *joy* is, it will only improve my life if I let it. When the word pops up on my phone, I look around me and try to find something that brings me joy. It might be the taste of the espresso I'm drinking or the breeze on my face or the sound of children laughing nearby.

4 My friend from the lake asked me a few days ago if this word had changed my life. Actually, it has, at least a little. I pay more attention to the world around me, and I'm able to forget my worries for a short time. Two thousand years ago, the Roman poet Horace described "words sent out" as taking "wing beyond recall." By this I think he meant that that words are like birds, with a life of their own.

5 So, I'm sending out the word *joy*. What word would you choose to send out?

WRITING SKILL Using reported speech

Writers express the ideas of others through paraphrasing, direct quotes, and reported speech. If you want to use ideas from several writers or several ideas from one writer, using reported speech helps you avoid lengthy quotes and provides greater sentence variety.

You can use reported speech to:

- present a position you want to comment on or argue about.

  I agree with the saying "A picture is worth a thousand words."

- show that an authority supports your point of view.

  Like Nelson Mandela, I believe that education is the most important weapon we can use to change the world.

- present rich or unusual language or context.

  "Ask not what your country can do for you—ask what you can do for your country."

7 ASSESS Answer the questions about the blog post. Then discuss your answers with a partner.

1 How many ideas does the writer present in reported speech?

2 What is the purpose of each example? Do they accomplish more than one thing?

3 Which do you think is the best use of reported speech?

4 In how many of the examples did the writer change the tense? Why do you think she made this choice?

GRAMMAR IN CONTEXT Reported questions

In reported questions, we report what someone has asked. We use verbs such as *ask, want to know,* and *wonder.* We generally use an object pronoun after *ask.*

We usually use the past tense of the reporting verb, e.g., *asked* or *wondered,* and change the tense as we do in reported statements.

To report a *wh-* question, we use:

ask + (object) + question word + clause (with affirmative word order)

"Why didn't I enjoy myself?" (past tense) → *I wondered why I hadn't enjoyed myself. (past perfect)*

Note that the subject comes before the verb, and we do not use the auxiliary verb *do.*

To report a *yes/no* question, we use:

ask + (object) + *if* or *whether* + clause (with affirmative word order)

"Has this word changed your life?" → *My friend asked me if this word had changed my life.*

See Grammar focus on page 166.

8 IDENTIFY Correct the error in each sentence.

1 Maria asked me she could borrow my tablet.
2 He wondered why they hadn't add the word to the dictionary yet.
3 She asked us what were we listening to.
4 They wanted to know I was interested in the speech.
5 The teacher asked Hao he hadn't finished his presentation by the deadline.
6 Tom asked if could he come with us to the lecture.

9 INTEGRATE Complete the reported questions. Use the verbs in parentheses to help you.

1 "Why haven't you read the speech?" (ask, you)
   I _____.
2 "Did she enjoy the trip to the lake?" (ask)
   He _____.
3 "Why did Ella choose that quote?" (wonder)
   Elisa _____.
4 "What have you learned about Chief Joseph?" (ask, we)
   He _____.
5 "What are you both studying?" (want to know)
   They _____.
6 "Do you want to improve your lives?" (ask, we)
   She _____.

10 PREPARE Read the quotations. Plan to write a blog post of your own related to one of the quotes from this exercise, another from this unit, or one you choose.

> *"One child, one teacher, one book and one pen can change the world. Education is the only solution. Education first."*
> Malala Yousafzai b.1997, Pakistani education campaigner: speaking to the United Nations General Assembly, New York, July 12, 2013
>
> *"Words are chameleons, which reflect the color of their environment."*
> Learned Hand 1872–1961, American judge (1948)
>
> *"We must be the change we wish to see in the world."*
> Mahatma Gandhi 1869–1948, Indian statesman: not traced in Gandhi's writings but said to be a favorite saying; attributed (1989) in *Yale Book of Quotations*

Do one of the following tasks:

• Say how the quote relates to your own life.
• Say whether you agree with the quote (respond positively or negatively).

Then follow these steps:

1 Choose a quotation and make notes of your ideas and opinions related to it.
2 Plan the paragraphs of your blog post.
   • introduction: State your main idea or thesis about the quote.
   • body paragraphs (1–3): Develop your idea using supporting details, explanations, arguments.
   • informal conclusion: Engage the reader with a question to answer or a task to do.
3 Consider how you could use reported speech to make your post more interesting.

11 WRITE Write a draft of your blog post. While you write, refer back to your notes from Exercise 10 and the information in the Writing Skill box.

12 IMPROVE Read your blog post and correct any grammar and spelling mistakes. Check for examples of what you have learned.

Writing Checklist

☐ Did you express your ideas or views based on the quotation?
☐ Did you include one main point in each paragraph?
☐ Did you engage directly with the reader?
☐ Did you use examples of reported speech to support your ideas?
☐ Did you have an introduction and conclusion?

13 SHARE Read a classmate's blog post. Say which ideas and views you agree with and what they have done well.

8.3 Stand and Deliver

1 **ACTIVATE** Look at the photo. Which of the following do you think are important in giving a good speech? Rank them in order of importance (1–6). Share your ideas in a small group.

___ telling a story

___ creating a picture with words

___ asking questions

___ using rhyme or rhythm

___ using famous quotes

___ speaking with emotion

___ using unusual words or word order

2 🔊 **ASSESS** Listen to the first part of a radio interview. According to Simone Adams, why do some people need speechwriters? What should a speechwriter think about?

3 🔊 **INTEGRATE** Listen to the next part of the interview. Answer the questions. Then share your ideas with a partner.

1 What makes a good speech?

2 According to Simone, what should a great speech "sound" like?

3 What clever speechwriting tricks does Simone mention?

🎧 LISTENING SKILL Recognizing paraphrase

We often report what someone has said by paraphrasing it. This means we refer to the person and their words but we do not quote them directly. Instead, we use some or all of our own words to explain or express what was said.

You can identify paraphrase by listening for:

• reported speech: name + reporting verb (*suggested, declared, announced, revealed*).

• words and phrases such as:
According to (name)…
(Name) believed / expressed / spoke about…
(Name) once said (that)…
(Name) is famous for saying…

4 🔊 **IDENTIFY** Listen to the excerpt from the interview. List three examples of paraphrase or mixture of paraphrase and quotation.

5 **ASSESS** Work with a partner. Follow the steps.

1 Share your ideas about the examples of paraphrase in the excerpt. Explain how you chose the examples.

2 Identify an example of a complete quotation in the text.

3 What is the difference between the paraphrase and quotation? Discuss your ideas.

🎧 PRONUNCIATION SKILL Spoken punctuation

🔊 In presentations and speeches, we use pauses in a similar way to how we use punctuation in writing. Pauses can have several functions. For example, they can separate the points in a list, add emphasis, allow the audience time to process an idea, or allow the speaker to take a breath. A speaker will often pause between thought groups—groups of words with a single idea. Prepositional phrases, noun phrases, and verb + object combinations are examples of common thought groups.

I'd like to make a point about education.
I'd like / to make a point / about education.
Identify your purpose, consider your audience, and deliver a powerful speech.
Identify your purpose / consider your audience / and deliver / a powerful speech.

Learning how to use pauses effectively and practicing using them will help you improve your fluency and get your message across to your audience clearly.

6 🔊 **IDENTIFY** Work with a partner. Imagine you are going to deliver these phrases in a speech. Mark where you might put the pauses. Then listen and check your answers.

1 It's essential that your message is heard and understood.

2 It isn't just the historical context that makes a speech memorable.

3 There's no shame in taking inspiration from other sources.

4 Memorable speeches sound like poetry, and poetry is easy to remember.

5 Do you have the power to inspire and enthuse, or will your words go down like a lead balloon?

7 **INTERACT** Take turns practicing the sentences in Exercise 6 with a partner.

VOCABULARY DEVELOPMENT
Discussing a quotation or paraphrase

When talking about the words of others, speakers use a variety of reporting verbs. These verbs have slightly different meanings. We are more likely to use some in certain contexts than others.

Neutral reporting verbs describe speech in factual terms (*say, report, point out, confirm, acknowledge, express*).

Weak reporting verbs are less certain (*suggest, remark*).

Strong reporting verbs indicate that the speaker is saying something forcefully (*declare, reveal, deny*).

8 BUILD Read the sentences. Choose the meaning of the reporting verb.

1 The man **denied** that he had copied the speech from someone else.
   a say is true
   b say is false

2 The police **reported** that more than a million people attended the speech.
   a give an account of
   b ask the listener to consider

3 The press secretary **confirms** that the president will speak at 1 p.m.
   a refuse to admit something is true
   b state with certainty that something is true

4 I **suggested** there might be another explanation.
   a give an account of
   b ask the listener to consider

5 The two sides **declared** they had reached an agreement.
   a say something in a serious, sure manner
   b make a suggestion

6 He **remarked** that he was tired.
   a say something very forcefully
   b mention, comment

7 The woman **revealed** that she had actually written the president's remarks.
   a make something known that was hidden
   b make a suggestion

8 The politician **acknowledges** that he may not win the election, but he's still going to continue his speaking tour.
   a comment
   b accept the truth of

℗+ Oxford 5000™

9 USE If you get some information from a social media site, how do you try to confirm it? Discuss with a partner.

GRAMMAR IN CONTEXT Reported speech

We use reported speech to explain what someone has said.

*T. S. Eliot once **remarked that** average or "mediocre" writers borrow the words of others…*
*A client once **told me** to imagine myself in the situation.*

In reported speech, we usually change the verb by moving it back one tense into the past.

present tense → past tense

"I admire Maya Angelou."
*She said she **admired** Maya Angelou.*

present perfect → past perfect

"So I've always wondered—what makes a great speech?"
He said he'd always wondered what makes a great speech.

will → would   can → could   must → had to
may → might

"Politicians may not have time to write their own speeches."
*She said that politicians **might** not have time to write their own speeches.*

We *do not* change the verb if what the person says is still true, relevant, or important.

*Everyone **wants** to write a speech that will motivate and inspire people.*

See Grammar focus on page 166.

10 IDENTIFY Choose the correct example of reported speech for each sentence.

1 "I've never wanted to speak to large groups of people."
   a He said to me he had never wanted to speak to large groups of people.
   b He said he had never wanted to speak to large groups of people.

2 "We might go to the lecture."
   a They said they might have gone to the lecture.
   b They said they might go to the lecture.

3 "Many speeches try to persuade the listener."
   a Jake said many speeches try to persuade the listener.
   b Jake said many speeches tried to persuade the listener.

4 "We could begin with a quote."
   a She suggested we can begin with a quote.
   b She suggested we could begin with a quote.

5 "I'll be in London on the 27th."
   a He told us he'd be in London on the 27th.
   b He said us he'd be in London on the 27th.

11 WHAT'S YOUR ANGLE? Discuss the questions with a partner. Then find a new partner and use reported speech to share your first partner's answers to one question.

1 What famous quote do you find inspiring? Why?
2 Who has been a role model for you?
3 Which famous person do you most admire? Why?

ENGLISH FOR REAL

1 ACTIVATE Look at the situations in the box. Have you given bad news about yourself in any of these situations in the past two weeks? What kind of news was shared?

| at work | at home | at school | social situation | with strangers |

2 ASSESS Look at the pictures. Discuss the questions with a partner.

1 Who is in the video?
2 How do you think they are feeling?
3 What do you think they might be saying?

3 ▶ IDENTIFY Watch the video and answer the questions.

1 What is the name of the grant that Max wants to apply for?
2 Why does he feel disappointed?
3 How does Emma cheer him up?

REAL-WORLD ENGLISH Sharing news about yourself

When we share news about ourselves, especially difficult news, we can follow several steps.

First, let the listener know a serious matter will be discussed.
Do you have a minute?
Can I talk to you about something?

Then, give background to orient the listener.
So, you know....?
Remember that...?

Finally, deliver the unexpected news.
Well, it turns out...
Well, I can't / didn't / won't...

The listener will often try to comfort the speaker by expressing sympathy, saying what the speaker does well or giving hope.

4 ▶ **INTEGRATE** Watch the video again. Who says each expression, Max (M) or Emma (E)?

Scene 1

1 Do you have a minute? ___
2 Sure, what's up? ___
3 So, you know that International Arts Grant I wanted to apply for? ___
4 Well…Dave is going to submit his application and Professor Armstrong says I can't apply. ___
5 Oh, no! That's awful. ___
6 Well, apparently my Art History grade isn't as high as Dave's. ___
7 Don't be so down on yourself, Max. ___
8 There will be other opportunities. ___
9 I'm just feeling really discouraged. ___

5 **ANALYZE** Match each expression in Exercise 4 with its purpose(s). Some may be used more than once, and some might not be used. Discuss your answers with a partner.

a express sympathy ___
b give hope ___
c start a conversation about a difficult topic ___
d accept the invitation to talk ___
e express difficult feelings or news ___
f give background, orient listener ___

6 **ANALYZE** With a partner, compare the two scenes. In what ways are the conversations similar? How are the interactions different? Why?

7 **PREPARE** You are going to practice giving bad news about yourself. Follow the steps.

1 Choose one of the situations in the list (or make up a situation of your own).
- You interviewed for your dream job, but you didn't get it.
- You failed your driving test.
- You slept late and missed an important exam.
- Your application to your first choice of college wasn't successful.
- Your team lost the championship game.
2 Prepare to explain your unfortunate situation. Take notes on background information to orient the listener.
3 Read through the other situations in the list. Consider how you could comfort your classmates if they have chosen these situations.

8 **INTERACT** When you are ready, get up and walk around the class. Greet a classmate and then ask, "Do you have a minute?" Share the difficult news. Then switch roles. Find new partners and share your news.

9 **SHARE** Have a class discussion. What news is harder to share? Why? What kind of background information is helpful to give? What kind of response is most comforting?

 GO ONLINE
to create your own version
of the English For Real video.

8.5 Just a Misunderstanding

1 ACTIVATE Describe the photos. What kinds of stories do you think are being told? How do you think the listeners or audiences are feeling?

2 **IDENTIFY** Listen to a student telling an anecdote about a misunderstanding she had. What was the misunderstanding?

SPEAKING Telling a story

When we tell stories, we engage and entertain our audience by conveying mood, describing the scene and the people, and making the listener feel "close to the action."

Use tenses to orient the listener and make them feel involved in the story.

- The dramatic present makes the action seem more immediate.

  The weather is hot and humid, there's the constant whine of mosquitoes in Beijing who seem to think I'm delicious, and something in the air tickles my throat all the time.

- Use narrative tenses to transport the listener back in time in a "flashback."

  I'd been there for a few weeks and had made a few friends.

- Use future tenses to show a person's predictions.

  I was thinking, "If I go over there, they're going to walk away."

Future tenses can also be used to jump forward in time.

If you think it's bad now, just imagine what it will be like in 2060!

Use reported or quoted speech to show a person's thoughts and feelings or present conversation.

Someone calls out, "Where are you going? Come here."

Use descriptive language to describe the characters' appearances or personalities, their feelings, their actions, and the setting.

An is kind and friendly, with a smile for everyone.
Now I'm completely confused, and my face is warm with embarrassment.
I yell "Hi" to them and wave to get their attention.
The weather is hot and humid.

---

3 **IDENTIFY** Listen to the anecdote again. Match the descriptive words (right) to the thing they describe. Check your answers with a partner.

1	quad ___	a	confused, embarrassment
2	vendors ___	b	crowded and noisy
3	meat ___	c	hands down, flap fingers
4	weather ___	d	hot and humid
5	mosquitoes ___	e	shouting
6	air ___	f	sizzling
7	gesture ___	g	tickle
8	the speaker's feelings ___	h	whine

4 ASSESS Work with a partner. What do the words in the first column in Exercise 3 mean? What parts of speech are they? Use a dictionary to check your answers.

5 **ANALYZE** Match the excerpts from the story to their functions.

1	___	a	describing a person's personality
2	___	b	making a prediction
3	___	c	describing a person's feelings
4	___	d	setting the scene
5	___	e	flashback
6	___	f	using dramatic present

6 PREPARE Prepare to describe a misunderstanding that you have experienced. It can be real or imaginary, serious or humorous. Take notes on the following, including descriptive language.

- main events   • people involved   • setting

7 SHARE Work with a partner. Practice telling your story and giving feedback. Make it as engaging as possible. Use your notes from Exercise 6 (including descriptive language) and dramatic present tense, narrative tenses, and future tense as appropriate.

8 IMPROVE When you are ready, use feedback to revise your story. Then work with a new partner to tell your stories.

9 WHAT'S YOUR ANGLE? Why do we tell stories? What qualities make a good story or storyteller? Do you know anyone who is a good storyteller? Why?

Now go to page 154 for the Unit 8 Review.

9 Investment

UNIT SNAPSHOT

In what ways can you invest in yourself?   101
What are the features of a good logo?   106
How are goats a good business investment?   110

How does investment benefit people?

Is investment always a good thing?

What do you invest time in?

BEHIND THE PHOTO

Answer the questions. Then discuss the answers in a small group.

1   How important is money to individuals, families, cultures, and society in general?
2   How important is it to invest in the future? What are you doing to invest in yours?
3   In what ways does what you invest in reflect who you are?

REAL-WORLD GOAL

Go online and find an example of an unusual business idea

9.1 Your Best Investment

1 ACTIVATE Look at the ways you could spend or invest your money. Which do you think would give you the greatest benefit over time?

gym membership	job skills class
share in a new business	savings account
membership in a networking organization	life or career coach

2 IDENTIFY Read the sentences. Match the word in bold in each sentence to its definition.

1 Some people earn income additionally by investing money in other businesses. ___
2 I don't have many assets—just a car and a nice bicycle. ___
3 Economists don't always agree on financial policies. ___
4 Entrepreneurs often work long hours as they try to get their businesses going. ___
5 New laws might potentially affect the prices of certain goods. ___
6 My time is very precious to me, so I don't like to waste it. ___
7 I don't invest in the stock market. I think it's too risky, so I choose safer options. ___
8 Do you want to attend this seminar on saving for retirement with me? ___
9 The government sometimes takes action that will stimulate the economy by creating new jobs. ___
10 The idea of failure terrifies me. I'm so afraid of not succeeding. ___

ℱ+ Oxford 5000™

a a useful or valuable thing (n.)
b as an extra factor or to introduce a new argument (adv.)
c an expert in economics or the branch of knowledge concerned with wealth
d able to develop or happen in the future
e of great value (adj.)
f a conference or other meeting for discussion or training
g encourage development or increased activity in
h full of the possibility of danger, failure, or loss
i cause to feel extreme fear
j someone who sets up a business that might fail in the hope of earning a profit

3 WHAT'S YOUR ANGLE? Answer the questions. Then discuss your answers with a partner.

1 What is more precious to you: money or time?
2 Do you think entrepreneurs need a certain kind of personality?
3 What is something risky you have done in the past year?
4 Does anything terrify you? If so, what?
5 What seminars, if any, have you attended?
6 What activities do you do to stimulate your mind?

4 IDENTIFY Decide if the sentences are true (T) or false (F).

1 A single class can change your life. ___
2 It's better to save your money than to spend it on activities you enjoy. ___
3 Exercise improves your physical health but doesn't do much for your mental health. ___
4 People in their twenties rarely change jobs, so skill development isn't as important as it will be when they're older. ___
5 A good way to invest your money is to buy yourself more time. ___

5 ASSESS Read the article on the next page. Then check your answers to Exercise 4.

6 INTEGRATE Answer the questions about the article.

1 What did Warren Buffet spend $100 on?
2 How does participating in wellness programs affect workers?
3 Why should people do sports like running?
4 How many times on average do U.S. workers change jobs over their lifetimes?
5 How many hours per week do entrepreneurs usually work?
6 What is a benefit of daydreaming?

Invest in Yourself

Billionaire investor Warren Buffett has often encouraged people to invest in themselves, saying it is their best investment. As a young man, he paid $100 to take a course to help him with something that terrified him—public speaking. The class changed his life in more ways than one. In fact, in the middle of the course, he had gained so much confidence that he proposed to the woman who would become his wife. A small investment provided a big reward.

When we invest, we use our precious resources of time and/or money to improve our situation in life, usually to increase wealth. But experts, including many economists, suggest we should be investing more in ourselves. The rewards are potentially much greater (although they're not always financial), and it is much less risky than investing in some businesses.

So how can you invest in yourself? First, invest in your physical and mental health. A recent study showed that workers who participated in wellness programs increased their productivity as much as one extra workday per month. Getting more exercise, even standing, can help students study more and employees get more work done. Exercise not only improves your physical health, it also boosts your mental health. People who participate in activities like running are better at cognitive tasks, live longer, and are less likely to get dementia or other mental problems as they get older. Eating healthy food and getting more sleep are also important ways to improve

the quality of your life. If you want to protect your most important asset, you, then it's important to stay healthy.

Additionally, you can invest in yourself by learning and acquiring new skills. Free online classes and seminars are available on the Internet, or you can attend one at a local college or university. The time and money you spend will only make you more valuable in the job market. If you need to find a new position, you will have skills employers want. In the United States, workers will change jobs on average 12 times in their lifetimes (and four times before they are 32 years old). Taking a class or taking up a new hobby that is mentally stimulating can help you improve problem-solving skills.

Improving your health and increasing your skill set may be obvious ways to invest in yourself. However, many people don't consider giving themselves more free time as a way to increase their overall worth. A recent study showed that entrepreneurs generally work more than 50 hours a week. As a rule, they believe that working more will help their small businesses succeed. However, hiring more people can give a business owner more time. What should you do with more free time? Daydreaming can lead to greater creativity. More time for self-reflection can help you refocus on your goals. Taking the time to organize your life can let you produce more. Volunteering for good causes can make you more optimistic.

The bottom line? Investing in yourself is a wise way to spend your time and money.

READING SKILL
Recognizing and understanding generalizations

A generalization is a broad statement used to describe what a group of people or things have in common. It uses information or observations to make a statement. Valid generalizations are based on factual information and logical thinking.

To recognize valid generalizations, look for facts and specific words and phrases: *in general, generally, generally speaking, as a rule, the majority of, a small minority of, many, most.*

A recent study showed that entrepreneurs **generally** *work more than 50 hours a week.*

To recognize words and phrases that might signal faulty generalizations, look for *all, every, everyone, no, no one, always,* and *never.*

7 **IDENTIFY** Work with a partner to match the parts of the sentences that use valid generalizations. Then identify the words or information that makes the generalization valid.

1 But experts, including many economists, ___
2 A recent study showed that workers who participated in wellness programs ___
3 Getting more exercise, even standing, can help students study more and employees ___
4 In the United States, workers will change jobs ___
5 However, many people don't consider giving themselves ___
6 A recent study showed that entrepreneurs ___
7 As a rule, they believe that ___

a generally work more than 50 hours a week.
b get as much as 75 percent more work done according to a university study.
c on average 12 times in their lifetimes and four times before they are 32 years old.
d suggest we should be investing more in ourselves.
e working more will help their small businesses succeed.
f increased their productivity as much as one extra workday per month.
g more free time as a way to increase value.

8 **EXPAND** Work with a partner. Discuss ways to change the faulty generalizations to valid ones.

1 All entrepreneurs work too hard.
2 No one thinks you should invest in yourself.
3 People who run a lot are always healthier than those who do not.
4 Everybody will change jobs four times before they reach 32 years of age.

GRAMMAR IN CONTEXT
Structures with infinitive

Want and *allow* are followed by object + *to* infinitive.
Billionaire investor Warren Buffett **wants people to invest** *in themselves*
It **allows them to develop** *better skills.*

Want can also be followed by the infinitive with *to*
If you **want to protect** *your most important asset, you, then it's important to stay healthy.*

Make and *let* are followed by object + infinitive without *to*
My desire to improve my life **makes me invest** *time and resources in myself.*
Taking the time to organize your life can **let you produce** *more*

See Grammar focus on page 167.

9 **IDENTIFY** Complete the text with the correct form of a verb from the box. Some verbs can be used more than once.

make	want	allow	let

Investment is the use of resources to
¹ _____ more money or goods.
Businesses ² _____ to spend a certain amount of money or other resources in order to grow the business. They plan to construct new buildings, buy machinery, and purchase supplies, all of which costs money. Economists often ³ _____ governments to build roads and bridges as a way to create jobs and make the country more productive. Individuals often take classes or training because it ⁴ _____ them to develop better skills. The development of better skills often ⁵ _____ workers earn more money. If they learn to do new things, they can often get better jobs. To grow, businesses need to replace damaged or worn-out equipment and adopt new technology. New technology will ⁶ _____ them to produce more.

—adapted from *Oxford Encyclopedia of Economic History*, edited by Joel Mokyr

10 **APPLY** Answer the questions. Then ask and answer them with a partner.

1 What would more free time allow you to do?
2 What should people plan to do to protect their most important assets?
3 In what ways can you expect your career to change over your lifetime?
4 What will learning new skills help you do?
5 In your country, how many times does the average person change careers? Why is this?

9.2 Smart Investments

1 ACTIVATE Work with a partner. Which of the following do you think governments should invest in? Rank them in order of importance (1 = most important, 7 = least important).

___ energy   ___ agriculture

___ small businesses   ___ roads and bridges

___ science   ___ security

___ education

2 IDENTIFY Read the persuasive essay that responds to the following prompt. How does the writer complete the following sentence prompt?

The government should invest in…

The Best Government Investment

On September 12, 1962, John F. Kennedy said, "We choose to go to the moon, not because it is easy, but because it is hard." His words gave us something to dream about. Before the decade was over, humans would not only go into space multiple times but actually walk on the moon. Because of government investment in space programs in the United States, the Soviet Union, and other countries, we can actually aim for the stars. Space exploration is just one way in which science has expanded our horizons. Government investment in different types of scientific research will benefit people in several important ways.

First, by investing in medical research, governments can solve health problems around the world. With increasing globalization, people and diseases can travel quickly from one country to another. New diseases such as SARS, HIV, and Ebola have had deadly consequences. It often takes drug companies a long time to develop medicines and vaccines that will treat and prevent such diseases, and it can be very expensive. Private companies may not want to invest time and money in research that will not make a profit. If governments provide funding for this research, it can speed the process of researching and developing medical treatments.

Investment in climate research will also benefit people around the world. Studies suggest that the climate is changing, with potentially disastrous results. Polar ice is melting, and sea levels are rising. This is dangerous for cities on the coast. Additionally, climate change may be causing more severe storms. Terrible hurricanes and tsunamis have destroyed cities around the world from Indonesia to Haiti. If governments know more about climate change, they can respond better to natural disasters and develop plans to help people who live in areas at risk. The best way to prevent problems is to learn as much as possible about what causes them.

Finally, scientific research may help us find new ways or new places to live. As our world changes and populations grow, we may run out of room. Scientists could help us figure out how to live on or below the water or on the moon or another planet. Governments have already established an international space station, put satellites in orbit, and launched spacecraft that have landed on Mars, so anything is possible. Although finding a new world to live in may seem too unlikely to worry about in the near future, this kind of exploration will need years if not decades to plan.

When Kennedy promised to go to the moon more than a half century ago, he put his faith in scientific research, and the U.S. government paid for it. Without government funding, the moon landing wouldn't have happened. If governments invest in science, they will be better able to solve medical and environmental problems and find solutions to an overcrowded world. The government should invest in science in order to deal with the hard problems we face.

WRITING SKILL
Writing main and supporting arguments

Like all essays, a persuasive essay has three parts: introduction, body paragraphs, and conclusion.

Introduction:

- Thesis: The main argument, or thesis, is usually stated in the introduction and is often the last sentence. The main argument presents the writer's position on a topic.

  The government should invest in…because…
  Government in…is necessary…because
  The government needs to…
  Government investment will…

- Hook: The introduction often begins with something that will grab the reader's attention, like a story or a quote.

Body paragraphs: Each paragraph contains:

- Topic sentence: presents one supporting argument

- Includes facts, examples, reasons, explanations

Conclusion:

- Restates the thesis or main argument

- Often gives a brief summary of supporting arguments

Arguments are more persuasive when they include facts and acknowledge opposing arguments.

3 ASSESS Work with a partner. Decide whether each argument is a main argument (M) or a supporting argument (S). Then group the arguments, and decide how you could organize them in a persuasive essay.

1 In addition, business investment in the community is a form of advertising. ___

2 By giving your time, you build relationships with people who feel the same way. ___

3 Volunteering can help you learn new skills. ___

4 Community leaders and local government will be more supportive of the business. ___

5 Businesses should invest in the local community. ___

6 When you volunteer to help, you can see how the organization works. ___

7 Research suggests that such investment results in a happier workforce. ___

8 It's better to give your time than your money to good causes. ___

4 INTEGRATE Complete the outline with information from the essay.

I. Introduction
   Hook (check all that are present):
   ___ quote   ___ rhetorical question
   ___ story   ___ interesting fact
   ___ simile or metaphor
   Thesis: _____

II. Body paragraph 1
    Topic sentence:
    _____

    A. Examples/facts:
    _____

    B. Reasons why government should invest:
    _____

III. Body paragraph 2
     Topic sentence:
     _____

     A. Examples/facts:
     _____

     B. Reasons why government should invest:
     _____

IV. Body paragraph 3
    Topic sentence:
    _____

    Examples/facts:
    _____

    Reasons why government should invest:
    _____

V. Conclusion (check all that are present):
   ___ restatement of thesis   ___ summary of main points
   ___ tie back to intro

5 EXPAND Discuss the questions about the essay with a partner.

1 Why does the writer begin with John F. Kennedy?

2 Why does the writer mention the diseases SARS, HIV, and Ebola?

3 Which argument(s) do you find most persuasive? Why?

4 Imagine you hold the opposite point of view—you think government should *not* invest in scientific research. What are your reasons?

5 Does the writer argue against any of your reasons in the essay?

GRAMMAR IN CONTEXT Infinitive constructions

We use the *to* infinitive with nouns and adjectives in addition to verbs (+ objects) and in purpose clauses. These constructions include:

• adjective or noun + *to* infinitive.
  *It often takes drug companies a **long time to develop** medicines and vaccines that will treat and prevent such diseases, and it can be very expensive.*

• noun + *be* + *to* infinitive.
*The best way to prevent **problems is to learn** as much as possible about what causes them.*

• *something, nothing, anything,* etc. + *to* infinitive.
  *His words gave us **something to dream** about.*

• *too* + adjective + *to* infinitive.
  *Although finding a new world to live in may seem **too unlikely to worry** about in the near future, this kind of exploration will need years if not decades to plan.*

See Grammar focus on page 167.

A young girl shares her food in Cuvette, Republic of Congo

6 IDENTIFY Complete the conversation using the prompts from the box.

option, invest	anything, report	risky, invest
interesting, read	advice, invest	reason, worry

Boss: John, last week, you agreed to find out about investment opportunities. Have you got [1] _____?

John: Well, there are many choices. Firstly, I'd say the best [2] _____ ethically. I identified a potential company and sent you information about them. I haven't looked for any new opportunities because I thought this would be the best.

Boss: Yes, it was [3] _____ their business profile.

John: Yes, my [4] _____ before someone else does.

Boss: I see. I am interested. But isn't it a bit too [5] _____ now with the markets as they are?

John: I don't think you'd have any [6] _____. They have a unique product that is likely to sell well.

Boss: OK, I'll give it some serious consideration. Let's meet again tomorrow at 9.

7 INTEGRATE Finish the sentences so they are true for you. Then work with a partner. Share your sentences and ask each other follow-up questions.

My best investment advice is to talk to a professional financial advisor.

1 My best investment advice is to
_____.

2 When I don't have anything to do,
_____.

3 In my situation, investing is too
_____ to
_____.

4 I find _____ really difficult to understand.

5 For a good return on your time investment, your best option is to _____.

8 PREPARE Choose an idea from Exercise 1 or your own idea. Make a list of arguments for and against that government investment. Discuss your lists with a partner. Then complete the sentence prompt.

The government should invest in…

9 DEVELOP Complete the outline for your persuasive essay. Check the hook you will use in the introduction and the ideas you will include in your conclusion.

I. Introduction
   Hook (check all that are present):
   ___ quote   ___ rhetorical question
   ___ story   ___ interesting fact
   ___ simile or metaphor
   Thesis: _____

II. Body paragraph 1
   Topic sentence:
   _____

   A. Examples/facts:
   _____

   B. Reasons why government should invest:
   _____

III. Body paragraph 2
   Topic sentence:
   _____

   A. Examples/facts:
   _____

   B. Reasons why government should invest:
   _____

IV. Body paragraph 3
   Topic sentence:
   _____

   Examples/facts:
   _____

   Reasons why government should invest:
   _____

V. Conclusion (check all that are present):
   ___ restatement of thesis   ___ summary of main points
   ___ tie back to intro

10 WRITE Write your essay. Then answer these questions.

1 Does it clearly state your position on government investment?
2 Does it grab the reader's attention? How?
3 Do you have supporting arguments?
4 Do you use facts to support each of your arguments?
5 Does your conclusion restate your argument and give a brief summary?

11 SHARE Exchange essays with a classmate. Answer the questions in Exercise 10 about your classmate's essay.

12 IMPROVE Rewrite your essay to incorporate feedback.

9.3 What's Your Logo?

1 ACTIVATE What is the purpose of a logo? What do these logos represent? Share your ideas with a partner.

2 VOCABULARY Read the sentences. Choose the correct meaning of the word or phrase in bold orange.

1 I recognized his face **instantly**. It was my old friend Ben.
   a anxiously
   b immediately
2 The **logo** for Twitter is a bird.
   a product
   b symbol
3 Most companies pay attention to what their **competition** is doing.
   a a contest people want to win
   b opposition or people you want to be better than
4 A good ad has certain **features**. It shows the product and it's easy to remember.
   a a distinctive attribute or aspect of something
   b a part of the face
5 That company's products **stand out** from others because they rarely break.
   a be clearly better
   b project from or come out of a surface
6 In our online ad, we should **highlight** our design and price.
   a underline with a special marker
   b draw special attention to
7 Entrepreneurs often have a **unique** idea—that's what makes it risky.
   a very interesting
   b one-of-a-kind

🍃+ Oxford 5000™

3 INTERACT Work with a partner. Brainstorm the features of a good logo.

4  **ASSESS** Watch the video. Which of your ideas did the speaker mention?

@
> **LISTENING SKILL**
> **Listening for main ideas and key details**
>
> When people give a talk or lecture, they usually present one or more main ideas and support each with key details. Speakers often tell listeners the structure of the talk and how many main ideas there will be.
> *Today, I'm going to talk about four features of a good logo.*
>
> Then the speaker may signal each main idea with words and phrases like *first of all, secondly, finally, another feature is,* or *in addition to.*
>
> Supporting details can include explanations, specific information, examples, and reasons.
> *They should be able to see it from far away and instantly know what it is.*

5 IDENTIFY Watch the video again. Put the main ideas in order.

___ The logo needs to be timeless.
___ The logo needs to communicate something about the company.
___ Now I'm going to show you some examples of good logo designs.
___ People need to be able to recognize your logo.
___ You want to make sure your logo looks good in different sizes.

6 ASSESS Read the key details. Write the number of the main idea from Exercise 5 next to the detail.

___ They should be able to see it from far away.
___ They shouldn't have to read it.
___ Global, fast, friendly, old-fashioned.
___ Don't use an old, outdated style.
___ Too many details can be hard to see.
___ Make sure it looks good in black and white.

7 IDENTIFY Note the answers to the questions and then compare answers with a partner.

1 How has the Wendy's logo changed over time?
2 Why does the lecturer think the Twitter logo is a good example?
3 Why does the lecturer think the Nike logo is effective?

8 WHAT'S YOUR ANGLE? Are you familiar with the logos from the lecture? What makes a logo eye-catching to you? Do you have a favorite logo? Why do you like it?

GRAMMAR IN CONTEXT
Purpose clauses with infinitive

We can use infinitives in purpose clauses. Purpose clauses answer a "why" question. Phrases such as *in order to*, *so as to*, and *so that* are used to give the reason why someone does something.

In order to make money, your company has to stand out from the competition.

The logo needs to be timeless *so as to* avoid looking old or outdated.

The shape of the logo is very simple *so (that)* it is recognizable.

To make the negative form, we use *so as not to* and *in order not to*.

Make sure your logo has few details *so as not to / in order not to* be difficult to see.

But we can't use *not to* on its own.

The company's new owners kept the logo the same *so as not to* confuse their customers.

(NOT ~~The company's new owners kept the logo the same not to confuse their customers.~~)

Note: If we put the purpose clause first, it sounds more formal.

So (that) it is recognizable, the shape of the logo is very simple.

See Grammar focus on page 167.

9 **IDENTIFY** Choose the correct option.

1 *In order to / So that* avoid paying too much tax, he made his wife a shareholder.

2 We hired a designer *in order to / so that* our logo looked professional.

3 We changed the design of the logo *so as to / so that* avoid it looking similar to another brand's.

4 I had saved money *so that / in order to* go to college.

5 We invested in the company early *so that / so as not to* miss the opportunity.

6 Could you write that down *so that / so as to* I can see the spelling, please?

10 **INTEGRATE** Complete each sentence with a suitable purpose clause from the box.

| in order to | so as to | so (that) | so as not to |
| in order not to | | | |

1 The clothing had had its labels removed _____ the brand couldn't be identified.

2 The company changed its logo _____ attract new customers.

3 _____ find an effective logo, the organization held a competition.

4 Some athletes remove labels from their clothing _____ be associated with a particular brand.

5 _____ we could review the product, we requested the company send us some samples.

6 I'm going to save my money _____ I can afford a better-quality brand.

PRONUNCIATION SKILL Linking two consonants

In English, we often link words when the same consonant (or sound) ends one word and begins the next.

*What's the idea that you wan**t t**o highlight?*

Sometimes the linking changes the sound of the letters. For example, the /t/ sound between two vowels changes to a /d/ sound when the words are linked.

We also link a /d/ and /t/ sound.

*We ge**t t**o register early.*

get to sounds like "geddoo"

*First of all, people nee**d t**o be able to recognize your logo.*

Remember that linking refers to sounds, not spelling.

*I don't have enou**gh f**riends.*

🔊 Listen to the examples and repeat them. Learning how to link words and practicing saying them will help you improve your fluency.

11 🔊 **IDENTIFY** Listen to the excerpts. Identify examples of linking in each sentence. Then practice saying the sentences to a partner using linking.

1 They should be able to see it from far away and instantly know what it is.

2 Finally, you want to make sure your logo looks good in different sizes.

3 Look for a style that will last.

4 It suggests speed, so it's perfect for a company that makes running shoes.

12 **INTERACT** Work with a partner. Choose two or three famous logos. Imagine you work for the company that designed the logos. Say why you designed the logo in that way. Think about:

- Type of customer
- Recognizability
- Company identity
- Timelessness
- Design

13 **WHAT'S YOUR ANGLE?** Work in a small group. Discuss how important a role brands or logos play in your purchasing decisions.

1 Do you always buy brand name products?

2 Do you want logos to show? Why or why not?

3 Have you ever bought something because of its brand and then regretted it?

9.4 Know Your Rights

ENGLISH FOR REAL

1 ACTIVATE Think about how and when you complain. Choose how often you do each of the following (1 = never or almost never, 5 = very often).

1 complain about a service to the provider	1	2	3	4	5
2 complain about a product to the company	1	2	3	4	5
3 complain to someone you work or live with about what they do	1	2	3	4	5
4 complain to someone about another person	1	2	3	4	5

2 ASSESS Look at the pictures. Discuss the questions with a partner.

1 Who do you think Andy is talking to? Why is he talking to the person?
2 Is Max's experience more or less pleasant than Andy's?
3 Why do you think so?

3 ▶ IDENTIFY Watch both scenes, and answer the questions.

1 What does the tech representative think the problem is?
2 What is Andy's response? What does he think the problem is?
3 What actions does Andy want?
4 Why is Max frustrated when he first talks to Andy?
5 How does he resolve the problem?

REAL-WORLD ENGLISH Complaining

When we complain, we let someone know there is a problem we tried to resolve and make a demand in the form of a question.

I took out the battery, and it's still beeping. Can't you fix it now?

If our problem hasn't been resolved, we might make a subtle threat to move things along.
A: It's really simple. Let's walk through the steps again.
B: No, thanks. This is broken. I think I'm going to have to take my business elsewhere.

If a resolution has been offered that still isn't to your liking, you may express your disappointment with a statement of doom.
A: I'm sorry we are completely booked up. We have open appointments to see you tomorrow.
B: No, thanks. This beeping is driving me crazy, and I can't wait until tomorrow.

4 ANALYZE Read the sentences and decide what complaining strategies Andy used with the tech person.

demand	subtle threat	statement of doom

1 I tried and it didn't work. Can't you look it up?
_____

2 No, thanks. I think there's a problem with this router. I think I'm going to return it. _____

3 No, that's too late. Thanks anyway. Bye!
_____

5 ▶ IDENTIFY Watch the video again. What examples can you identify of Max complaining to Andy?

6 ANALYZE Read the conversation. Keeping in mind the complaining strategies from the Real-World English box, how would you change what Speaker A says or does?

A: Hi, I'm calling about a problem I'm having with my cable service.

B: I'm sorry to hear you're having a problem. Can you tell me what's happening?

A: Well, it's been out for three days, and the technician didn't show up yesterday for the appointment.

B: I'm really sorry about that. Let's see if we can resolve this. Can you give me your address and phone number?

A: You can see my phone number on your screen, can't you? That's just typical. No wonder your service is terrible! [A hangs up on B]

A: Oh, I just had the worst conversation with the cable company!

C: Were you polite? You know how annoyed you get on the phone.

A: Thanks a lot for your sympathy. You call them then. I'm done dealing with them.

C: Well, maybe you have a point.

7 PREPARE You are going to role-play a conversation between a customer and a sales representative. Work with a partner to follow the steps:

1 Choose one of the situations in the list (or make up a situation of your own).
   • You bought a new phone and it isn't working.
   • You reserved a table at your favorite restaurant, but when you arrive, there are no tables available.
   • Your roommate or family member has borrowed something of yours without asking again.
   • Your boss or co-worker has made a mistake and you have to work late to fix it.

2 Decide who is the person making the complaint and who is the person receiving the complaint. Prepare to complain about or defend your situation.

8 INTERACT When you are ready, have your role play. Then swap roles and do it again.

9 ANALYZE Join another pair and watch each other's role-plays. Discuss whether you complained and responded to each other appropriately.

GO ONLINE
Go online to create your own version of the video discussion.

9.5 Banking on Success

1 **ACTIVATE** Listen to the presentation about an idea for a business. What problem does this business solve? What benefits does it provide?

SPEAKING Using data to support a point of view

When giving your point of view, it is important that you support your ideas with facts from reliable sources.

- Provide statistics (e.g., dates, numbers, and percentages)

- Provide facts

- Reference reliable sources: *According to…, As supported by…*

- Give examples: *Take _____, for example. A good example of this is _____. To demonstrate,…*

2 **IDENTIFY** Work with a partner. Discuss the examples of facts and statistics in each sentence. What point of view or idea is the presenter using them to support? Listen to the presentation again if needed.

1 According to the Bureau of Land Statistics, as many as a million people work in the landscaping industry.
2 Landscaping workers earn $10–20 per hour.
3 Goats eat shrubs and problem plants like poison ivy.
4 According to some calculations, 38 goats can clear 50,000 square feet in a day.
5 The city of Turin saved 30,000 euros using sheep in three city parks.

VOCABULARY DEVELOPMENT
Collocations with *get*, *have*, *make*, and *take*

Collocations with *get*, *have*, *make*, and *take* are very common in English. Their meaning changes some depending on the expression. *Have* becomes passive. *Take* means the subject has an active role, but the object is not changed. *Make* implies that the subject has caused something new. *Get* often describes a change in the subject's state. All are often followed by a noun, and *get* is often followed by an adjective.

have: a bath, lunch, a problem, time, an argument
take: a break, a look, notes, a walk, a risk, a photo
make: a difference, trouble, progress, room, friends
get: a job, the impression, angry, ready, motivated

The best way to learn collocations is to memorize them, so you can recognize them in texts and while listening.

3 **IDENTIFY** Complete each sentence with the correct form of *get*, *have*, *make*, or *take*.

1 Green space usually means grass and shrubs, which require maintenance. Now you _____ a problem.
2 Now imagine you can _____ the job done more cheaply and in a quieter and more ecofriendly way.
3 I _____ interested in the idea when I saw a herd of goats in a city park one day and immediately started to explore this opportunity.
4 I think you'll agree that this is a business idea that _____ a lot of sense.
5 I hope you'll _____ a chance on our company.

4 **PREPARE** Choose a business you want people to invest in. Answer the questions.

1 What is your business idea and how will it work?
2 What problem will it solve?
3 Why hasn't the problem been solved before? How is your idea different?
4 What facts, statistics, and sources support your business idea?
5 Why should people invest in this idea?

5 **INTERACT** Work with a partner. Take turns presenting your business plans. Use feedback to revise your presentation as necessary.

6 **IMPROVE** When you are ready, work with a new partner and present your case.

7 **WHAT'S YOUR ANGLE?** Complete the prompts to make statements that are true for you. Share your ideas in a small group.

1 One problem I think most people have is…
2 A business that I think will make money is…
3 One kind of risk I'm comfortable taking is…

Now go to page 155 for the Unit 9 Review.

10 Theories

UNIT SNAPSHOT

What are agoraphobics afraid of? 113
What do groups do after forming? 115
What kind of people like spicy food? 118

How do theories help people?

How are theories tested?

Is it human nature to need explanations?

BEHIND THE PHOTO

Answer the questions. Then discuss your answers with a partner.

1 What do you think people used to fear in the past? How have our fears changed over time? What do people tend to be afraid of now?

2 Who is responsible for finding answers to the world's mysteries? Why?

3 Is there a mystery in your country or the wider world that you find especially interesting? Why?

REAL-WORLD GOAL

Watch a video explaining a theory; then tell someone about it

Facing Your Fears

1 ACTIVATE Discuss the photos and the questions with a partner.

1 Do you associate the images with positive or negative feelings?
2 Why do you think people often fear these things?

2 INTEGRATE Discuss the questions in a small group.

1 What other phobias (strong fears about things that aren't really dangerous) do people have?
2 Why do you think people have phobias?
3 How do you think phobias are formed?

3 IDENTIFY Review the main ideas from an academic article about phobias. Check the ones you discussed in Exercise 2.

☐ Fear type is age dependent, but response is not. ___
☐ Exposure to the object of fear can help treat the phobia. ___
☐ Phobias are not useful nowadays. ___
☐ Fear of what other people think is a common phobia. ___
☐ One typical phobia is a fear of busy places. ___
☐ Phobias are learned rather than inherited. ___
☐ Phobias may have been of use in the past. ___

4 INTEGRATE Read the article on the next page quickly and number the main ideas from Exercise 3 in the order they appear in the text.

5 IDENTIFY Read the article again and answer the questions.

1 Why do agoraphobics not like crowded public spaces?
2 What do agoraphobics think might happen if they cannot leave these places?
3 How do social phobics deal with their fear?
4 How are children's phobia triggers different from adults?
5 Have phobias ever been helpful for humans? How?
6 What influences whether a person develops a phobia?
7 What are the basic principles of the treatment for phobias?

> **READING SKILL Recognizing and understanding complex sentences with subordinate clauses**
>
> Writers use complex sentences with subordinate clauses to add extra details and make a text more interesting and informative for the reader. Recognizing and decoding these will help you to understand higher-level texts.
>
> *Agoraphobics fear crowded public spaces where escape is difficult.*
>
> *Whereas now it is sensible to be fearful of cars or weapons, in the distant past open spaces and heights presented real-life threats.*
>
> A subordinate clause connects to the main clause with words such as *before*, *after*, *unless*, *where*, and *when*. These words show the reader the logical connection between the two ideas.
>
> When you come across a complex sentence, read the clauses carefully to work out the logical connection between the ideas presented in the sentence.

1   Fear is a helpful emotion; it stops us entering or remaining in dangerous situations. The feeling is justified. A phobia, on the other hand, is not helpful. It is irrational and unjustified and can be harmful, limiting the ability of the sufferer to lead a normal life. Unfortunately, about one in nine people are known to suffer from phobias at some point.

2   Phobias can take many forms. One common type is "agoraphobia." Agoraphobics fear crowded public spaces where escape is difficult, such as public transport and elevators. A sudden feeling of overwhelming anxiety, known as a *panic attack*, often accompanies this phobia. Sufferers believe that they could suddenly collapse or die unless they escape the situation. Sufferers' lives become increasingly restricted as they choose to stay at home rather than risk the consequences of going out.

3   Another common phobia is "social phobia." Social phobics fear the negative judgments of others. They worry that people will notice they are nervous, and they fear "making a fool of themselves." For some, the fear is confined to specific situations, such as public speaking, while for others it is more general. In both cases, the sufferer often finds that the only way to **cope** is by restricting where they go and what they do.

4   Phobias can be triggered in many different ways, depending to some extent on age. Common triggers for adults include animals (such as spiders and snakes), heights, air travel, confined spaces, and storms. In children, monsters and the dark are common triggers, although these usually resolve before adulthood. For any age group, however, the fear is extreme, causing a raised heart rate and rapid breathing. This reaction often creates a powerful desire to escape, which cannot be easily **resisted**.

5   Although phobias are, by definition, irrational, they may once have served a useful purpose. It is said that phobias, like fears, may have evolved as a strategy to cope with potentially dangerous situations, which were common for our early ancestors. Whereas now it is sensible to be fearful of cars or weapons, in the distant past open spaces and heights presented real-

life threats. Similarly, fear of spiders would have been useful in places where there was a significant risk from dangerous species; this fear only appears to be a phobia in places where spiders are harmless.

6   The mechanism behind phobias is a complex area that is not yet fully understood. Phobic responses are thought to be controlled by the amygdala, the primitive brain structure, and are not consciously controlled. They are not considered to be strongly inherited; children of phobic parents are not necessarily more **at risk** of developing phobias than others. It is believed, instead, that phobias must be "learned." Research has shown that this learning may be influenced by factors that include a person's emotional state, stage of development, and expectations as well as how the trigger for the phobia is encountered.

7   From a practical point of view, the most important area of study is how phobias can be treated. Cognitive behavioral therapy, or CBT, which involves **facing up to** the fear rather than trying to **run away**, is claimed by many to be key. Sufferers are exposed to their particular trigger gradually and over a long period of time, which leads to reduced anxiety. Many sufferers are eventually able to **get over** their phobias. It is claimed by researchers, therapists, and ex-sufferers themselves that through CBT phobias can be successfully overcome without any obvious downside.

—adapted from *The Oxford Companion to the Mind*, 2nd ed., by Richard L. Gregory

🕮+ Oxford 5000™

6 APPLY Match the subordinate clauses to their main clauses. Then check your answers in the article.

a   although these usually resolve before adulthood

b   as they choose to stay at home rather than risk the consequences of going out.

c   unless they escape the situation.

d   where there was a significant risk from dangerous species.

e   that is not yet fully understood.

f   which leads to reduced anxiety.

1   Sufferers believe that they could suddenly collapse or die ___

2   Sufferers' lives become increasingly restricted ___

3   In children, monsters and the dark are common triggers, ___

4   Similarly, fear of spiders would have been useful in places ___

5   The mechanism behind phobias is a complex area ___

6   Sufferers are exposed to their particular trigger gradually and over a long period of time, ___

7 WHAT'S YOUR ANGLE? Discuss the questions in a group.

1 What experience do you or people you know have of the phobias mentioned in the article?

2 Have you or they tried to overcome the phobia? How? How successfully?

GRAMMAR IN CONTEXT
Passive reporting verbs

Passive reporting verbs are common in formal written English such as academic articles and news reports. We use them to describe general ideas and beliefs and when we don't know or don't want to say who the information came from. Examples include *believe*, *claim*, *consider*, *know*, *report*, *say*, and *think*.

We use reporting verbs in the passive with the subject pronoun *it*.

It + be + past participle + (that)

It is believed that *phobias had a purpose once.*
It is felt that *fears are helpful to us.*

We can also use reporting verbs in the passive after other subjects.

Subject + be + past participle + to infinitive

Many people are reported to suffer *from phobias.*
Many of us are believed to have developed *phobias as children.*

See Grammar focus on page 168.

8 APPLY Complete the sentence heads with the reporting verb in parentheses in the present passive. Use the information in the article.

1 One in nine people _____ to _____. (know)

2 It _____ that phobias, like fears, _____. (say)

3 Phobic responses _____ to be _____. (think)

4 Phobic responses _____ to be _____. (not consider)

5 It _____ instead that phobias must be _____. (believe)

6 CBT _____ by many to be _____. (claim)

9 INTEGRATE Work with a partner. Use the sentence heads from Exercise 8 to write the information about phobias from the article. Then check your information with the article.

10 VOCABULARY Complete each sentence with a word or phrase from the box.

run away	face up to	at risk
get over	resist	cope

1 I find it easy to _____ with stressful situations.

2 I always _____ difficult situations as soon as they arise.

3 Sometimes I want to _____ when life gets too hard.

4 I _____ problems quickly by telling myself not to worry and to move on.

5 I can't _____ sharing my problems with all my friends.

6 I know when I'm _____ of getting stressed, and I take more care of myself.

11 WHAT'S YOUR ANGLE? Which of the statements in Exercise 10 are true for you? Share your answers with a partner.

12 INTEGRATE Complete the sentence prompts to express your own theories.

1 People who do get help with a phobia are at risk of…

2 The best way to cope with fear is to…

3 The most effective way to get over a phobia is to…

4 Running away from a problem can lead to…

5 Some people resist help when they have a problem because…

6 Facing up to problems can be especially hard when…

13 WHAT'S YOUR ANGLE? Compare and discuss your theories in Exercise 12 in a group. How similar or different are your views?

1 ACTIVATE Look at the infographic. Answer the questions.

1 What process is being described?
2 How many stages are there in the process?

TUCKMAN'S THEORY OF
GROUP WORK

Forming:
getting together as a group

Storming:
challenging each other

Norming:
understanding the rules

Performing:
getting the job done

Mourning:
saying goodbye

2 WHAT'S YOUR ANGLE? Discuss the questions with a partner.

1 Which groups are you part of at the moment (for example, at work or in college)?
2 What stage is each group at according to Tuckman's theory?

3 IDENTIFY Read the essay about a theory of group work and answer the questions.

1 Which two stages are the most positive?
2 Which two stages are the most negative?
3 Is this theory agreed on by everyone?
4 Notice the bold phrases. What other phrases in the essay show the stages of the process?

1 There are several theories of the process of group work, but the most influential is probably Tuckman's, which he published in 1977. In this theory, **there are five basic stages** that groups tend to go through from when they first come together to when the work they are doing is completed.

2 **The first stage** is called *forming*. **This is where** the group first comes together, and people get to know each other. They may bring ideas of rules of behavior from previous experience, and **at this stage**, they often assume that the rules will be the same in the new group. **This is generally a positive stage**, and people feel happy and comfortable.

3 Tuckman called the second stage *storming*. By *storming*, he meant that there would be conflict or difficulties. For example, the leader may be challenged, and the rules that people assumed were valid at the forming stage might be questioned. People will probably have started to compete for power within the group, and the initial feelings of happiness may have disappeared as people realize that they aren't necessarily going to be allowed to do things in the way they would prefer.

4 The third stage is *norming*. By this stage, members of the group will have come to an understanding on a number of issues, such as their personal role or status, the rules of the group (in relation to deadlines and communication, for example), and so on. Typically, these will now be made more explicit, and what is or is not normal behavior will be agreed upon—hence the description *norming*.

5 Next, the group enters the *performing* stage. As the name suggests, this is when the real work is done. Individuals within the group will have been integrated and should now be generally comfortable with their particular role. This phase will last until the work is completed.

6 The final stage in this theory is known as either *mourning* or *adjourning*. The word *mourning* implies a period of sadness that the group has finished its work, while the word *adjourning* would be used when the breakup is more temporary, for example, if a particular team project has finished and a new one not yet started. The group may reflect on its performance at this stage, and members will perhaps express their feelings about the work they have accomplished.

7 While Tuckman's theory is popular, it has been attacked by some critics, for example, for being too general, and many alternatives have been suggested, but it remains a useful framework with which to evaluate group work.

Make sure you include significant details in your writing, especially when describing a process. You cannot assume that your reader will know what you know. To do this:

- Give definitions of key terms, especially if these are specific to the topic.

  By storming, *he meant that there would be conflict or difficulties.*

- Give detail, especially when you are describing a process or concept that your readers may be unfamiliar with.

  The group may reflect on its performance at this stage, and members will perhaps express their feelings about the work they have accomplished.

- Use a variety of examples to illustrate and strengthen key points or main ideas.

  …such as their personal role or status, the rules of the group, and so on.

4 IDENTIFY Read the essay again. Identify three examples of the following.

- definitions
- details (for example, explaining what happens as a result of something)
- examples

5 INTEGRATE Sentences a–d give more details. Each sentence goes at the end of one of the paragraphs in the essay. Decide where each one goes and write the paragraph number.

a Understanding that each phase is absolutely normal can help participants maintain perspective in what can be a challenging part of working life. ___

b This stage can be very uncomfortable, but it cannot be avoided, so it must be managed carefully. ___

c In this essay, I will outline the main characteristics of each phase. ___

d This is a good time for group leaders to focus participants on the process that has been completed. ___

 6 WHAT'S YOUR ANGLE? Work with a partner. Think of a time when you have worked in a group. Did you experience all the stages described in the essay? Tell your partner, giving details and examples if possible.

GRAMMAR IN CONTEXT Passive future

We form the future passive in various ways:

- *will*

  *In many cases, these **will** now be made more explicit, and what is or is not normal behavior will be agreed upon.*

- *be going to*

  *…as people realize that they **aren't** necessarily **going to** be allowed to do things in the way they would prefer.*

- future perfect

  *Individuals within the group **will have been accommodated** and should now be generally comfortable with their particular role.*

See Grammar focus on page 168.

7 IDENTIFY Complete each sentence with a future passive form of the verb in parentheses.

1 I don't think the theory _____ until larger studies are conducted. (prove)

2 You _____ if any new evidence is discovered. (inform)

3 The professor's claims _____ into consideration during the investigation. (take)

4 The study _____ by the end of the year. (not / complete)

5 _____ the findings _____ by scientists? (acknowledge)

8 INTEGRATE Rewrite the sentences. Use the correct future form of the passive. Then compare answers with a partner.

1 We won't need these documents for the next stage of the project.

_____

2 They aren't going to publish the research.

_____

3 They are going to release the next book in the scientific theory series soon.

_____

4 No one will have proved the theory by the time we need the results.

_____

5 They will have warned journalists not to release the story too soon.

_____

9 **PREPARE** You are going to use Tuckman's theory to describe a group you are or were in. Follow the steps.

1 Identify the group to focus on.
2 Note the key stages of the process your group is going through or went through.
3 Decide whether you need to give any definitions of key or specific terms.
4 Note details and examples of things that happened at each stage.
5 Think about words and phrases you can use to connect ideas and show the sequence of the stages.
6 Note your answers to these questions:
Will the group's goals be achieved by the group's end?
What else will have been achieved by the time the group ends?
Are friendships between group members going to be maintained once the group has ended?

10 **WRITE** Use your notes to write about the group's work process.

11 **IMPROVE** Read your description and correct any grammar and spelling mistakes. Check your work.

☐ Have you included definitions, details, and examples?
☐ Have you used passive structures?
☐ Are words and phrases that describe sequence or process included?

12 **SHARE** Read other students' descriptions of group work processes.

1 How similar is their description of the process of group work?
2 How much do you agree with Tuckman's theory of group work?

Members of a creative team share their ideas at an advertising agency in New York, the United States

10.3 Some Like It Hot

1 ACTIVATE Read the glossary terms. Working with a partner, brainstorm a short list of activities that could be described as risky, scary, or thrilling. Then discuss the questions.

risky: full of the possibility of danger, failure, or loss
scary: frightening; causing fear
thrilling: causing excitement and pleasure; exhilarating

1 How would you describe each activity?
2 Which of the activities have you done? Why?
3 What risky, scary, or thrilling activities would you like to do? Why?

2 WHAT'S YOUR ANGLE? Describe your personality to a partner. Use the sentence prompt and include the adjectives from Exercise 1. How similar are you to each other?

I'm a person who…

I'm a person who enjoys scary experiences because…
I'm a person who hates anything risky because…
I'm a person who loves thrilling experiences because…

3 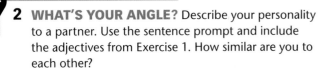 IDENTIFY Listen to the first part of a science podcast and answer the questions.

1 Which activities from Exercise 1 are discussed?
2 How does the host feel about these activities?

4 INTEGRATE Listen again and complete the diagram with information about how each person feels about the two "constrained risk" activities.

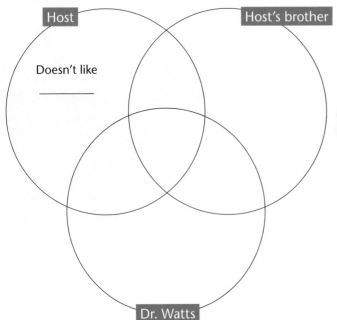

Host
Host's brother

Doesn't like
_____

Dr. Watts

LISTENING SKILL
Listening for main ideas and supporting evidence

When listening for the main ideas, we also need to listen for the supporting evidence. This evidence tells us more about the main idea. It also helps make the main idea stronger.

Supporting evidence may include:

- general examples that illustrate the main idea in action.
  One theory is that liking spicy food may be connected to personality types.

- specific examples such as information from studies or research.
  Rozin and Schiller, two scientists who were investigating this theory back in 1980, compared the way…

5 IDENTIFY Review the four main ideas included in the science podcast. Then match the supporting evidence (a–d) to the main ideas. Listen again to check your answers.

1 Researchers are interested in why not everyone likes spicy food.
2 People who like risky, thrilling activities are more likely to enjoy spicy food.
3 Riding roller coasters and eating spicy foods are both constrained risks.
4 Constrained risk theory is not proved in everyday life.

a There are examples of people who enjoy spicy food but do not like other forms of constrained risks. ___
b One theory is that liking spicy food may be connected to personality types. ___
c Rozin and Schiller claimed a link between eating spicy food and riding on roller coasters. ___
d They both stimulate a physical response to danger, but then the person realizes there is no real threat. ___

6 WHAT'S YOUR ANGLE? Discuss the questions in a group. Support your opinion with examples from your personal experience.

1 How similar and different are you on spicy food and roller coasters? Complete a diagram similar to the one in Exercise 4.
2 What do you think of the theory that liking spicy foods may be linked to personality type?

7 🔊 **INTEGRATE** Listen to the second part of the science podcast. Are any of your ideas from Exercise 6 included?

8 🔊 **IDENTIFY** Listen again to the second part of the science podcast. Complete the notes on the main ideas and supporting evidence.

> Alternative theory for liking spicy food
> Main idea 1: _____ influences liking of
> _____
>   Supporting evidence: eat food _____
>   in our culture
> Main idea 2: Lots of _____ →
> preference for spicy food.
>   Supporting evidence: eat a lot → _____
>   Supporting evidence: _____ = eat a
>   lot → get used to spicy food
> Main idea 3: no _____ for liking spicy
> food
>   Supporting evidence: theories linking to biological,
>   environmental + _____

See Grammar focus on page 168.

GRAMMAR IN CONTEXT
Passive voice

The passive voice focuses attention on an action or process. We can omit the agent (the person or thing that does the action) when it is obvious, unimportant, or not known. If we include the agent, we use *by*.

*Your pain receptors **are stimulated** (by the spicy food).*

We can also use modals in the present passive.

*Roller coasters **can be seen** as a "constrained risk."*

When a verb has two objects, there are two possible passive structures.

*Your taste buds sent **your brain strong signals**.*
***Your brain** was sent **strong signals** (by your taste buds).*
***Strong signals** were sent to **your brain** (by your taste buds).*

Change the verb *be* to change the tense of the passive structure.

*Spicy food **has been investigated** by researchers.*

9 🔊 **INTEGRATE** Complete each excerpt from the podcast with the correct passive form. Use the sentence prompt in parentheses to help. Listen and check.

1 (It has set my mouth on fire…)
   I feel like my mouth _____ on fire.

2 (They have investigated the idea…)
   This idea _____ by scientific researchers a lot in the past decade.

3 (They are carrying out research…)
   Further research _____ out at the moment.

4 (We usually acquire our eating habits…)
   Our eating habits and preferences _____ from a very young age by observing our parents' eating behavior.

5 (If your family eats spicy food…)
   So, basically, if spicy food _____ by your family, you'll eat it, too.

6 (Studies have demonstrated…)
   And it _____ by studies that the more often we eat spicy foods, the less our body reacts to them.

VOCABULARY DEVELOPMENT
Alternatives for the word *thing*

We often use the word *thing* to replace a noun if we do not want or need to mention the specific noun or if we cannot describe or name the specific item or concept we are referring to.

*It's the **thing** that everyone's talking about just now. (thing = topic)*
*What's that **thing** over there? (thing = object or item)*

The use of *thing* is generally considered to be informal. It is especially common in spoken English and in informal writing. Nouns that can replace *thing* include *concept, principle, alternative, objective, issue, topic, trait, feature, attribute, item, matter, point,* and *incident*.

*This seems like an obvious **concept**.*
*Given these **alternatives**, it's difficult to know which to believe.*

10 **IDENTIFY** Review the words in italics. They are more precise words we can use to describe things. Choose the correct one to complete the sentence.

1 I understand the *concept* / *alternative* of personality type linking to food preferences, but I don't agree with it.

2 There was an *objective* / *incident* when I ate very spicy food when I was young and couldn't cope.

3 I would like to hear an *incident* / *alternative* to culture theory and constrained risk theory.

4 My main *concept* / *objective* in life is to stay safe rather than do risky but also thrilling activities.

5 The *matter* / *incident* of why some people enjoy risk taking is of great interest to me.

6 I agree with the *principle* / *matter* that what we like as adults is influenced by our childhood experiences.

👤⁺ Oxford 5000™

11 **WHAT'S YOUR ANGLE?** Which of the statements in Exercise 10 are true for you? Compare your views in a small group.

1 ACTIVATE Discuss the three situations with a partner. What would your initial reaction be? What would you say? What wouldn't you say?

1   Your best friend tells you they have just landed a dream job abroad.

2   Your favorite teacher tells you they are retiring next semester.

3   Your boss tells you that you have been chosen to lead a team on a difficult project.

2 ASSESS Look at the pictures. Discuss the questions with a partner.

1   What do you think Kevin, Max, and Andy are talking about?

2   How do you think each one feels?

3 ▶ IDENTIFY Watch the video. Answer the questions and then share your ideas with a partner.

1   What are Kevin, Max, and Andy talking about?

2   What reasons do Max and Andy give for not wanting Kevin around?

3   What do Max and Andy decide to do in the end?

REAL-WORLD ENGLISH Expressing reaction

How we react to news depends on a range of factors. For example, it depends on how surprising or unexpected the news is and how serious it is. It also depends on how well we know the person who is affected and how much we care about them.

less formal: *You're kidding. Wow!*

more formal: *I'm delighted for you!*

The emotions we show in a reaction could be positive, negative, or neutral, and the way we respond has an important effect on the listener. When we react, the intonation and stress we use can carry as much meaning as the actual words we say.

A: *I can't wait.*   B: *Me neither!*

A: *I can't wait.*   B: *You don't mean that, do you?*

4 🔊 **INTEGRATE** Listen and decide which reactions are positive and which aren't. Then listen and repeat, expressing the same reaction.

1   It's going to be great!
2   I can't wait!
3   That's interesting.
4   Really? That's fantastic!
5   You're kidding me!
6   Really? Erm…
7   Right…OK.
8   That's interesting.

5 ▶ **ANALYZE** Watch the video again. Discuss the questions with a partner.

1   How does Kevin feel about his news?
2   How do Max and Andy react to Kevin's news?
3   Why do you think they have reacted in this way?
4   How do you think Kevin feels about Max and Andy's reactions?

6 🔊 **APPLY** Who said each phrase? Is their reaction positive, negative, or neutral? Listen again and repeat, expressing the same reaction.

1   You're kidding me! That's awful.
_____

2   Really? Erm…
_____

3   Yeah! I've already filled out the application!
_____

4   Wow…Kev. Good luck with that.
_____

5   Yeah, um, Kevin…that's great.
_____

6   Right. Shouldn't have said that!
_____

7 **WHAT'S YOUR ANGLE?** Discuss the questions with a partner.

1   Do you think Max and Andy should have pretended to be happy for Kevin?
2   If you were in Max and Andy's position, would you like to live near Kevin?
3   If you were Kevin, would you go ahead and put in your application for the apartment? Why or why not?
4   Have you ever been in a similar situation to Max and Andy? What did you do?

8 **INTEGRATE** Prepare to give and express reactions to news. Choose a piece of news from the list (or use an example of your own).

- Your boss tells you he or she is leaving the company.
- Your best friend announces that he or she is getting married.
- Your rival boasts about winning an important competition.
- Your brother tells you he is moving out of the country next month.
- Your real estate agent announces that he or she has just sold your house.
- A student you don't get along with tells you he is moving into your apartment building next week.

9 **ANALYZE** Work in a small group. Discuss the level of seriousness and your relationship to the speaker with regards to each piece of news from Exercise 8. What type of positive or negative reaction would be appropriate in each situation? Note a few phrases you will use to express your reaction.

10 **INTERACT** Work in a small group to role-play giving news and reacting to it. One person gives the news you discussed in Exercise 9, and the others give positive and negative reactions.

11 **IMPROVE** Work with another group and watch their role play. Afterward, talk about how effectively you expressed your reactions and whether others responded appropriately considering the level of seriousness and relationship to the speaker.

 GO ONLINE to create your own version of the English For Real video.

10.5 What's the Risk?

1 ACTIVATE Work with a partner. Look at the photo and the lesson title. What do you think "throw caution to the wind" means?

2 **IDENTIFY** Listen to the discussion. With a partner, discuss what activities and personality types the people talk about.

3 **INTEGRATE** Listen again and decide whether each idea is stated by Neil (N), Chao (C), or Elisa (E).

1 ___ People avoid risk despite their personality type.
2 ___ Climbing is not a risky activity.
3 ___ Flying is safer than driving.
4 ___ Personal experience shapes what we are afraid of.
5 ___ There is no connection between thrill-seeking personalities and preference for spicy foods.

SPEAKING Expanding ideas with related points and examples

Expanding your ideas by adding related points and examples shows that you have spent some time considering your thoughts. To expand your ideas, state your main idea and follow it with relevant support.

Main idea + related points + examples

I think people who are outgoing usually have adventurous hobbies. Things like climbing, bungee jumping, and mountain biking, for example. At least they do from my experience. I'd say I have a pretty outgoing personality, but I'm not interested in extreme sports. I'm not shy—in fact, I love socializing and meeting new people. I really admire people who rock-climb, but I wouldn't be brave enough to do it myself…

4 **IDENTIFY** Listen to the discussion again. Note related points and examples that Neil, Chao, and Elisa use to support their main ideas in Exercise 3.

5 WHAT'S YOUR ANGLE? Do you agree with the views of Neil, Chao, and Elisa? Why or why not? Share your ideas in a small group. Refer to their examples and add examples from your own knowledge and personal experience.

PRONUNCIATION SKILL Intonation for uncertainty

We can use intonation to show certainty and uncertainty. This helps the listener understand how sure we are even if we do not use specific words to show it.

• Unsure

Really? Are you sure? (rising intonation = uncertainty)

• Sure

Yes, I am.   *Of course.*
Absolutely (falling intonation = certainty)

We often use tag questions when we express certainty or uncertainty.

Outgoing people are more likely to try new things, aren't they? (rising intonation = uncertainty)
Outgoing people are more likely to try new things, aren't they? (falling intonation = certainty)

Learning how to show certainty and uncertainty will help you express your ideas and concerns and negotiate more effectively.

6 **IDENTIFY** Listen and decide if the speaker is sure (S) or unsure (U). Then listen again and repeat.

1 Absolutely, I take risks. We all do, don't we? ___
2 Really? Are you sure about that? ___
3 You like mountain biking, don't you? ___
4 Of course, you've done many risky things, haven't you? ___

7 PREPARE In a small group, prepare to contribute to a group discussion. Choose one of the following topics, and outline the main ideas with related points and examples.

• Children should be encouraged to do risky activities so that they can learn to face up to their fears.
• It's fine to throw caution to the wind if the results of your actions won't hurt anyone else.
• People are responsible for themselves. If they want to do a risky leisure activity, whatever it is, they should be allowed.

8 INTEGRATE Have your group discussion. Make sure you:

• present your main ideas clearly.
• expand on your ideas using related points and examples.
• use intonation to show how sure or unsure you are.

9 WHAT'S YOUR ANGLE? Which ideas in the group discussion interested you the most? How well did you and others express your views? Make notes. Then discuss with your group.

Now go to page 156 for the Unit 10 Review.

11 Lifestyle

UNIT SNAPSHOT

What does having an '80s lifestyle involve? 125
Where can you find a garden high off
the ground? 127
Why do animals live in groups? 130

What are life's necessities?

Why do people change lifestyles?

What or who has the biggest impact on your life?

BEHIND THE PHOTO

Read the quotation. What do you think it means? Do you agree? What are your priorities in life? Why? Discuss your ideas in a small group.

"Your time is limited, so don't waste it living someone else's life."
—Steve Jobs, selected from *Oxford Essential Quotations*, 5th ed., edited by Susan Ratcliffe

REAL-WORLD GOAL

Take photos to show different lifestyles where you live

1 ACTIVATE Discuss the questions and photos in a group.

1 What type of lifestyle does each picture represent?

2 What type of person do you think would have a lifestyle like this? How old would they be? What priorities might they have?

2 WHAT'S YOUR ANGLE? Compare your views in your group. Which lifestyle would you prefer? Why?

3 ACTIVATE You are going to read about two different lifestyles. First, discuss the questions in a group.

1 Do you think it is possible to live without money?

2 Do you think it is possible to live without technology?

4 APPLY Read the article on the next page and number the main ideas in the order they appear in the article.

___ The couple had a good experience and met many kind people.

___ The people began doing things the way they were done in the past.

___ The people decided their family was too dependent on technology.

___ They decided to continue their new lifestyle in their home country.

___ Their life became more relaxed and easier.

___ Their lifestyle does not affect the environment negatively.

___ They work hard to promote the benefits of the lifestyle.

___ They removed modern technology from their home.

READING SKILL
Understanding reason and consequence

Writers express reason and consequence in a variety of ways. When reading, look for:

- linking words indicating reason: *because, as, since, due to, when* (something happened).

- linking words indicating consequence: *so, consequently, subsequently, as a result, result in*

- related vocabulary: *happen, occur, affect, influence, have an impact on, this means* (*that*).

To understand reason-and-consequence relationships within a text, apply your own knowledge and experience when considering the context and clues. For example:

- If someone changes something or takes action, there must be a reason.

- A change in situation or an action will always have a consequence (either positive or negative).

As you read ask yourself "why?" to determine a reason and "what?" to determine the consequence.

5 IDENTIFY Look at the underlined sentences in *Living in the Past*. Which part of each sentence is reason, and which part is result? Which words helped you decide?

6 INTEGRATE Read the rest of *Living in the Past* again. What were the consequences of Blair and Morgan's lifestyle choice for the following?

1 Their house and the things they owned

2 Their friends and colleagues

3 Their relationships with each other

4 Their children

7 IDENTIFY Compare answers for Exercise 6 with a partner. Explain where and how you found each consequence.

Lifestyle Choices

A Living in the past

How many times have you checked your cell phone or gone online today? Can you imagine life without technology? In 2013, a Canadian couple, Blair and Morgan, decided to **adopt** a new, simpler lifestyle and banned technology from their home. Well, almost— they banned all technology that had been developed after 1986, the year Blair was born. The pair made the decision to try this new lifestyle for a year after they recognized that their children, then ages 2 and 5, had become addicted to using their smartphones and tablets. The reality struck Blair one day when he invited his son to play in the garden but had his offer ignored. The children would not or could not look up from their screens. They were spending hours on these each week, and as a result, they had lost all interest in playing outside.

So, how was their "old" twenty-first-century lifestyle **affected** by their "new" '80s one? Well, in their home, which was built in the '80s, there was no longer any Internet connection or cable TV, and there were no computers, tablets, or smartphones. The family had an old-fashioned box-style TV, an '80s-model video game console, a video recorder to watch movies on, and a plastic cassette player for music. They did their banking in person, used paper maps instead of GPS, and used an old-fashioned camera. (They had a professional develop their film and print the photographs on paper.)

What impact did their alternative lifestyle have on them? The main challenge was getting their friends and colleagues to understand that their new lifestyle resulted in wanting to **lead** a quieter life and that they weren't going to be so easily contacted via email or cell phone. However, the family believes that using less technology changed their lives for the better. Since making the change, their lifestyle has become less **hectic**—they feel more relaxed and have become closer because they communicate more. They have also found that the children are less influenced by advertising and technology than they had been previously, and they are better able to amuse themselves with imaginative games and outdoor activities.

B Life without currency

Raphael Fellmer met Nieves Palmer while he was traveling with friends from Europe to Mexico without money. During their adventure, they were inspired by the many people they met along the way who showed them kindness by giving them rides and sharing their food. After traveling for 15 months in more than 500 vehicles, the couple returned to Berlin, Germany, where they now live with their baby daughter. They say that their **nomadic** lifestyle during the trip resulted in a complete change of perspective on life, making them feel unwilling to participate in modern society with its extreme consumerism. So, they made the decision to **maintain** their moneyless lifestyle in order to raise awareness of the damage that consumerism does to humans and the environment. But just how easy is it to live in this society with no money? How do you afford life's essentials such as accommodations and food?

The couple say they have everything they need and do not feel that living frugally has negatively affected their lifestyle at all. They live rent-free in the basement of a friend's house in exchange for doing jobs around the house and garden. They **support** their basic lifestyle by sharing, borrowing, lending, reusing, and recycling. They eat rejected food that is going to be thrown away by supermarkets, even though it is still safe to eat. They wear secondhand clothing, and when they travel, they either go by bicycle or hitch a ride. This means that they cause minimal damage to the environment. If they want to get something done, they either do it themselves or exchange their skills. For example, if someone wants to have their house painted or a building renovated, they will work as a team to get the job done.

Raphael and Nieves are so passionate about sharing their lifestyle that it has become their full-time job. They organize work events; give lectures at schools, universities, and conferences; write articles; and do interviews for the media in order to highlight the benefits of leading a more considerate, community-minded, more active, and less wasteful lifestyle.

🔑+ Oxford 5000™

8 INTEGRATE Work with a partner. Complete the notes to show some of the reason and consequence relationships in *Life without Currency*.

Reasons ➡	Consequences
lived a _____ with no money while traveling	the way they saw life _____
back home, no longer wanted to _____ in the way most people do	decided to _____ without money
live in a friend's house and _____ things	their lifestyle has no _____ on the environment
believe strongly in _____ lifestyle	_____ about their lifestyle with others

VOCABULARY DEVELOPMENT Collocations for *lifestyle*: Verb + noun; adjective + noun

The word *lifestyle* is often used in collocations such as *busy lifestyle* (adjective + noun) and *adopt a lifestyle* (verb + noun).

When you learn vocabulary, learn collocations for the words, too. Using correct collocations makes your English sound natural. Remember, some word combinations sound "wrong" to native English speakers even if they seem grammatically correct. For example, we can say *adopt a lifestyle* but not *adopt a life*.

9 INTEGRATE Choose the correct verb or adjective for the lifestyle collocation. Then use the article to check your answers.

1 The Canadian couple decided to *take / adopt* a new, simpler lifestyle and banned technology from their home.

2 How was their "old" twenty-first-century lifestyle *affected / led* by their "new" '80s one?

3 What impact did their *other / alternative* lifestyle have on them?

4 Since making the change, their lifestyle has become less *excited / hectic*—they feel more relaxed.

5 They say that their *nomadic / travel* lifestyle during the trip resulted in a complete change of perspective on life.

6 They made the decision to *maintain / keep* their moneyless lifestyle.

7 They *make / support* their basic lifestyle by sharing, borrowing, lending, reusing, and recycling.

8 They organize events to highlight the benefits of *leading / running* a more active and less wasteful lifestyle.

10 IDENTIFY Work with a partner. Identify collocations of the word *lifestyle* + verbs or + adjective in Exercise 9.

11 INTEGRATE Complete the sentences so they are true for you. Then compare and discuss your sentences with a partner.

I _____ an active lifestyle.

I would like to lead more a(n) _____ because _____.

It can be difficult to maintain a(n) _____ where I live because _____.

Many people in my country nowadays enjoy a(n) _____ lifestyle.

Most young people I know have a very _____ lifestyle.

I _____ a change of lifestyle because _____.

GRAMMAR IN CONTEXT
have / get something done

We use *have / get something done* to describe what someone does for us, usually when we have arranged it. We do not say who does the action. (We tend to use *get* in more informal situations.)

*If they want to **get something done**, they do it themselves or exchange skills.*

*If someone wants to **have their house painted**, they will work as a team.*

See Grammar focus on page 169.

12 APPLY Rewrite each sentence using the correct structure of the words in parentheses. Then tell a partner which sentences you agree with or are true for you.

1 It's easy to (my point of view / get / across) regarding my lifestyle to my friends.

2 To avoid waste, I usually (repaired / things / have) rather than buy something new.

3 For example, I (get / mended / my torn clothes) when they get ripped.

4 I also (fixed / get / my electronics).

5 To avoid fast food, I usually (for the week / all of my food / have / cooked).

6 This means I have to plan in advance and (get / done / all my grocery shopping / in one day).

7 I (my shopping lists / have / prepared) so I don't buy things I don't need when I go to the store.

13 WHAT'S YOUR ANGLE? Discuss your lifestyles in a group. Do you do the things in the box yourself, or do you have them done by someone else? Why? What are the advantages and disadvantages of this?

1 ACTIVATE Describe the photos of this urban green space. Where do you think it is? How are the people using it?

2 INTERACT Work in a small group. How important do you think it is to have green space in cities? Give reasons, examples, and evidence to support your views.

3 ▶ NOTICE Watch the video. Where is this urban green space? Were any of your ideas from Exercises 1 and 2 mentioned? Share your ideas with a partner.

4 ▶ IDENTIFY Watch the video again. Answer the questions and then compare answers with a partner.

1 Where is the High Line? What type of place is it?
2 When was the High Line built? What was it initially used for?
3 What were some of the disadvantages of the High Line when it was first built?
4 What happened in the early 1960s that affected the High Line?
5 How long was the High Line abandoned for?
6 When was the High Line developed into a green space?
7 How has the development of the High Line area affected the New York economy?

5 WHAT'S YOUR ANGLE? Discuss the questions in a small group.

1 What are the public spaces in your town or city like?
2 Are these public spaces "green" enough?
3 Is there an abandoned structure or space in your area that you feel could be developed? How?

6 INTERACT Read the essay question and then answer the questions with a partner.

What are the economic benefits of developing abandoned urban areas or structures into public green spaces?

1 What change is the writer analyzing?
2 What information and facts from the video do you think the writer should include?

7 **IDENTIFY** Read the essay and share your views with a partner.

1. How well has the writer answered the question?
2. Did the writer mention any of the information or facts you thought of in Exercise 6?
3. What kind of businesses do you think would be successful in the High Line district? Why?

Developing Green Spaces

Green spaces in cities are absolutely essential to our well-being, helping to reduce stress and promote healthier lifestyles within an urban environment. This direct benefit to people's lives is significant, but perhaps the most important benefit, at least for city planning authorities, is the quite considerable boost it gives the local economy.

Adding a new green space by developing an existing urban structure or abandoned area brings immediate opportunities to **make money**. One example is the High Line park in New York City. According to city authorities, the development of the old High Line railway line, which runs through Manhattan, into a park has generated approximately $2 billion for the city's economy to date.

Such areas have a particularly positive effect on the economy due to the fact that any development that improves a part of a city becomes **in demand** as a place to live and do business. The areas around abandoned industrial structures or disused land tend to be less **desirable** as residential locations. However, when new, attractive green spaces are developed on previously undesirable sites, people are drawn to the lifestyle that living near them can offer. Developers come in and restore existing buildings or build new dwellings. Housing in the area suddenly becomes more requested by buyers, and as a result, real estate values increase. In addition, the area draws in businesses hoping to take advantage of new opportunities.

Another way in which green spaces such as the High Line generate income for the economy is through tourism. Parks in major cities are always popular with tourists, especially if, like the High Line, they have the fashionable factor of being transformed from an **abandoned** industrial structure into an attractive modern space. Often such spaces are enhanced with gardens and art installations, so they become interesting sightseeing destinations. Cafés, restaurants, and shops benefit from tourists as well as from locals, who frequent these businesses regularly. As a result, money is fed back into the local community where it can be used to continue its improvement.

For all these reasons, developing urban green space has become a particularly attractive option for cities hoping to solve the problem of what to do with disused urban spaces. The success of the High Line has already prompted several major U.S. cities, including Chicago and Philadelphia, to consider converting forgotten areas into new green spaces. Undoubtedly, the number of developments like this will increase as their benefits, both economic and social, are recognized. This demand for green space and improved lifestyle for residents will grow in cities across the world.

We can use synonyms to avoid repeating the same words over and over. This makes our writing more cohesive and sophisticated.

This immediate and direct **benefit** *to people's lives is* **significant**, *but it is also just one of many benefits. Perhaps the most important, for city planning authorities at least, is the* **considerable boost** *it gives the local economy.*

Notice how writers use synonyms in texts, and underline these words in the articles you read. This study technique creates a kind of visual "web" that can illustrate more clearly how words (as well as grammar) make texts cohesive.

8 **IDENTIFY** Read the text again. Identify a synonym in the text for each of the bold words.

Bold word	Synonym
_____	_____
_____	_____
_____	_____
_____	_____
_____	_____

9 **INTEGRATE** Replace the bold words in the text with synonyms from the box to avoid repetition.

residents	improve	opportunity
good	life	forgotten

As cities grow larger, green spaces are increasingly in demand. City **inhabitants** want to have a healthier, more active lifestyle. Green spaces allow them the **chance** to do activities such as biking, jogging, and sports. They are also **beneficial** because they offer inhabitants the chance to relax and escape from their stressful **lifestyles**. City authorities have found that developing **abandoned** areas into green spaces has also been beneficial to the local economy. For this reason, many large cities are also looking to develop abandoned areas and **develop** existing housing around those areas in order to boost the economy and improve inhabitants' lifestyles.

10 **ASSESS** Compare answers to Exercise 9 with a partner. Then discuss the meanings of the word pairs listed. Are they exactly the same, or is there slight variation in meaning? If so, what's the difference?

inhabitants—residents
chance—opportunity
beneficial—good for
lifestyles—life
abandoned—forgotten
develop—improve

We use adverbs to say *how much*.

Gradable adjectives describe qualities that you can measure, e.g., *intelligent*, *interesting*. For example, we can say a person is more or less intelligent. We use gradable adverbs with this type of adjective.

*That program was **particularly interesting** last week.*

Non-gradable adjectives describe qualities that are absolute or extreme, e.g., *ideal*, *terrible*. They cannot be used as comparative adjectives. We use non-gradable adverbs with these.

*The result was **absolutely awful**.*

The adverb *quite* can be used with both types of adjectives.

*They were **quite difficult**.*
*The experience was **quite amazing**.*

See Grammar focus on page 169.

11 **IDENTIFY** Identify four more examples of intensifying adverbs in the essay.

12 **APPLY** Choose the best follow-up for each sentence.

1 I think that city is particularly interesting.
   a But it's not my 100 percent favorite.
   b It's absolutely amazing.

2 His lifestyle is absolutely terrible.
   a He needs to change it immediately.
   b He could make some changes to it in the future.

3 I find the city gardens quite peaceful.
   a I can never relax there.
   b They are great places to relax.

4 Using space in this way is absolutely fantastic.
   a I can't understand why we didn't do it before.
   b I just about understand the point of it.

13 **PREPARE** Plan to write a text of your own that answers the following essay topic, and follow the steps.

What are the lifestyle benefits of developing public green spaces in cities? Give examples.

1 Note two or three lifestyle benefits of developing public green spaces and consider both personal and social perspectives.

2 Write at least one example, explanation, or extra piece of information to support each main idea (benefit) you have chosen.

3 Consider which key words or phrases you could paraphrase by using a synonym.

4 Identify places to add intensifying adverbs.

14 **WRITE** Write a draft of your text. While you write, refer back to your notes and the information in the Writing Skill box.

15 **IMPROVE** Read your text and correct any grammar and spelling mistakes. Check for examples of what you have learned.

Writing Checklist

☐ Did you include facts and information from the video?
☐ Did you include new vocabulary from the unit?
☐ Did you use synonyms to avoid repetition?

16 **SHARE** Read a classmate's text. How similar are your views?

A student reads at home in the Mekong Delta Region, Vietnam

11.3 Living Together

1 ACTIVATE When and why do you spend time with other people? Discuss your experiences with groups with a partner.

2 VOCABULARY Match the words in the box to the definitions.

status	split up	join in	identify with
get along with	gather	exclude	depend on

👤⁺ Oxford 5000™

1 _____ participate in group activities
2 _____ have a good relationship with
3 _____ deny someone access to a group or place
4 _____ relative social position
5 _____ trust or rely on someone
6 _____ an ending of a connection or relationship
7 _____ get together with others in a group
8 _____ regard oneself as sharing the same characteristic or thinking as someone else

3 WHAT'S YOUR ANGLE? Complete the sentences so they are true for you. Share your sentences with a partner.

1 I depend on my _____ for _____.
2 I find it difficult to join in when _____.
3 My status in a group is _____ to me.
4 I really identify with _____.
5 Many of my _____ have split up.
6 My friends and I usually gather _____.
7 I _____ been excluded from a group.
8 I get on best with _____.

4 APPLY Work with a partner. What do you know about the animals in the photos and how they live? Discuss the pictures using words from Exercise 2.

LISTENING SKILL Dealing with longer listening

Before listening to a presentation or lecture, it is useful to:

• preview the topic. Consider the title and think about what you already know about it, relating it to your own general knowledge and experience.

• consider how you will structure your notes. A useful way to do this is to write down some questions that you would expect to be answered by the speaker.

When you listen, in your notes:

• use bullet points to note key words, facts, and statistics.

• use abbreviations to make your notes shorter and to the point.

5 IDENTIFY You are going to listen to the talk advertised here. Discuss the questions with a partner.

1 What do you know about the topic?
2 What questions do you think the talk will answer? Make a list of at least three.

Group life

A talk by Mia Palubiski

The gathering of animals — the different ways animals depend on the group for survival

6 🔊 **INTEGRATE** Listen to the start of a talk. Add to and adjust your questions.

1   Which of your questions do you think the talk will answer?

2   Which other questions do you think it will answer?

—adapted from the *Encyclopedia of Evolution*, edited by Mark Pagel

7 🔊 📖 **IDENTIFY** Listen to more of the talk. Which of your questions from Exercise 6 did the talk answer?

8 **APPLY** Work with a partner. Plan abbreviations for the following words the speaker uses in the talk.

1   group _____
2   animal _____
3   predator _____
4   member _____
5   individual _____

9 **INTEGRATE** Use the outline for the talk to take notes. Compare your notes with a partner. Then listen again. Finalize your notes and compare them with a different partner.

Group life _____

The gathering of animals—the different ways animals depend on the group for survival

_____

A talk by Mia Palubiski

_____

Animals in groups—overview

_____

A choice? _____
Basic needs _____
Being attacked _____
Staying safe _____
Identifying the enemy

_____

10 **WHAT'S YOUR ANGLE?** Discuss the questions with a partner.

Which information in the talk:
• did you know?
• was the most surprising?
• do you want to find out more about?

See Grammar focus on page 169.

🔊 **GRAMMAR IN CONTEXT Conjunction clauses**

We can use conjunctions, such as *unless* and *in case*, time conjunctions, such as *when*, *as soon as*, and *while*, to link two ideas in the same sentence.

When *animals gather, it is often around food.*
Unless *something unusual is happening, it is best to stay in the group.*

The conjunction clause can go first or second.

As soon as *they saw the predator, they ran.*
They ran **as soon as** *they saw the predator.*

When talking about the future, these conjunctions are not usually followed by a future tense. The main clause can be a present or future form.

Tonight, they **will protect** *each other while they will sleep.*

---

11 🔊 **IDENTIFY** Choose the correct option. Then listen to the excerpts from the talk and check your answers.

1   *When / Unless* I've introduced the main themes, I hope you'll join in the discussion afterward, as usual.

2   *As soon as / In case* some of you can't stay, I've put some useful links for further reading on the website.

3   After all, *while / unless* the benefits do outweigh the costs, the animals wouldn't exhibit this behavior.

4   Basically, in nature, *in case / as soon as* a good source of food is identified, groups of both related and unrelated animals will arrive.

5   *While / As soon as* it is clear that birds in some ways choose to fly together when they migrate, other life forms, such as tiny, newly hatched squid, are powerless to stop their distribution by ocean currents.

12 **INTEGRATE** Complete the sentences with your own views.

1   It is always best to join in with a group unless _____.

2   As soon as _____, we need to depend on _____ for _____.

3   It is natural for _____ to exclude _____ when _____.

4   It is best to try to get on with _____ in case _____.

5   While many of us identify with _____, some _____.

13 **WHAT'S YOUR ANGLE?** Share and discuss your sentences from Exercise 12 in a group. Find out who agrees. Try to convince those who don't agree.

Nice of You to Say So!

1 ACTIVATE Discuss the situations and questions in a small group. How similar are your responses?

1 You cook a meal for friends, and they tell you it is delicious. What do you say?
2 Your friends admire your new haircut. What do you say?
3 You give a speech at a friend's going-away party. Everyone says it is good. What do you say?
4 You paint a picture, and your friends say it is fantastic. What do you say?

2 ASSESS Look at the pictures. What do you think of the art work? What would you say to a friend if she or he were the artist? Discuss the questions with a partner.

3 ▶ IDENTIFY Watch the video and answer the questions.

1 What does Kevin think about Max's artwork?
2 How does Max respond to his compliments?
3 How does Andy compliment Max?
4 How does Max respond?

REAL-WORLD ENGLISH Giving and responding to compliments

The way we give and respond to compliments depends on the situation and our relationship to the speaker. We give compliments with phrases such as:

I really like your…   Your…looks great!   I love your…   Wow, that's amazing!

We tend to compliment achievements (for example, an exam result), possessions (a car), clothes and style (a new jacket, a cool look). Avoid complimenting physical attributes (for example, *You look great for your age*). Types of responses can include the following.

- Compliment elaboration

  Thanks. At first the preparation was a little stressful, but once I got into the swing of things, it was fine.

- Return of compliment

  That's very kind of you.   Thanks. Yours is good, too.

- Compliment evaluation

  This dish is balanced with just the right amount of sweet and savory. And the texture is just right!

- Compliment downgrade

  I don't think my entry is as good as the others.

Paying attention to how people give and respond to compliments can help you to respond appropriately in real-life situations. In most situations, English speakers try to maximize agreement between themselves and the person who has complimented them while, on the other hand, they minimize self-praise, "playing down" their achievement.

ENGLISH FOR REAL

4 **ANALYZE** Work with a partner. Read Max's responses to the compliments in the video. Match them to the four types of compliment responses (A–D) from the Real-World English box.

A Compliment elaboration	B Return of compliment
C Compliment evaluation	D Compliment downgrade

1 Thanks, Kevin…That's a nice compliment. I know you aren't a fan of art. ___

2 Yeah…those colors are true to life. ___

3 Yeah. It's been a lot of work…and so stressful. ___

4 Aw…really, Kevin. I wouldn't say that. ___

5 Thanks, Andy, but I'm not sure my work is as popular as Dave's. ___

5 **WHAT'S YOUR ANGLE?** Discuss the questions with a partner.

1 Did Max respond appropriately to the compliments he received?

2 Are there any differences between how Max responded and how someone might respond in your culture? If so, what are the differences?

6 **PREPARE** You are going to practice giving and receiving compliments. First, choose one of the situations in the list (or make up a situation of your own). Then predict the type of compliments you might receive in this situation.

You have:

• just won a competition.

• dressed up, and you look awesome!

• produced a really great piece of work.

• bought a new car.

• changed your lifestyle for the better.

7 **APPLY** Prepare four compliment responses, one of each type from the Real-World English Box. Then prepare a couple of compliments to give people in the other situations in Exercise 6.

8 **INTERACT** Tell a partner about the situation you chose in Exercise 6, e.g., "Hey, guess what! I've just won a competition" or "Look at me, I'm all dressed up." Listen to their compliments and respond appropriately. Then swap roles.

9 **IMPROVE** Interact with at least three other people in the class, complimenting and responding to compliments.

10 **EXPAND** Discuss the questions in a group.

1 What was your favorite compliment you received? Why?

2 How do you tend to respond to compliments in everyday life (e.g., elaboration or downgrade)?

3 Is there a best way to respond to a compliment? Why or why not?

GO ONLINE
to create your own version
of the English For Real video.

11.5 Pros and Cons

1 ACTIVATE Think about living on a farm, on a houseboat, or in a high-rise apartment. What type of lifestyle would each situation offer? Which appeals most to you? Why?

2 **IDENTIFY** Listen to the first part of a discussion about lifestyles. What lifestyle is mentioned?

3 **INTEGRATE** Listen to the full discussion. Which advantages and disadvantages are discussed? Which would you enjoy or not enjoy? Discuss with a partner.

SPEAKING
Talking about advantages and disadvantages

In discussions, it is often important or relevant to consider a topic or situation from both sides. This is an important critical thinking skill that we can use to communicate our ideas and negotiate with others. When discussing advantages and disadvantages, you can do the following:

1 Use words and phrases to describe advantages and disadvantages: *pros…cons, positives…negatives, an upside…a downside, a plus…a minus.*

2 Use words and phrases that show contrast: *conversely, actually, in contrast, on the one hand…on the other hand, then again, however, but, although, in spite of, despite*

3 Relate the situation to your own preferences or personal experience: *for me…, I would like…, wouldn't like…*

4 Use vague language to "soften" your tone and sound less "direct": *perhaps, but…, it seems to me that…*

4 **IDENTIFY** Work with a partner. Complete the excerpts from the discussion. Use no more than three words in each blank. Listen and check.

1 On _____, sure, you might be lonely, but on _____, if you go to a small community, there will be no escape from your neighbors.

2 It would be a definite _____ for me.

3 But _____, I think that everyone knowing everyone else's business could also be a _____.

4 _____, I'm sure I'd find living a rural lifestyle incredibly boring.

5 _____ have a simpler, more outdoor lifestyle. It'd be so nice to have a slower pace of life.

5 IDENTIFY Match the excerpts from the discussion in Exercise 4 to the functions in the Speaking box. Share your ideas in a small group.

PRONUNCIATION SKILL
Using intonation to soften language

When we are discussing our views with others, we usually try to soften our tone. This helps us avoid sounding too direct or certain (particularly if we're basing our views on personal opinion rather than facts). Including intensifying adverbs or modal verbs and hedging language in speech can have a softening effect.

I think that's <u>unfair</u>.
———→ *I think that's <u>a bit</u> **unfair**.*
Yes, but *I do like a nice meal in a restaurant.*
———→ **Perhaps that's true**, <u>but</u> *I do like a nice meal in a restaurant.*

When we say words and phrases to soften our language, we tend to use a rising then falling intonation to soften our tone, too.

———→ *I think that's **a bit** unfair.*

———→ **Perhaps that's true**, *but I do like a nice meal in a restaurant.*

6 **IDENTIFY** Read the examples. Choose the sentences with softer language. Listen and mark the intonation. Then listen again and repeat.

1 ☐ I think that's unfair.
☐ I think that's a bit unfair.

2 ☐ But some people don't find those things very interesting.
☐ Maybe, but some people might not find those things very interesting.

3 ☐ Perhaps that's true, but I do like busy cities.
☐ Yes, but I do like busy cities.

4 ☐ You like it, but others don't.
☐ On the one hand, you like it, but on the other hand, others don't.

7 PREPARE Prepare to discuss the advantages and disadvantages of a lifestyle from the unit. Make notes on what they are. Think about intensifying adverbs and vocabulary you can use.

8 INTERACT Work with a partner. Practice presenting one or two of the advantages and disadvantages from your list. Try to soften your language where appropriate.

9 INTEGRATE When you are ready, have your discussions in a small group.

10 WHAT'S YOUR ANGLE? How do you soften statements in your language? What words and intonation do you use?

Now go to page 157 for the Unit 11 Review.

12 Character

UNIT SNAPSHOT

What makes us different from each other?   137
What can you do about poor accommodations? 139
What do 41 percent of people who move wish? 142

How are young people different from old people?

Do places have characters?

What is your national character?

BEHIND THE PHOTO

Imagine you are choosing the following. What is important about the character of each one for you?

- A friend
- A person to work on a project with
- Someone to share accommodations with
- A person to sit next to at work or in class

REAL-WORLD GOAL

Watch a documentary about a famous person you admire

12.1 What Makes You, You?

1 ACTIVATE Look at the photos and discuss the questions with a partner.

1 What do you think the people's relationships are?
2 What type of personalities do you think they have? Why?
3 What adjectives would you use to describe their characters?

2 IDENTIFY Complete the characteristic definitions with the words in the box. Use a dictionary to help.

jealous	emotional	logical
professional	awkward	humorous

ℙ⁺ Oxford 5000™

1 The _____ person is confident and skilled in what they do in their workplace.
2 _____ people feel unhappy and angry because they want something that someone else has.
3 An _____ person feels uncomfortable and shy around other people.
4 _____ people make you laugh and are fun to be with.
5 An _____ person has and expresses strong feelings.
6 _____ people think clearly with good reasoning.

3 APPLY Complete the quiz from a psychology website.

Who Are You?	Yes, that's me.	Yes, that's at least one of my parents.
You like to be professional in everything you do, whatever it is: cooking a meal, wrapping a present, learning guitar…		
You sometimes get jealous for no real reason. You often find yourself wanting what a classmate, colleague, or friend has.		
Others consider you to be a humorous person; you enjoy sharing a joke with friends, and what's more, it's often you who makes the others laugh.		
You get emotional watching movies, especially when they are based on real life.		
You are basically conventional in your tastes. You prefer to do what other people around you do; you read the same books, watch the same movies, and are conservative in the way you dress.		
You pride yourself on being logical. When you argue, you like to prove you are right by reasoning. If you knew you were wrong about something, you would happily admit it.		
You feel awkward with people or in situations that are new to you. For this reason, you wouldn't go to a party unless a lot of your family or friends were there.		

4 INTEGRATE Compare your answers to Exercise 3 with a partner. Ask questions to find out more.

5 INTEGRATE Discuss the questions in a small group.

1 How do you think a person's character forms?
2 What can influence a person's character?
3 What influenced your character?

6 IDENTIFY Read the article that accompanies the quiz in Exercise 3. How many of your ideas from Exercise 5 are included in the article?

7 INTEGRATE Read the article again. Decide if the statements are true (T), false (F), or not given (NG) according to the writer.

1 Only a few people have several similarities with family members. ___
2 Genetics is frequently identified as the cause of habits, success, and physical appearance. ___
3 Most people believe that culture and experience are not as important as family. ___
4 Male twins are the most useful for revealing whether nature overcomes nurture. ___
5 Research indicates that nurture is a stronger influence than nature. ___

 READING SKILL Recognizing and understanding addition and contrast linking words

Writers use conjunctions or "linking" words and phrases to:

- add information: *what's more, moreover, furthermore.*
- contrast ideas: *even though, on the other hand, in spite of.*

When reading, notice the function of linkers. What connections is the writer trying to make?

8 IDENTIFY Look at the example in the first column of a linking phrase from the quiz. Then read the article again. Identify four more examples of linking phrases in the article. Identify the original information and the information being added or contrasted.

Linking word	Original information	Information added or contrasted
what's more	you enjoy a joke	you make people laugh

 9 WHAT'S YOUR ANGLE? Are you a product of nature or nurture? Work in a small group. Share and explain your views, adding and contrasting information.

 ## To Be or To Learn

Now look at your answers to the quiz. How many times was there a check in both columns?

For most people, there will be quite a few. More than four, and it looks like you're just like your older family members...but is that nature (you take after them) or nurture (you learned from them)? If you've ever wondered whether you were born like them or if you learned to copy them, don't worry, you're not alone—it's a debate that's been going on for decades.

Nature versus nurture: The great debate

We live in an age of genetics. We blame genetics for our bad habits, our height, and our poor grade on last week's math exam. But can we blame them for our personality (the nature theory)? Or did we learn to be who we are (the nurture counterargument)? This is the subject of a very serious debate.

The nature argument is simple; we inherit most of our individual characteristics from our genes—in other words, from our parents and ancestors. If we'd had different parents, we would have developed different personalities. But if the nature argument is true, it presents a troubling philosophical problem. If we are preprogrammed by our genes, do we actually have free will, the thing that many

believe makes us human? Furthermore, if we aren't free, can we be blamed for our actions? On the other hand, there are many who believe the nurture argument; they claim that in spite of the fact that we obviously inherit genes, we are more than just a copy of older family members. We become ourselves through living. It is our early experiences, the cultural attitudes we experience, and what we are taught that make us what we are. In other words, if we had grown up in a different place with different influences, we wouldn't have become who we are now.

To test this, psychologists study identical twins, who have the same genetic makeup. The idea is that if twins were brought up in different places, by different parents, and in different cultures, they would reveal the extent to which nature overcomes nurture. But even though there has been lots of research, the results are inconclusive. The best guess is that we are partly nature and partly nurture.

So, take a look back at the questions you answered before you read this. Can you say for sure whether you learned to be "you" or you inherited "you"?

—adapted from *A Dictionary of Education*, 2nd ed., edited by Susan Wallace

GRAMMAR IN CONTEXT
Second conditional versus third conditional

The second conditional describes an imaginary or unlikely situation in the present or future along with its imagined result.

If I **did** it again, I **would do** it differently.
If my children **weren't** the same as me, I'**d be** disappointed!

The third conditional describes unreal situations in the past. The condition is imaginary because it didn't actually happen. Consequently, the result is impossible.

I **would have been** a different person if I **had had** a different family.

We can replace *would* with other modals in both second and third conditional sentences.

If you **heard** me speaking, you **might** think I was my sister since we sound the same.

We can use *unless* in second conditional sentences but never in third conditional sentences.

I wouldn't do it **unless** there was a very good reason.
~~I wouldn't have been there unless he had called.~~

See Grammar focus on page 170.

10 IDENTIFY Use the prompts to write the complete sentences from the quiz and article. Check your answers in the text.

1 if / know you are wrong about something / happily admit it

2 not go to a party / unless / there / be / a lot of your friends or family there

3 if / have different parents / have developed different personalities

4 if / grow up in a different place / not become who we are now

5 if / twins / be brought up in different places / reveal the extent to which nature overcomes nurture

11 INTEGRATE Work with a partner. For each sentence in Exercise 10, discuss which conditional is used.

12 APPLY Complete the prompts with your own ideas to make second or third conditional sentences.

1 If I had lived in a different place,…

2 I wouldn't have met my best friend if…

3 I wouldn't argue with the nature-nurture theory unless…

4 If I spent more time with my family,…

5 If I had had a different childhood,…

13 INTERACT Compare your sentences in Exercise 12 with a partner. How similar or different are they? Again, for each third conditional sentence say what actually did or didn't happen. For each second conditional, say what the real situation is.

PRONUNCIATION SKILL
Sentence stress in conditional sentences

In conditional sentences, we can change the meaning or add emphasis by stressing certain words.

If I had the <u>time</u>, I'd read <u>more</u> about the theory. (= I wish I could read more about it.)

If <u>I</u> had the time, <u>I'd</u> read more about the theory. (= the person who has the time hasn't done what I would have done)

I'd do it <u>myself</u> if I had the <u>skills</u>. (= I asked someone else, but I wish I could do it)

I'd do it <u>myself</u> if <u>I</u> had the skills. (= I'm commenting that someone else has the skills but isn't doing it themselves)

14   INTEGRATE Listen and mark the stress in the sentences. Match the sentences with their implied meanings (a–e) according to the stressed words. Then say a sentence and ask a partner to identify which one it is.

1 If I had more money, I'd buy a new car. ___

2 If I had more money, I'd buy a new car. ___

3 If I had more money, I'd buy a new car. ___

4 Perhaps they could change if they worked really hard at it. ___

5 Perhaps they could change if they worked really hard at it. ___

a I wouldn't waste it like he has!

b But I doubt they will.

c It might be possible.

d I wouldn't rent one.

e I wish I had enough money.

15 WHAT'S YOUR ANGLE? Imagine you could make changes to your character. Discuss the questions with a partner.

1 What would you change about yourself?

2 What parts of your character would you choose to keep?

1 ACTIVATE Look at the photos. Where were they taken? What typical facilities would you expect to find in places like these? Discuss your ideas with a partner.

2 WHAT'S YOUR ANGLE? Have you ever stayed in places like these? If so, what were they like? If not, say whether you think it would be a good experience. Share your ideas with a partner.

3 INTEGRATE Read the email and discuss the questions with a partner.

1 Which setting from Exercise 1 is it about?
2 Who is it written to?
3 What is it about?

from: <BoHuang21@campus.net>

to: <housing_director@campus.net>

date: August 16, 2017 at 2:46

subject: Issues with student accommodations

Good morning,

   I have recently moved into my campus housing. Unfortunately, I have some issues with the room I have been assigned and the standard of the facilities. I'd appreciate it if you would consider my concerns and take action to resolve them as soon as possible.

   In my application, I requested a single room. In spite of this, upon moving in, I found that I'm in a quad room, sharing with three others. If I hadn't asked for a specific type of room, I wouldn't be bothered by this. However, I asked for a single because I find it distracting and noisy having lots of people around.

   I had also expected to have a room with an attached bathroom, but this is not the case. This means I have to walk to the end of the corridor to shower, which I do not find acceptable. Furthermore, neither the bathroom nor shared kitchen facilities are particularly clean. If I knew I wasn't going to get the type of room I wanted, I would have found alternative accommodations.

   Even though my new roommates are very friendly, our shared space is already becoming messy, and this is something that I personally find difficult to deal with. With all this in mind, I'd like to request that you review my application and allocate me a more suitable room.

   Thank you very much in advance for your assistance. I look forward to hearing from you.

Best wishes,

Huang Bo

Student ID: Y1F76490268

WRITING SKILL
Using addition and contrast linking words

Writers often use linking words to:

- add information: *moreover, furthermore, what's more.*

- express contrast: *even though, on the other hand, despite, in spite of.*

These can be used at the beginning or middle of a sentence to improve the cohesion of a text and make sentences more complex.

Notes: *furthermore* and *moreover* are more common in formal writing, such as letters of complaint, official letters or documents, emails, and academic coursework.

What's more is used in more informal contexts, such as emails, informal letters, and stories.

Even though is considered less formal than *although*.

We can write *and furthermore* and *what's more*, but we do not write *and moreover*.

4 APPLY Complete the sentences with a suitable linking word or phrase from the box.

even though	what's more	moreover
on the other hand	furthermore	

1 I would like you to note that the bed is very uncomfortable, and _____, the sheets are very old.

2 I'm moving out of my student accommodations. _____ I like it, it's just too expensive.

3 As a well-known hotel, I would expect you to deal with the issue immediately. _____, I feel I should be given a partial refund.

4 I'm not sure whether I want to share an apartment with Pauline. She's really nice, and she's a really good cook, but _____, she can be really messy.

5 They gave me an upgrade on my hotel room, and _____, I've been offered an extra night for free!

5 IDENTIFY Compare your answers to Exercise 4 with a partner. What do you think the situation for each question is: formal or informal? Why?

6 INTEGRATE Work with a partner. Identify four examples of linking words in the email. What does each show: addition or contrast?

7 WHAT'S YOUR ANGLE? Discuss the questions and share your experiences in a group.

1 Have you ever been in a situation where accommodations (at college, on vacation, or on a business trip) wasn't good enough?

2 What was the situation?

3 How did you handle it?

4 Was it resolved to your satisfaction?

GRAMMAR IN CONTEXT Mixed conditionals

We use mixed conditionals to describe an unreal situation, either a past condition with a present result or a present condition with a past result.

In a mixed conditional, the time reference in the *if* clause is different from the time reference in the main clause.

To describe an unreal situation in the past that has a present result, we use *if* + past perfect + *would* + infinitive.
If I hadn't asked *for a specific type of room,* ***I wouldn't be*** *bothered by this.*

To talk about the possible past result of an unreal situation in the present, we use *if* + past tense + *would have* + past participle.
If I were *rich and famous, I* ***would have been given*** *the exact room I wanted.*

We can use other modal verbs in the main clause, especially *could* and *might.*
Huang ***could have found*** *alternative accommodations if he'd known about the room.*

See Grammar focus on page 170.

8 APPLY Choose the correct option in each sentence.

1 I wouldn't have paid for the more expensive room, even if I *have / had* had the money.

2 If she had heard about the other accommodations, she *would have / would* taken them.

3 If she *were / is* more sociable, she would have applied for shared accommodations.

4 Would you have taken the room if it *was / is* in a better location?

5 If they *were / would have been* unhappy with the room, they would have complained about it.

6 If I'd rented an apartment with friends, I *would / would have* probably be enjoying college more.

9 INTEGRATE Complete different people's comments about Huang's situation. Use the correct form of *would* and a suitable verb from the box in each sentence.

read	got	understand	receive	have

Huang: I ¹ _____ be able to work more easily if I ² _____ a single room.

Huang's roommate: If you ³ _____ more detailed information, you ⁴ _____ be so disappointed now.

Huang's resident advisor: If you ⁵ _____ his application, you might ⁶ _____ what he was talking about.

Huang's housing director: If you ⁷ _____ my letter, you ⁸ _____ be so upset.

10 PREPARE Plan to write an email of your own. Follow these steps.

1 Think of a problem or issue you had with accommodations, for example, on campus, rented from a landlord, on a business trip, or on vacation.

2 Plan to write an email requesting that a housing director, hotel manager, or apartment owner fix the issues you have.

3 Consider which linkers of addition and contrast you could use.

4 Think about how you could include an example of a mixed conditional.

11 WRITE Write a draft of your email. While you write, check your work by referring back to your notes and the information in the Writing Skill box.

12 IMPROVE Read your email and correct any grammar and spelling mistakes. Check for examples of what you have learned.

Writing Checklist

☐ Have you included linkers of addition and contrast?

☐ Do you have an example of a mixed conditional?

☐ Is there vocabulary related to accommodations?

13 SHARE Read a classmate's email. Help them correct any errors, and say what they have done well in their email.

14 INTEGRATE Read other classmates' emails. Which accommodations issue was the worst in your opinion? Which email was the most effective? Why?

A home in Swaziland

12.3 Stay or Go?

1 ACTIVATE Look at the photos of people's homes. If you were moving, which of these would appeal to you the most? Why? Discuss your ideas with a partner.

2 WHAT'S YOUR ANGLE? Discuss the questions in a small group.

1 Have you ever moved?

2 If yes, what were the challenges? Is there anything you wish you'd done differently?

3 If you have never moved, what do you think the challenges would be?

3 INTEGRATE Read the information about the radio call-in show. Then work with a partner to think of three reasons people might have for wishing they hadn't moved.

Wednesday about town

Have you moved? Sometimes wish you hadn't? Share your views on our weekly show — we're always interested, whatever you have to say.

Today Radio

4 🔊 IDENTIFY Listen to the radio call-in show. What do the callers wish they had or hadn't done? Did you discuss these regrets in Exercise 3?

> **LISTENING SKILL**
> **Recognizing and understanding vague language**
>
> We often use vague language in informal conversation, especially when we can't think of or don't want to spend time thinking of specific words to describe something.
>
> *It's **kind of** interesting, **you know**, that people think that.*
>
> Recognizing this vague language will help you identify the important information in what the person is saying. When describing, the speaker can use vague expressions such as the following:
>
> | | | | |
> |---|---|---|---|
> | *kind of* | *sort of* | *pretty (adv.)* | *whatever* |
> | *I don't know* | *like* | *you know* | *I guess* |
>
> When we use *sort* or *kind of*, we often add *-ish* or *-y* to the following adjective.
>
> *It's **sort of** blu**ish**. It's **kind of** big**gish**.*
>
> When a speaker is listing or categorizing, you often hear phrases such as the following:
>
> | | | |
> |---|---|---|
> | *and so on* | *etcetera* | *that kind / sort of thing* |
> | *stuff like that* | | |

5 🔊 IDENTIFY Listen and complete each excerpt from the talk show with vague language.

1 _____, we wanted to make sure that we could visit every day if necessary.

2 There was a cool, _____ relaxed, airy feeling about the place.

3 There's nowhere to walk, no cafés _____.

4 …the guy was _____ convincing…

5 It's _____…it _____ enabled us to see much more of each other.

6 🔊 APPLY Listen to excerpts from the radio call-in show. Write the main point of each excerpt.

1   It's boring.

2 _____

3 _____

4 _____

5 _____

7 🔊 **INTEGRATE** Listen to the radio call-in show again. Then discuss and answer the questions with a partner.

1 Why is moving an important event for many people, according to one of the hosts?

2 What changes did Jeremy's move bring about in his life?

3 What was the difference in character between the two places where Jeremy lived?

4 What did Freida like about the character of the new place when she heard the radio ad?

5 How has the way Freida's family lives changed since moving?

6 What does Marie like about her new place?

GRAMMAR IN CONTEXT *I wish…*

We use *wish* to say that we want things to be different from how they are or were.

To talk about the present, we use *wish* + past tense.
*I **wish** I **listened** to some other radio station!*

To express regrets about the past, we use *wish* + past perfect.
*I **wish** we'd **chosen** somewhere a bit more interesting.*

Note: *would* cannot have the same subject and object.
I wish the house was bigger. (NOT ~~I wish the house would be bigger.~~)

We can use *if only* instead of *wish* in all these situations. *If only* is more emphatic.
***If only** I hadn't!*

See Grammar focus on page 170.

8 **IDENTIFY** Identify the four sentences with errors and rewrite them to be correct.

1 If only we didn't move when I was younger.

2 I wish I would have a bigger home.

3 I like my home, but I wish it will be in a different place.

4 I wish I had gotten to know my neighbors better before they moved.

5 If only we have more time to consider whether to buy or rent.

9 **INTEGRATE** Use the prompts to write sentences with *wish* or *if only*.

1 have / a bedroom each / when I was growing up (if only)

2 I / have / a garden when I was a child (wish)

3 I / rent / more modern apartment (wish)

4 I / the neighbors / not make so much noise (wish)

5 we / afford / dream home (if only)

10 **WHAT'S YOUR ANGLE?** Which sentences do you relate to the least from Exercise 9? Tell a partner.

VOCABULARY DEVELOPMENT
Prefixes *inter-*, *pre-*, *trans-*, and *pro-*

You can form new words by adding a prefix to a root word.

international   *prepacked*   *transport*   *ensure*

Each prefix has a general meaning. This combines with the meaning of the root word to give the definition of the new word.

Prefix	Meaning	Examples
inter-	between	intersection, interchangeable
pre-	before	precaution, predates
trans-	across	transformed, transatlantic
en-	make	ensure, enabled

11 🔊 **IDENTIFY** Listen to the excerpts and complete each phrase. Add the words to the Vocabulary Development box. Then discuss and check the meaning of all the words in the box with a partner.

1 Her mother's been sick so as a _____caution, we decided to move nearer to her…

2 You know, we wanted to _____sure we could visit every day if necessary.

3 …it's right at an _____section of two big roads…

4 Whether it's a _____atlantic move or you're just moving around the corner,…

5 Anyway, it feels like, you know, really modern, even though it actually _____dates our old place.

6 I feel like my life has been _____formed for the better.

7 It's funny how a home—four walls—can actually _____rich your life…

8 I thought homes were kind of _____changeable…

12 **APPLY** Complete each sentence with your own ideas.

1 The best way to enrich your life is to
_____.

2 I think _____ are completely interchangeable.

3 My friendship with _____ predates
_____.

4 When I leave the house, I always take the precaution of
_____.

5 I transformed my home by
_____.

13 **WHAT'S YOUR ANGLE?** Compare your sentences from Exercise 12 in a group. How similar are they?

With All Due Respect...

1 ACTIVATE Discuss the questions with a partner, using the prompts to guide your answers.

1 When was the last time you criticized someone? Describe who, when, where, why, and how.

2 When was the last time someone criticized you? Describe who, when, where, why, and how.

2 ASSESS Look at the pictures. Discuss the questions with a partner.

1 What do you think Max, Andy, and Kevin are talking about?

2 How do you think they might be feeling?

3 What do you think they could be saying in each situation?

3 ▶ IDENTIFY Watch the first scene of the video. Then answer the questions.

1 What happened to Kevin?

2 How does Andy feel about this?

3 Does Max agree with Andy?

4 Why does Max decide to talk to Sam?

4 ▶ IDENTIFY Watch the second part of the video. Discuss the questions with a partner.

1 What general criticism do Max and Andy have of Kevin?

2 What specific criticisms do they make?

REAL-WORLD ENGLISH Giving criticism

Criticism can be uncomfortable, but at times, we need to give or receive it. Being polite and considerate of the other person's feelings makes this easier. Follow these tips.

Avoid criticizing the person. Focus on the action instead.

~~You give bad presentations.~~   *The presentation needs some improvement.*

Start with a positive.

~~You are always late.~~   *It's always fun once you arrive, but that's often late.*

Use phrases to introduce criticism.

With all due respect, *I don't think this is the right approach.*

Let me put it this way: *you need to do more to help.*

Use phrases to soften the criticism for the listener.

Don't get me wrong, *I enjoyed it. I'm just not sure I would do it again.*

He is really noisy, but **to be fair**, *he is also a lot of fun.*

5 ▶ **INTEGRATE** Watch the second part of the video again. Evaluate how polite and considerate Max and Andy are of Kevin's feelings.

6 **APPLY** Rewrite Max and Andy's criticisms using the information and phrases in the Real-World English box.

1. Uh, Kevin? Sorry, buddy, but you're *not* a quiet person.
2. It's true, mate, you're, erm, kind of noisy.
3. Well…you're a bit heavy-footed. Your feet *pound* on the floor, like this.
4. Right. And your voice can be really loud sometimes.

7 **INTEGRATE** Work with a partner. Take turns in the role of Kevin. Practice giving the softer, more polite criticism.

8 **PREPARE** First choose one of the situations in the list (or make up a situation of your own). Then prepare to give criticism appropriately in the situation.

- Your friend is always late when you meet up.
- Your teammate hasn't completed the tasks they should have (again!).
- Your roommate leaves the kitchen a mess after cooking.
- You are a tutor, and one of your students didn't get a good grade.

9 **ANALYZE** Review the other situations in the list in Exercise 8. Consider how you could respond to criticism in each situation.

10 **INTERACT** Work with a partner to do a role play. Tell your partner what the situation is, e.g., you did not get a good grade on your essay. Then give appropriate criticism, e.g., *This kind of essay takes a lot of work. I'm not sure you did enough this time.* Listen to your partner's response and develop the discussion. Then change roles.

11 **ANALYZE** Get together with another pair. Describe and discuss your role play from Exercise 10. Was the criticism appropriate? How did the person respond? Did the follow-up discussion reach a positive conclusion?

GO ONLINE
to create your own version
of the English For Real video.

12.5 Finding Common Ground

1 ACTIVATE Look at the photos. How would you describe the character of the building and of the room? Share your views with a partner.

2 WHAT'S YOUR ANGLE? Discuss the questions in a small group.

1 Have you lived in a place like the one shown at right?
2 If yes, what did you like and not like about it?
3 If no, would you like to live somewhere like this? Why or why not?

3 ▶ IDENTIFY Watch the start of the video. Then discuss the questions with a partner.

1 How does Kate describe the apartment?
2 What do Kate and Maria have in common?
3 Why is Kate visiting the apartment?
4 What do you think they will talk about during the rest of Kate's visit?

4 ▶ INTEGRATE Watch the rest of the video and check your predictions from question 4 in Exercise 3.

> ### SPEAKING Eliciting and making relevant comments on the opinions of others
>
> Conversations often involve finding out what another person thinks and giving our own opinion at appropriate points in the conversation. By exchanging opinions, we can connect with others, learn about each other's views, negotiate, and establish common ground.
>
> To elicit opinions and comments and the reasons for them, we ask directly.
>
> *What do you think about…?*   *What's your view on…?*
> *How about you?*   *In what way?*
>
> We can prompt indirectly by making a comment that encourages the other person to respond with their view.
>
> *A: That kind of thing really bugs me. [inviting the other person to say what annoys them]*
> *B: Totally! What bugs me is…*
> *A: That's awful! [inviting the other person to agree with you]*
> *B: Oh, me too…*
>
> When making relevant comments you can (1) use phrases to acknowledge the other person's opinion, (2) express agreement, and (3) relate the situation to your own experiences or ideas.
>
> | | | |
> |---|---|---|
> | 1 *I get it.* | *Uh-huh.* | *I hear you!* |
> | 2 *Absolutely!* | *That's great!* | *Good for you.* |
> | 3 *Me too!* | *I love / hate it when…* | |

5 ▶ IDENTIFY Watch the video again. Work with a partner to list phrases that Kate and Maria use to elicit each other's opinions and make relevant comments.

6 ▶ INTEGRATE What opinions did Kate and Maria share in their discussion? Watch again if needed.

7 PREPARE Prepare to discuss your opinions. Working with a partner, choose a place you both know, such as your classroom, a library, a nearby cafe, or another public place in the area.

8 INTEGRATE On your own, make notes on your opinion of the place you chose in Exercise 7. Use the questions to guide you.

• What do you like about it? Why?
• What do you dislike about it? Why?
• What experiences, good or bad, have you had there?

9 APPLY Discuss the place with a partner. Share your opinion and experiences with each other. Use phrases from the Speaking box and the video.

10 IMPROVE Work with a different partner. Share your opinions and ideas with each other. How much common ground did you find with each person?

11 WHAT'S YOUR ANGLE? Discuss the questions in a small group.

1 What strategies and phrases did you find useful for eliciting opinions?
2 How do we benefit from sharing opinions and experiences?

Now go to page 158 for the Unit 12 Review.

Unit Reviews

Unit 1

VOCABULARY

1 Complete the news report with the collocations in the box.

a cause damage	e educate the public
b having an impact	f monitor the situation
c protect the environment	g spread a messaged
d suspended activity	h take responsibility

A group of about 500 protesters gathered in Pliny Park on Saturday to stand up against the construction of the new chemical plant. Archer Parks, a spokesperson for the protesters, said that the group's goal is to [1] ___ about the dangers of living near a factory that produces dangerous chemicals. They want to [2] ___ to area residents that the chemical plant will [3] ___ to the surrounding land. "As citizens, we need to do what we can to help [4] ___ in our town and in the world," said Parks. "If local government officials won't [5] ___ for protecting citizens from toxic chemicals, we will." At least for now, it seems the group is [6] ___ since the chemical company building the plant has temporarily [7] ___ at the building site. We will continue to [8] ___ and give updates.

 GO ONLINE to play the vocabulary game.

GRAMMAR

2 Complete each question with *for*, *on*, or *against*. Then ask and answer them with a partner.

1 What's a lifestyle choice that you insist _____?
2 Some hotel owners argue _____ more tourism at the Great Barrier Reef. What do you think?
3 Would you stand up _____ a stranger if someone was unkind to them?
4 Do you think about social interaction when you are deciding _____ a place to live?

3 Complete the conversation with the dramatic present form of the verbs in the box. Some verbs may be used more than once.

be	get off	go	have	pick up
notice	ride	see	sit	think

A: Hi Karen! I heard you got an interview at that famous art gallery on 22nd Street.
B: I did! It's a crazy story. [1] _____ the subway last week, and this older man [2] _____ next to me.

After he [3] _____ the train, I [4] _____ he's left a package behind.
A: What was it?
B: Well, it was wrapped in paper, and as I [5] _____ the package, I [6] _____ that it [7] _____ the art gallery's name written on it. So, now [8] _____ the package [9] _____ probably a painting that's worth a lot of money.
A: So, what happened?
B: Well, I [10] _____ the train at the next stop and I [11] _____ straight to the gallery…

4 Choose the correct words to complete the paragraph.

After finishing college, I've [1] *took / taken* time off to travel. [2] *Since / For* February, [3] *I've been / I was* to two countries! I was in Malaysia [4] *since / for* a month, and I'm now in Thailand, where I've been [5] *working / worked* as a volunteer in an elephant rescue center. There's no Internet here, so I haven't [6] *contacted / contacting* my family much.

 GO ONLINE to play the grammar game.

DISCUSSION POINT

5 Read the quote. Do you agree with it? Share your ideas with the class.

"A good man and a good citizen are not the same thing."
—selected from the *Oxford Dictionary of Quotations*, 8th ed., edited by Elizabeth Knowles

 GO ONLINE and listen to a podcast. Then add your comments to the discussion board.

ZOOM IN

6 What about you?

Task 1 Talk about an issue that you think people should stand up for (or against).
Task 2 Write a paragraph about how to deal with a social or environmental issue.
Task 3 Find an image of someone being a good citizen. Share your opinion on it.

7 How did you do in the tasks? Complete the prompts.

I found Task ___ easy because…
I found Task ___ difficult because…
I need to improve _____. To do this, I'm going to…

Unit 2

VOCABULARY

1 Read each sentence. Add the correct noun suffix from the box.

-ship	-ion	-ism	-ness	-ry

1. My grandparents were the most wonderful people. They treated everyone with kind_____.
2. My father wanted me to study chemist_____ in college, but I chose art instead.
3. Today, I finally got a gym member_____.
4. The way you bite your bottom lip is a manner_____ that reminds me of my best friend from high school.
5. The destruct_____ of my elementary school during a flood is one of my saddest memories.

2 Choose the correct vocabulary word to complete each sentence.

1. Certain foods are known for *departing / boosting* people's brainpower.
2. My family moved around a lot when I was young, but we settled *accurately / permanently* when I was in high school.
3. What do you think is the best *strategy / trigger* for remembering information for a test?
4. My computer doesn't have *adequate / astonishing* memory for me to add this program.
5. My first year of college was not very enjoyable for me. I didn't have any friends, and I had a lot of *anxiety / strategy*.
6. The hotel we stayed in in Italy was very *colorful / charming*, and so were the owners.

 GO ONLINE to play the vocabulary game.

GRAMMAR

3 Complete the narrative with appropriate forms of the verbs in parentheses.

Last Tuesday, Greg Hessel [1] _____ (come) home from work at the usual time. He [2] _____ (be) home for about 15 minutes when he [3] _____ (decide) to take a bike ride. About 6 p.m., when Greg's wife Ariel [4] _____ (get) home, she saw that Greg [5] _____ (leave) her a note on the kitchen table. It said simply, "Out for a ride." Greg [6] _____ (go) on many evening rides before, so she wasn't worried. But about an hour [7] _____ (pass) when Ariel's phone rang. She immediately [8] _____ (know) something was wrong. When she answered her phone, a voice on the other end said, "This is the Springfield Police. Your husband Greg is OK, but he [9] _____ (be) in a biking accident and is at the hospital." While waiting to see Greg at the hospital, Ariel [10] _____ (wonder) what [11] _____ (happen) to him. By the time she saw him, he was all cleaned up and doing fine except for a few scratches. Greg explained that he [12] _____ (not know) how he'd crashed. He [13] _____ (wake up) in the hospital with no memory of the accident.

4 Complete the prompts about habits and routines from your past.

1. In high school, whenever I had to study for a test,…
2. On vacations when I was young,…
3. When I first started studying English,…
4. Every summer when I was a college student,…
5. During family vacations when I was a kid,…

 GO ONLINE to play the grammar game.

DISCUSSION POINT

5 Read the quote. Do you agree with it? Share your ideas with the class.

> *"Your memory is a monster; you forget—it doesn't. It simply files things away. It keeps things for you, or hides things from you—and summons them to your recall with a will of its own. You think you have a memory; but it has you!"*
> —John Irving, selected from *Oxford Essential Quotations*, 5th ed., edited by Susan Ratcliffe

 GO ONLINE and listen to a podcast. Then add your comments to the discussion board.

ZOOM IN

6 What about you?

Task 1 Talk about a time when your memory played a trick on you.

Task 2 Write a paragraph describing how to memorize information before a test.

Task 3 Find an image of someone doing something that looks memorable. Share your opinion on it.

7 How did you do in the tasks? Complete the prompts.

I found Task ___ easy because…

I found Task ___ difficult because…

I need to improve _____. To do this, I'm going to…

Unit 3

VOCABULARY

1 Complete the text with adjective-noun collocations from Unit 3. Use the first letters to help you.

Developments in health and hygiene have prevented the
^{1} c_____ d_____ of mankind
as a result of the spread of diseases like the bubonic plague.
The plague was a disastrous epidemic that caused
^{2} w_____ p_____ in London
and southeast England in the 1600s. The rapid spread of
the disease resulted in ^{3} u_____
d_____ across the city as residents fled to
the countryside where the disease was less prevalent. About
a fifth of London's population died. Once a busy center of
commerce, London came to an economic standstill, and the
city's economy was left in ^{4} t_____
r_____ for several years.

—adapted from *A Dictionary of World History*, 2nd ed., edited
by Edmund Wright

2 Add one or more particles from the box to complete the phrasal verbs in the sentences. Some particles can be used more than once.

about	at	out	up	with

1 Do you think scientists will ever come _____
_____ a cure for cancer?

2 The professor pointed _____ the fact that the study
was still ongoing.

3 How did you end _____ working in that research
lab?

4 I'd like to participate in a dream study, but I'm not sure
how to go _____ contacting the researchers.

5 The meeting went on for hours before we finally arrived
_____ a decision.

GO ONLINE to play the vocabulary game.

GRAMMAR

3 Correct the bold errors in the contrast clauses. Sometimes more than one answer is possible.

1 **In spite** the fact that they had the technology,
researchers couldn't access the site.

2 **Whereas** the houses had been damaged by the flood,
the people were able to live in them.

3 One team worked at the site, **although** the other
worked in the laboratory at home.

4 **Even though** the heat, we continued to work.

5 We continued our hike to view the Nazca Lines **despite**
we were exhausted.

4 Complete each sentence with a word or phrase from the box. Different answers are possible.

each of	every one of	either of	neither of

1 Only two volunteers applied to take part in the study,
and _____ them was suitable.

2 _____ the archaeologists on the team
got sick because of the heat.

3 I'm afraid I don't agree with _____ you.

4 I wanted to attend the lecture, but _____
the tickets had been sold.

5 Complete the sentences with *the* or Ø for no article.

1 Scientists at _____ Humboldt State University in
_____ California made an amazing discovery.

2 Roman coins were found buried in _____ muddy
banks of _____ Thames River in _____ London.

3 _____ report was written by researchers at
_____ Oxford University.

GO ONLINE to play the grammar game.

DISCUSSION POINT

6 Read the quote. What do you think it means? Do you agree with it? Share your ideas in a small group.

*"The discovery of a new dish does more for the
happiness of mankind than the discovery of a star."*
—Jean-Anthelme Brillat-Savarin, selected from
Oxford Dictionary of Scientific Quotations,
edited by W. F. Bynum and Roy Porter

**GO ONLINE and listen to a podcast. Then add
your comments to the discussion board.**

ZOOM IN

7 What about you?

Task 1 Speak for one minute about the discovery you
think has contributed most to the "happiness of
mankind." Use supporting examples and evidence.

Task 2 Write a 250-word summary of a news story you
heard or read about that reports a recent discovery.

Task 3 Find a picture that represents a discovery or recent
research. Share your opinion of how important it is.

8 How did you do in the tasks? Complete the prompts.

I found Task ___ easy because…

I found Task ___ difficult because…

I need to improve _____. To do this,
I'm going to…

Unit 4

VOCABULARY

1 Use the words in the box to complete the article.

accomplish	clarify	consequently	expertise
exploited	forum	icon	invasions

How many times a day do you click the Internet
¹ _____ on your phone or computer? The Internet
is a convenient tool that can help us ² _____ a lot
of tasks quickly. We use it to shop and to ³ _____
information when we have a question. It can also be a
great ⁴ _____ for social interaction and sharing ideas.
However, the more we use the Internet and the more
personal information we share online, the greater the
chances that we may be ⁵ _____ by cybercriminals.
According to those with ⁶ _____ on the subject, the
average person with Internet access owns three or more
electronic devices that can connect to it. Many websites
request that users enter personal information. ⁷ _____
there is a lot of opportunity for people who want to use
that information for criminal activity. However, despite
warnings about personal security, research shows that
only 9 percent of teenagers feel very concerned about
cybercrime or ⁸ _____ of privacy.

2 Complete the phrases for clarification.

1 Social media doesn't rule my life. That is to _____,
I don't spend a lot of my time on it.

2 I wasn't happy my boss yelled at me for receiving
personal emails at work. In other _____, I quit!

3 It's important that employees obey the office Internet
use rules. Just to _____, no one is allowed to use
social media while at work.

4 I don't appreciate drones flying everywhere. To put it
_____, I don't want them flying over my yard!

5 I've decided to stop being friends with Gerald—on
social media, _____ is.

 GO ONLINE to play the vocabulary game.

GRAMMAR

3 Choose the correct modal to complete each conversation.

1 A: I heard you lost your wallet. What do you *must /
have to / can* do in that situation?

B: Well, you *can / must / need to* call the police if you
want to, but you *have to / shouldn't / don't have to.*
There isn't much that they can do.

2 A: I don't like these cameras all over the place. Do the
police really *need to / must / can* watch us all the
time?

B: The police *can / can't / must do* their jobs somehow.
They *don't have to / can't / can* be everywhere at
once. That's why I think they *can't / need to / don't
have to* have cameras.

4 Complete the prompts with a modal of regret (*should have*
or *shouldn't have*) and your own ideas. Compare your work
with a partner.

1 Jana said all her friends blocked her on social media.
She really…

2 Last summer several residents of that apartment
building reported seeing a drone outside their
windows. The police…

3 My credit card information was stolen from a website I
used to rent a car. I knew I…

4 The songwriter told the court that his new song had
been stolen by another artist. He had put the recording
on his computer at work. I guess he…

5 I don't know why James left the company suddenly. He
was a private person, and I didn't get to know him very
well. I…

 GO ONLINE to play the grammar game.

DISCUSSION POINT

5 Read the quote. What do you think it means? Do you
agree with it? Share your ideas in a small group.

 *"Civilization is the progress toward a society of
privacy."*
—Ayn Rand, selected from *Oxford Dictionary of
Quotations,* 8th ed., edited by Elizabeth Knowles

 **GO ONLINE and listen to a podcast. Then add
your comments to the discussion board.**

ZOOM IN

6 What about you?

Task 1 Talk about a time when you did something online
that you regretted later.

Task 2 Write a paragraph giving an argument for and a
counterargument against advertising companies
using browsing data to target consumers.

Task 3 Find an image of people using Internet devices in
public. Share your opinion of it.

7 How did you do in the tasks? Complete the prompts.

I found Task ___ easy because…

I found Task ___ difficult because…

I need to improve _____. To do this,
I'm going to…

Unit 5

VOCABULARY

1 Choose the correct words.

1 Mathilda has been an excellent employee. We really should *contract* / *promote* her.

2 My part-time job *finances* / *contracts* my studies.

3 George didn't pass his exams, and his career *income* / *prospects* aren't good.

4 The *contribution* / *income* of people such as Tim Berners-Lee and Steve Jobs to the tech industry cannot be over-estimated.

5 Engineers and technicians are paid more *extensive* / *generously* than nurses and teachers.

2 Write predictions about the following things in the future. Use each of the adverbs of probability in your sentences.

definitely	doubtless	perhaps	unlikely	surely

1 Off-grid communities

2 Alternative therapies

3 Robot–human relationships

4 Attitudes toward alternative lifestyles

5 Sources of energy

 GO ONLINE to play the vocabulary game.

GRAMMAR

3 Choose the correct wording to complete each sentence. Sometimes both options are correct.

1 When *is the company changing* / *will the company change* its energy policy?

2 What *do we do* / *are we doing* in robotics class next week?

3 *We're going* / *We will go* to a meeting about off-grid communities this weekend.

4 Juanita *is studying* / *studies* alternative medicine in China next year.

5 The robotics conference *starts* / *is starting* on Monday.

4 Complete the brochure for an alternative therapy school. Use *will*, the future perfect, or the future continuous and the verbs in parentheses.

Thank you for your interest in Modern Tranquility Alternative Therapies.

As a student in our Beginner Therapist program, you
¹ _____ (study) under some of the most experienced experts in the field of alternative therapies.

During this one-year course, you ² _____ (learn) the history and basic principles of herbal medicine, massage therapy, and aromatherapy—the science of smell. You ³ _____ (get) real, on-the-job experience, and you ⁴ _____ (have) a chance to apply your learning with real patients in the Modern Tranquility Clinic.

By the time you graduate, you ⁵ _____ (master) the basic techniques for using these therapies to help people deal with a variety of physical and emotional problems including stress and anxiety.

Within just a few months after graduation, you
⁶ _____ (work) as an independent alternative therapist.

 GO ONLINE to play the grammar game.

DISCUSSION POINT

5 Read the quote. What do you think it means? Do you agree with it? Share your ideas in a small group.

 "History teaches us that men and nations behave wisely once they have exhausted all other alternatives."
—Abba Eban, selected from *Oxford Dictionary of Humorous Quotations*, 5ᵗʰ ed., edited by Gyles Brandreth

 GO ONLINE and listen to a podcast. Then add your comments to the discussion board.

 ZOOM IN

6 What about you?

1 Talk about the future. Which lifestyle change interests you: embracing technology or going off-grid? Why?

2 Write a description of a job that requires skills that a machine can't do.

3 Find an image of people who have an alternative lifestyle or job. Share your opinion on it.

7 How did you do in the tasks? Complete the prompts.

I found Task ___ easy because…

I found Task ___ difficult because…

I need to improve _____. To do this, I'm going to…

Unit 6

VOCABULARY

1 Complete each sentence with a term from the box. Which sentences do you agree with?

acquire	challenge (verb)	concentration
determination	opponent	stick to
under pressure		

1 You are never too old to _____ new skills.
2 Some people work very well _____.
3 One mistake can lose a match, so you need total _____ when you are playing tennis.
4 Playing against a(n) _____ who is better than you is the best way to improve your game.
5 A lot of people go to the gym for a few weeks but don't _____ it.
6 I like to _____ people to a game.
7 To finish a long-distance run, you need a lot of _____; most people give up.

2 Identify the three sentences with the correct intensifying adverbs. Correct the others by replacing the adverb with a suitable alternative.

1 Have you seen this movie? It's very amazing!
2 We all went bowling. It was totally fun.
3 Surely it isn't true. It's absolutely ridiculous!
4 The author of this book is really inspiring.
5 I wasn't totally popular at school.
6 Don't go near that old building. It's highly dangerous!

 GO ONLINE to play the vocabulary game.

GRAMMAR

3 Correct the errors in the sentences. Then compare answers with a partner. Say why the sentences are incorrect and explain any different meanings they have.

1 I'll never forget to walk out onto that beach for the first time.
2 I've tried play tennis, but I definitely prefer baseball.
3 I saw Reza walking home, so I stopped giving him a ride.
4 Sorry. I completely forgot replying to your email!
5 We tried to building a sandcastle, but it kept falling down.
6 I stopped to go to the gym after I hurt my knee.
7 Let's try reserve a table at Frankie's tonight!

4 Complete each sentence with the correct form of the verb in parentheses.

1 A: Are you interested in _____ (take) the job?
   B: Well, I'm not sure. It involves _____ (work) night shifts, and I like my sleep!
2 A: Oh no, there's not enough ice cream!
   B: That's OK. I'm OK with not _____ (have) any.
3 A: Did you get the house?
   B: No, we chose _____ (not buy) it in the end.
4 A: How do you feel about _____ (study) abroad?
   B: I like it, but I miss _____ (see) my family.
5 A: What happened after you finished _____ (complain) about the hotel?
   B: The manager agreed not _____ (charge) the full price.

 GO ONLINE to play the grammar game.

DISCUSSION POINT

5 Read the quote. Do you agree with it? Why or why not? Share your ideas with the class.

 "Never underestimate the vital importance of finding early in life the work that for you is play."
—Paul A. Samuelson, selected from *Oxford Dictionary of Quotations*, 8th ed., edited by Elizabeth Knowles

 GO ONLINE and listen to a podcast. Then add your comments to the discussion board.

ZOOM IN

6 What about you?

Task 1 Talk about something that you find fascinating about the world.

Task 2 Interview your classmates about their favorite free time activities. Then write a report of your findings.

Task 3 Find an image of someone having fun. Share your opinion on it.

7 How did you do in the tasks? Complete the prompts.

I found Task ___ easy because…
I found Task ___ difficult because…
I need to improve _____. To do this, I'm going to…

Unit 7

VOCABULARY

1 Choose the correct answers.

In the 1930s, in the United States and in much of the world, people experienced many economic problems. In the United States, this is known as the Great Depression. Many people lost their jobs and their savings. There is sometimes a(an) ¹ *perception / assistance* that when bad things happen to people, it might be their fault, but in the Depression, most people were hurting, and even wealthy people were not ² *immune / relieved* from these problems. The U.S. government needed to provide
³ *assistance / perception* so that people had shelter and food. As in hard times of the past, the government responded in ⁴ *conventional / innovative* ways by setting up soup kitchens and distributing meals, but it also tried some more ⁵ *innovative / conventional* ideas. Instead of just giving people food, the government provided jobs through new programs. People were hired to build roads and bridges but also to create art such as paintings and photos. Getting back to work helped ⁶ *heal / activate* people. The country began the process of ⁷ *recovery / assistance*. By the end of the 1930s, the United States was in a much better situation.

2 Correct the sentences by replacing the bold word(s) with a suitable opposite.

1 Oh no, I've left my purse in the office. Can you **borrow** me $20, please?
2 Walking will **reduce** your creativity by 60 percent.
3 I can't **leave** inside on a nice day, even if I have work to do.
4 In this unit, I **taught** that placebos actually work.
5 If you never leave the country, you **increase** your creativity.

 GO ONLINE to play the vocabulary game.

GRAMMAR

3 Choose the correct relative pronoun. Then decide if the pronoun can be omitted.

1 Describe a place *where / when* you used to hang out with friends.
2 Talk about a person *which / who* you admire for their creativity.
3 Explain the plot of a movie *when / that* you have seen recently.
4 Talk about an issue *that / who* you are passionate about.

4 Use the prompts to write sentences with participle clauses.

1 we didn't **realize** the time / we missed the last train home.
2 the woman who is presenting the prizes / do you **recognize** her?
3 Marcus **saw** the opportunity / he started his own business.
4 we didn't **hear** the bell / we carried on with what we were doing.
5 I didn't **read** the article / it describes placebo effects.

5 Write questions you can ask someone about his or her preferences regarding the items listed. Use *would rather*. Ask and answer questions with a partner.

1 watch a movie / play video games
2 go skiing / have a beach vacation
3 eat chocolate / cheese
4 play soccer / baseball

 GO ONLINE to play the grammar game.

DISCUSSION POINT

6 Read the quote. Do you agree with it? Share your ideas with the class.

 "Good management is the art of making the problems so interesting and their solutions so constructive that everyone wants to get to work and deal with them."
—Paul Hawken, selected from *Oxford Essential Quotations*, 5ᵗʰ ed., edited by Susan Ratcliffe

 GO ONLINE and listen to a podcast. Then add your comments to the discussion board.

ZOOM IN

7 What about you?

Task 1 Talk about an innovative product that you have bought or seen advertised recently.
Task 2 Write a letter to the expert you wrote to in the writing lesson. Thank them for their advice and explain how you overcame or reduced the problem.
Task 3 Find an image that illustrates a global problem or issue. Describe the issue and suggest one or two possible solutions.

8 How did you do in the tasks? Complete the prompts.

I found Task ___ easy because…
I found Task ___ difficult because…
I need to improve _____. To do this, I'm going to…

Unit 8

VOCABULARY

1 Complete the text with the correct form of a neologism in the box.

selfie	binge-watch	brunch	chillax
crowdsource	datahead		

On Saturday, I went to eat ¹ _____ with a few friends at a new restaurant. Then we decided to go to a picnic in the park. Of course, I took a ² _____ or two on my phone to record the experience. On Sunday, I actually had to work on a research project. I had my friend help me—she's a real ³ _____ and pretty much knows everything about the topic and about technology. She suggested that I ⁴ _____ some of the research. We could ask a question online and get a lot of information from people who responded. The report was due on Monday, so I worked hard. After that, I needed to ⁵ _____ a little, so I turned on the TV to ⁶ _____ a few episodes of my favorite show.

2 Choose the best reporting verb to complete each sentence.

1 The president *declared / commented* that the war was over!

2 The teacher *revealed / remarked* that the rain had stopped.

3 She *suggested / denied* stealing the money. She said she hadn't even seen it.

4 Ben *commented / acknowledged* that the story was true, but he seemed embarrassed.

5 I *confirmed / declared* the reservation at the restaurant.

 GO ONLINE to play the vocabulary game.

GRAMMAR

3 Complete the sentences. Use a reporting verb from the box and the prompts in parentheses.

deny	thank	advise
apologize	admit	refuse

1 Did you _____? (them / the present)

2 Journalists asked him for a statement, but _____. (he / comment)

3 The boss _____ and said it was the employee's fault. (he / make / a mistake)

4 The man has _____ and gone to the police. (steal / the painting)

5 Has Helen _____? She really should say she's sorry. (miss / the meeting)

6 The doctor has _____ for three weeks. (me / not play / basketball)

4 Write reported questions. Use the pronoun in parentheses where appropriate.

1 "Where are you going?" he asked. (me)

2 "Why didn't they show up at the meeting?" she wondered.

3 "Are you going to apply for the grant?" she wanted to know.

4 "Can I come to the theater with you?" Mai asked us.

5 "Why haven't you replied to my email, Steve?" I asked.

5 Work with a partner. Interview your partner about what they do in their free time. Then find a new partner. Report what your first partner said as well as what they asked you.

 GO ONLINE to play the grammar game.

DISCUSSION POINT

6 Read the quote. What do you think it means? Do you agree with it? Share your ideas in a small group.

 "Don't, Sir, accustom yourself to use big words for little matters."
—Samuel Johnson, selected from *Oxford Essential Quotations,* 5ᵗʰ ed., edited by Susan Ratcliffe

 GO ONLINE and listen to a podcast. Then add your comments to the discussion board.

ZOOM IN

7 What about you?

Task 1 Talk about language. What are the advantages of learning new languages and sharing words with other languages?

Task 2 Write a brief report of a statement or words said by a famous person. Say what they said (either quotation or paraphrase) and why it is significant.

Task 3 Find an image of someone telling a story or people having a conversation. What do you think they are saying? How do you think they are feeling? Share your ideas.

8 How did you do in the tasks? Complete the prompts.

I found Task ___ easy because…

I found Task ___ difficult because…

I need to improve _____. To do this, I'm going to…

Unit 9

VOCABULARY

1 Complete the collocation in each question with *get, have, make,* or *take.*

1 How do you _____ choices about the way you spend your time and money?

2 Do you _____ a plan for your retirement already?

3 What kinds of risks do you _____? Why?

4 What's the best way to _____ ready to start a new business?

5 When you _____ a problem with something, how do you usually solve it?

2 Ask and answer the questions in Exercise 1 with a partner. Give reasons and examples. Ask follow-up questions.

3 Complete the text with words from the box.

additionally	asset(s)	competition	entrepreneur
instantly	potentially	risky	seminar(s)
stimulated			

A(n) [1] _____ is someone who wants to start a business based on a new idea. This kind of business can be [2] _____ because it often hasn't been tried before. But if the idea succeeds, you can [3] _____ make a lot of money. Also, you may not have a lot of [4] _____ because no one else is doing the same thing. I recently attended a(n) [5] _____ on starting a new business. The evening [6] _____ my imagination, and I started to think of unusual business ideas. I know I will need money for any business I try to start up. I have some [7] _____ I can sell. [8] _____, my parents have given me some money. I'm excited. I know I won't make a lot of money [9] _____, but I might some day in the future.

 GO ONLINE to play the vocabulary game.

GRAMMAR

4 Complete the sentences with a word from the box and a suitable verb.

big	time	reason
something	option	easy

1 Cheer up. There's no _____ to _____ upset.

2 It's _____ to _____ for investors.

3 I think the best _____ is to _____ our own business.

4 Was that app _____ to _____?

5 I'll help. Just give me _____ to _____.

6 Do you think the company's getting too _____ to _____ successfully?

5 Choose the correct answer. Then compare ideas with a partner.

1 The "Small Is Big" loan allows businesses *to set up / set up* in the community.

2 Shopping at local businesses makes people *to feel / feel* part of their community.

3 Banks to not want customers *to change / change* banking products too often.

4 Our company lets us *claim / to claim* travel expenses.

5 The boss has allowed me *have / to have* a company credit card.

6 Complete the sentences. Then share your ideas with a partner.

We went to the bank so as to…

I'm saving money so that…

In order to succeed over the competition, I…

So that I make money, I'm going to…

 GO ONLINE to play the grammar game.

DISCUSSION POINT

7 Read the quote. What do you think it means? Do you agree with it? Share your ideas in a small group.

"Never invest in anything that eats or needs repainting."
—Billy Rose, selected from *The Oxford Dictionary of American Quotations*, 2nd ed., edited by Hugh Rawson and Margaret Miner

 GO ONLINE and listen to a podcast. Then add your comments to the discussion board.

ZOOM IN

8 What about you?

Task 1 Describe the benefits of investing in: education, medical research, and new technology.

Task 2 Write a persuasive essay giving reasons people should invest in a certain product or industry.

Task 3 Find an image of someone doing an activity that will invest in the future for them personally, their children, or the world. What are they doing? How are their actions an investment? Share your ideas.

9 How did you do in the tasks? Complete the prompts.

I found Task ___ easy because…

I found Task ___ difficult because…

I need to improve _____. To do this, I'm going to…

Unit 10

VOCABULARY

1 Read the definition of the word *theory*. Choose the best words to complete the text.

theory

noun (plural theories) a supposition or a system of ideas intended to explain [1] *something / some alternative*, especially one based on general [2] *principles / things* independent of the [3] *thing / incident* to be explained; a set of [4] *things / principles* on which the practice of [5] *a thing / an activity* is based: for example, a theory of education

[6] *an idea / a thing* used to account for a situation or justify a [7] *course / thing* of action: for example, *My theory would be that the place has been seriously mismanaged.*

phrases

in theory used in describing what is supposed to happen or be possible, usually with the [8] *thing / implication* that it does not in fact happen: for example, in theory, [9] *things / concepts* can only get better; in practice, they may well become a lot worse.

2 For each sentence, use a word from Exercise 1 to replace *thing*. Then complete the sentences with your own ideas. Compare your sentences with a partner.

1 For me, the most important thing is

_____.

2 People who don't _____ don't understand the most important thing about it.

3 The thing that worries me the most is

_____.

 GO ONLINE to play the vocabulary game.

GRAMMAR

3 Complete each sentence with a perfect or future passive form of a verb from the box.

warn	confirm	publish	welcome
inform	convince	tell	

1 The story _____ already _____, so it was too late to cancel it.

2 People aren't _____ easily _____ of the concept.

3 Tourists _____ of any reports of problems in the area.

4 We haven't _____ whether the sighting _____.

5 _____ the customers _____ about how spicy the food was?

6 The news _____ by scientists around the world.

4 Complete each sentence using the passive reporting verb in parentheses.

1 It _____ that the animals could still exist in remote areas. (think)

2 Until recently, it _____ that diesel cars were better for the environment than cars that run on gasoline. (believe)

3 It _____ that the matter will be investigated thoroughly. (agree)

4 The concept _____ to be the most revolutionary in modern science. (consider)

5 The theory _____ to be new, but it seems similar to what scientists have always argued. (claim)

 GO ONLINE to play the grammar game.

DISCUSSION POINT

5 Read the quote. Do you agree with it? Share your ideas with the class.

> *"When a distinguished but elderly scientist states that something is possible, he is almost certainly right. When he states that something is impossible, he is very probably wrong."*
> —Arthur C. Clarke, selected from *Oxford Essential Quotations*, 5th ed., edited by Susan Ratcliffe

 GO ONLINE and listen to a podcast. Then add your comments to the discussion board.

ZOOM IN

6 What about you?

Task 1 Talk about a thing that:
has been proved or agreed on recently,
many people believe but you don't, or
has been seen or claimed in your area or country.

Task 2 Write a description of a process that interests you, such as the way something happens, works, or is made.

Task 3 Find an image that illustrates an unusual phobia. Describe it to a partner.

7 How did you do in the tasks? Complete the prompts.

I found Task ___ easy because…

I found Task ___ difficult because…

I need to improve _____. To do this, I'm going to…

Unit 11

VOCABULARY

1 Choose the best lifestyle collocation for each sentence. Which sentences do you agree with?

1 People often choose to *adopt / support* a lifestyle that is different from their parents' lifestyle.

2 Not many people lead a(n) *nomadic / alternative* lifestyle; most people nowadays prefer a fixed home.

3 The demands of modern life often result in a *hectic / alternative* lifestyle with no time for rest and relaxation.

4 To *maintain / adopt* a healthy lifestyle over a long period of time requires self-discipline.

5 Most young people prefer a *busy / nomadic* lifestyle, going out and seeing friends rather than staying at home.

2 Complete each sentence with a word or phrase from the box.

identify with	depend on	status	get on with
gather	join in	split up	exclude

1 Most people _____ their brothers and sisters.

2 Most young people can _____ a famous person.

3 It is unusual for animals to _____ members from their groups when they get old.

4 Whenever animals _____ together, they fight.

5 Animals and humans _____ others to survive.

6 The _____ of a group member usually depends on their physical power or beauty.

7 When one animal attacks another, others usually _____.

8 It is best for a group of animals to _____ when they are attacked to make it difficult for the predator to catch more than one.

3 Which of the sentences from Exercise 2 do you agree with? Discuss with a partner.

 GO ONLINE to play the vocabulary game.

GRAMMAR

4 Complete the sentence prompts so they are true for you. Compare with a partner.

1 While I am on vacation, I usually…

2 As soon as I get up, I…

3 I tend to feel happy unless…

4 When I meet new people in a group, I…

5 I like to…in case…

5 Write sentences with *get* or *have something done*. Use the prompts as a guide.

1 Karl / laptop / stolen

_____

2 where / you / hair cut

_____

3 I / had to / tooth out

_____

4 we / the decorators / paint / house / decorate

_____

5 he / often / help / with the cooking

_____

 GO ONLINE to play the grammar game.

DISCUSSION POINT

6 Read the quote. What do you think it means? Do you agree with it? Share your ideas in a small group.

 "Study as if you were to live forever; live as if you were to die tomorrow."
—Edmund of Abingdon, selected from *Oxford Essential Quotations*, 5th ed., edited by Susan Ratcliffe

 GO ONLINE and listen to a podcast. Then add your comments to the discussion board.

ZOOM IN

7 What about you?

Task 1 Talk about changing one's lifestyle. Why do people do this? How difficult is it to do?

Task 2 Write a brief article on the positives and/or negatives of making your own lifestyle choices rather than following what's expected of you from family, peers, and society.

Task 3 Find an image of a type of animal in the wild. Tell your group about the living arrangements of this animal.

8 How did you do in the tasks? Complete the prompts.

I found Task ___ easy because…

I found Task ___ difficult because…

I need to improve _____. To do this, I'm going to…

Unit 12

VOCABULARY

1 Choose the best adjective to complete each sentence.

1 He has a very *emotional / humorous* character; you always know when he is upset.

2 I felt really *jealous / logical* when I looked around their beautiful new home. My place is really messy.

3 She is a good problem-solver and always approaches issues in a *logical / conservative* way.

4 Don't ask him if you want new ideas; he is very *humorous / conventional*.

5 He seems very *conventional / awkward* with new people but is much more relaxed with friends.

2 Add the correct prefix from the box to complete a word in each sentence.

trans	inter	pre	en

1 Where I'm from, we have to pay a lot to _____ (port) furniture when we move.

2 The place I live has a very _____ (national) feel to it, with people from all over the world.

3 I always take the _____ (caution) of finding out about people before becoming close friends.

4 Being friends with people of very different character can really _____ (rich) your life.

5 I try to _____ (sure) that there is a mix of people when I invite friends over.

3 Which sentences do you agree with? Tell a partner.

 GO ONLINE to play the vocabulary game.

GRAMMAR

4 Correct the bold errors in the sentences.

1 If I **didn't** applied for the apartment, I wouldn't be living in this city anymore.

2 We could have been early if the trains **are** reliable.

3 He'd have more opportunities to play soccer if he **chose** to study part time.

4 If I had more time, I **would have** visit for a week.

5 **Would you** bought the apartment if it was a bit closer to the city center?

6 If you'd **be** watching, you might know how to do it.

5 Write conditional sentences using the prompts and the pronouns in parentheses.

1 more time / learn to play / musical instrument (I)

2 meet / twin sister / might think she was me (you)

3 apply / for the apartment / have / good references (I)

4 they stayed longer / have / the opportunity (they)

5 give you / lift / into town / see you (I / you)

6 Write sentences using the prompts. Then share your ideas with a partner. Ask each other a bit more about each situation and the reasons behind it.

1 I wish I could…

2 I wish I hadn't…

3 If only I had…

4 I wish…wouldn't…

 GO ONLINE to play the grammar game.

DISCUSSION POINT

7 Read the quote. Do you agree with it? Share your ideas with the class.

 "Perhaps a man's character is like a tree and his reputation like its shadow. The shadow is what we think of it; the tree is the real thing."
—Abraham Lincoln, selected from *Oxford Essential Quotations*, 5th ed., edited by Susan Ratcliffe

 GO ONLINE and listen to a podcast. Then add your comments to the discussion board.

ZOOM IN

8 What about you?

Task 1 Talk about someone you know who has a very individual character.

Task 2 Write an advertisement for a roommate. Describe your home and the type of person you want to share with.

Task 3 Find an image of a room with character. Share your opinion on it.

9 How did you do in the tasks? Complete the prompts.

I found Task ___ easy because…

I found Task ___ difficult because…

I need to improve _____. To do this, I'm going to…

Grammar focus

Unit 1

Dramatic present in narratives

USE

We often use the simple present or present continuous to tell stories, anecdotes, and jokes. We use these present tenses to make our stories sound more dramatic and more immediate.

*It's about midnight when the phone **rings**, so I **go** downstairs.*

Television presenters also use the simple present to give a commentary on sports and news programs.

*And he **passes** to number 7, **shoots**, and **scores** the winning goal!*

We often use the present continuous to describe the background of the story.

*In the movie, the children **are living** at a boarding school during the school year and only **going** home over the school vacations.*

Present perfect and present perfect continuous

FORM

We form the present perfect with:

have + past participle.

*I've never **been** to Africa.*

We form the present perfect continuous with *have + been + -ing* form.

*It's **been raining** since ten o'clock this morning.*

USE

We use the present perfect to connect the past and the present.

*The cafe **has just opened**. (= It is open now.)*

We can often use either the present perfect or the present perfect continuous with *since* or *for* when something started in the past and continues now, or is repeated up to now.

*We've **lived**/'ve **been living** here for about a year now.*

PRESENT PERFECT VERSUS PRESENT PERFECT CONTINUOUS

We use the present perfect to focus on the result of an action, and we use the present perfect continuous to focus on the doing of the action itself.

*I've **been practicing** this piece for weeks but still **haven't learned** it.*

We use the present perfect to talk about how much or how many. When we focus on how long something has taken, we use the present perfect continuous.

*I've **done** three tests this term.*

*I've **been working** on this project for a month now.*

We use the present perfect continuous for repeated actions when we don't say how many times they have happened.

*I've **been trying** to contact him all morning.*

We usually use the present perfect, not the present perfect continuous, to talk about states rather than actions with verbs like *be, have, know, seem.*

*We've **known** each other since college. (NOT ~~We've been knowing each other since college.~~)*

We often use the present perfect, not the present perfect continuous, to announce news for the first time.

*Have you **heard**? Tom's **lost** his job.*

Question types: Subject, direct/indirect, with preposition

FORM

We form most questions by putting an auxiliary verb before the subject.

Does Sam speak French?

SUBJECT QUESTIONS

When we ask about the subject of a sentence, the word order is the same as in a statement and the question word replaces the subject. We do not use the auxiliary verbs *do/does/did.*

*What **happened**? (NOT ~~What did happen?~~)*

However, we use *don't/doesn't/didn't* in subject questions to ask about negative ideas.

*Who **didn't receive** the email?*

INDIRECT QUESTIONS

If we begin a question with a phrase like *Do you think…, Do you know…* and *Have you any idea…,* we do not put the auxiliary verb before the subject and we do not use the auxiliary verbs *do/does/did.*

*Do you know where **Dariusz works**? (NOT ~~Do you know where does Dariusz work?~~)*

QUESTIONS WITH PREPOSITIONS

When we are asking about the object of a preposition, the preposition usually goes at the end of the question.

*What are you looking **at**?*

We can, however, sometimes put the preposition at the beginning of the question, but this generally sounds very formal.

***For** how long did you wait?*

 GO ONLINE for the complete grammar reference.

159

Unit 2

Narrative tenses

USE

A narrative is a description of a past event. The main tenses we generally use in a narrative are the simple past, the past continuous, and the past perfect.

We use the simple past to describe the main events of the story.

> I **looked** out of the window and **saw** the Taj Mahal for the first time.

We use the past continuous to talk about a) background actions or situations that were in progress at the time of the main events, or b) two actions in progress at the same time.

> I **was waiting** for them to arrive when I heard the news.

We use the past perfect to show that a past action or situation took place a) before one of the main events or b) before the story began.

> We'd **been driving** all day and were totally exhausted.

Past perfect continuous

FORM

We form the past perfect continuous with:

had + *been* + *-ing*.

	Subject	had	been	*-ing*	
+	It	had	been	raining	hard.
−	I	hadn't	been	feeling	well for hours.

Positive and negative

USE

We use the past perfect continuous to talk about an action or situation that continued for a period of time before another action in the past.

> I'd **been living** in Italy for three years when we first met.

Past perfect simple versus past perfect continuous

PAST PERFECT

We use the past perfect to talk about actions that were completed before another action or situation in the past.

> Francis **had left** when we arrived.
>
> **Had** the meeting **started** by the time you got there?

We usually use the past perfect and not the past perfect continuous when we are talking about states rather than actions, with verbs like *be*, *have*, *know*.

> We'd **known** each other for about five years before we became friends.

PAST PERFECT CONTINUOUS

We use the past perfect continuous to talk about actions that continued for a period of time before another action or situation in the past. This action may or may not have continued up to the moment we are talking about it.

> I'd **been living** in Italy for three years when we first met.

Habits and routines—present

USE

To talk about present habits, we can use the simple present tense, often with an adverb of frequency, such as *usually*, *often*, *always*, etc.

> I **usually** watch TV for an hour or so in the evening.

We use *be used to* + *-ing* to say that we are, or aren't, familiar with or accustomed to something.

> I'm **used to getting** up early these days.

We use *get used to* + *-ing* to say that we are becoming, or have become, familiar with or accustomed to something.

> We're **getting used to living** here, but we've only been here three months

We can also use *be/get used to* + noun.

> I'm **not used to** the weather here.

We often use the present continuous with *always*, *constantly*, or *continually* to show that we are annoyed, angry, or frustrated by something that happens regularly.

> They're **always complaining** about my cooking!

Habit and routines—past

USE

We use *used to* + infinitive to talk about past habits and typical behavior, and states and situations that no longer exist.

> I **used to go** to bed around midnight when I was a teenager.
>
> We **used to live** in Wisconsin before we moved here.

 GO ONLINE for the complete grammar reference.

Unit 3

Contrast clauses

USE

Contrast clauses describe how something contrasts with information in another clause in a surprising or unexpected way. A contrast clause can come before or after the clause it contrasts. We separate the contrast clause from the main clause with a comma.

> He persuaded everyone that he was a doctor, **although** he had no medical training.

Contrast clauses often begin with *although*, *though*, and *even though*.

> She managed to survive the illness, **even though** her condition was very bad.

More formally, they can begin with *in spite of* and *despite*. There are different ways to follow these phrases:

- *despite/in spite of + the fact (that) + clause*

> Despite the fact that she had worked really hard all year, she still failed her exams.

- *despite/in spite of + -ing + clause*

> Despite having worked really hard all year, she still failed her exams.

- *despite/in spite of + noun*

> Despite her hard work all year, she still failed her exams.

We use *whereas* or *while* in a contrast clause to show a contrast in factual information to the main clause.

> Whereas her first job was a highly paid finance job, she now works for a charity on fairly low pay.

Articles

A/AN (INDEFINITE ARTICLE)

We use *a/an* when we don't specify which exact thing we are talking about. This is often when you first mention something.

> I saw an amazing movie last night.

THE (DEFINITE ARTICLE)

We use *the* when both the speaker and listener (or writer and reader) know the specific thing they are talking about.

> How was the concert last night?

We also use *the* with:

- superlative forms

> The Mall of America is **the biggest mall** in the US.

- rivers, valleys, deserts, mountain ranges, oceans, seas, groups of islands, and plural country names.

> How long is the Amazon?

- the names of theaters, movie theaters, hotels, galleries, and museums.

> Have you been to the Guggenheim Museum?

NO ARTICLE (OR THE ZERO ARTICLE)

We use no article in a number of ways. These include:

- to refer to something in a general sense (with plural or uncountable nouns).

> My daughter's always listening to **music**.

- with most country names, continents, states, lakes, and individual mountains.

> Have you ever been to **Australia**?

- with towns/cities, neighborhoods, and streets.

> Have you been to **Paris**?

Determiners and quantifiers

MANY, MUCH, SOME, ANY, A FEW, ETC.

We use *(too) many*, *(a) few*, *several*, *a number of*, and *hundreds/thousands of* with countable nouns.

> There are **several shared student houses** on my road.

We use *(too) much*, *(a) little*, *a great deal of*, and *a large quantity of* with uncountable nouns.

> "Did you do **much sightseeing** in Paris?"

We can use *a lot of*, *lots of*, *some*, *any*, and *enough* with countable and uncountable nouns.

> There are **a lot of cafes** in the area.

ALL, EVERY, AND EACH

We use *all*, *every*, and *each* to talk about all the items in a group.

All is used with plural nouns. You can use *all the/all (of) the...*

> **All visitors** must report to reception.

Every and *each* are used with singular nouns. You cannot use "each/every the..."

> **Every apartment** has been sold. (NOT ~~Every the apartment has been sold.~~)

Each refers to two or more. *Every* refers to three or more.

BOTH, EITHER, AND NEITHER

We use *both*, *either*, and *neither* to talk about two people or things.

> **Both David and Andrew** speak French.

Both is used with plural nouns and pronouns. Before a determiner (e.g., *the*, *my*, *these*) we can use *both* or *both of*. When we use a pronoun (e.g., *them*, *us*, *you*), we must use *both of*.

> **Both of them** speak French. (NOT ~~Both them speak French~~)

Either and *neither* are used on their own with a singular noun.

> I don't like **either house**.

We use *either... or* and *neither... nor* when there are two nouns.

> **Neither David nor Andrew** speaks German.

When we use a plural pronoun or a plural noun with a determiner, such as *the*, *my*, or *these*, we use *either/neither of*.

> I don't like **either of the houses**. (NOT ~~I don't like either the houses~~)

 GO ONLINE for the complete grammar reference.

Unit 4

Modal of necessity, obligation, and prohibition

USE

We use modal verbs (e.g., *must, can, could, might, should*) in a number of ways. We also use some non-modal verbs (e.g., *have to, need (to), ought to*) in similar ways. These uses include:

OBLIGATION AND NECESSITY

We use *must, shouldn't* and *have to* to talk about what we are obliged to do or what is necessary. We usually use *must* to talk about the feelings and wishes of the speaker. We usually use *have to* to talk about rules or obligations that come from somewhere else.

> You **must be** at work by 9 a.m. (= I am giving you an instruction.)
> You **have to sign** in before you can enter the building. (= This is a rule.)
> We **shouldn't be** late for the meeting.

Tip

The difference between *must* and *have to* is not very important. It is generally safer to use *have to* in speech.

LACK OF OBLIGATION AND NECESSITY

We use *don't have* to or *don't need to* to talk about what we are not obliged to do or what is not necessary. *Needn't* is also possible but is much less common. We do not use *shouldn't* in this way.

> You **don't have to wear** a tie at work. It's a personal choice.
> We **don't need to leave/needn't leave** until this afternoon.

PERMISSION AND PROHIBITION

We use *can* to talk about what is permitted or allowed. We also use *may*, but this is less common and more formal.

> Employees **can use** the gym for free.

We use *can't* to talk about what is not permitted or not allowed.

> You **can't smoke** in public buildings.

Modals of regret

FORM

We form past modals with:

may/must/can't/might/could + *have* + **past participle**.

USE

We use *should have* or *shouldn't have* + past participle to express regret or disapproval about something we or other people did or didn't do in the past.

> I **should have waited** before I sent the email.
> She **should never have posted** the letter.
> You **shouldn't have said** anything to him. He's really upset now.

Tip

In spoken English, we usually contract *have* to *'ve*.

> We **should've waited** a little longer.
> You **shouldn't've said** anything.

Past modals of deduction

PAST MODALS OF DEDUCTION

We can use past modals to make deductions about something in the past.

We use *must have* + past participle when we feel we are certain something happened or is true.

> James isn't in his office. He **must have just left**.
> I didn't know Olivia lived in Berlin. She **must've moved** there quite recently.

Tip

In speaking and informal writing we generally use *'ve* instead of the full form *have*.

> He **must've been** mistaken.
> They **might've gotten** lost.

We use *can't/couldn't have* + past participle when we feel we are certain something didn't happen or wasn't true.

> He **can't have known** about it.
> You **couldn't have seen** Alice earlier. She's in Dubai at the moment.

Tip

We can sometimes use *must not have* in the same way.

> They **must not have read** the notice.

We use *might/could/may have* + past participle when we think something possibly happened or was possibly true. We do not use *can have*.

> She's late. She **might've missed** the bus.
> I've looked everywhere for my phone. I suppose I **could've left** it in the taxi.
> They don't know what to do. They **may not have understood** the instructions correctly.

 GO ONLINE for the complete grammar reference.

Unit 5

Future forms

FORM

In English, there is no future tense. We use a number of different forms to talk about the future and each has its own meaning and use.

WILL

We use *will* to make a prediction based on personal knowledge, opinion, or feeling.

> *You'll really like the movie.*
>
> *Some children born today will probably live to be 120 years old.*

We also use *will* to make a instant choice or decision. This can include promises, offers, plans, refusals, and requests.

> *I think I'll leave work a little early today.*

GOING TO

We use *going to* to make a prediction based on evidence in the present.

> *Look at the traffic. We're going to be late!*

We also use *going to* to talk about plans we have made or intentions that we already have.

> *I'm going to look for a new job.*

SIMPLE PRESENT

We use the simple present to talk about an event on a schedule or timetable.

> *The conference is from April 11 to 15.*

PRESENT CONTINUOUS

We use the present continuous to talk about arrangements and fixed plans.

> *We're meeting at the restaurant at 7:30 p.m.*

ABOUT TO

We use *(just) about to* + infinitive to talk about an action in the immediate future. We do not usually give a time with *about to*. We don't use it for instant decisions.

> *Quick, hurry! The train's about to leave!*

Future perfect

FUTURE PERFECT

We form the future perfect with:

will + *have* + *past participle.*

> *The contractors won't have received the message yet.*

FUTURE PERFECT CONTINUOUS

We form the future perfect continuous with

will + *have been* + *-ing.*

She won't have been waiting long.

We often use the future perfect continuous with a time expression with *for* to focus on the duration of an activity.

> *I will have been working for ten weeks on this project by the time I finally complete it.*

We use the future perfect continuous to talk about a present action that will continue up to a particular time in the future. The future perfect continuous often focuses on the action in progress. Time expressions are normally used.

> *This is a very time consuming project. I'll have been working on it for ten weeks by the time I finally complete it.*

FUTURE PERFECT OR *WILL*?

We can use both the future perfect and *will* to predict events in the future. We use the future perfect to talk about the completion of an action in the future, usually by a certain time.

> *We'll eat our dinner at 7 p.m.*

Future perfect versus future continuous

FUTURE CONTINUOUS

We use the future continuous with a future time phrase to talk about an action that will be in progress at a certain time or over a period of time in the future.

> *This time tomorrow I'll be flying to Los Angeles.*

We also use the future continuous to talk about a future action that is fixed or decided. A time expression is not always necessary.

> *Will Pete be playing at the concert?*

We can also use the future continuous to talk about the present, when we are making a guess about something that is happening now. We sometimes use a time expression.

> *Sophia's on a business trip this week. I expect she'll be flying over the Atlantic right now.*

FUTURE PERFECT

We use the future perfect to talk about an action or event completed before a certain time in the future or still in progress up to a certain time in the future.

> *Do you think you'll have finished the report by the end of the week?*

We can also use the future perfect continuous with a similar meaning, although it is not common.

> *How long will you have been studying when you graduate?*

 GO ONLINE for the complete grammar reference.

Unit 6

Verb + *-ing* or *to* infinitive (same/different meaning)

USE

When one verb follows another verb, the second verb is either the *-ing* form or the infinitive, with or without *to*.

-ING FORM OR *TO* INFINITIVE?

Some verbs can take either the *-ing* form or the *to* infinitive, with little or no change of meaning: *attempt, begin, can't stand, continue, hate, like, love, prefer,* and *start.*

> *I love getting up late on Sundays.*
> *I love to get up late on Sundays.*

Some verbs are followed by *-ing* or the infinitive with *to* with a change of meaning. These include:

REMEMBER/FORGET

We use *remember/forget* + *-ing* to talk about memories.

> *He'll never forget meeting Alice for the first time.*

We use *remember/forget* + infinitive with *to* to say we do or don't do something.

> *I forgot to mail your letter. Sorry.*

REGRET

We use *regret* + *-ing* to express regret about an action in the past.

> *I really regret not speaking to her when I had the chance.*

We use *regret* + infinitive with *to* to express regret about something we are just about to do. This is used in formal contexts.

> *We regret to inform you that the train has been canceled.*

STOP

We use *stop* + *-ing* when we stop an action or habit.

> *I stopped playing computer games when I was about 30.*

We use *stop* + infinitive with *to* when we stop an action in order to do something else.

> *Sorry we're late. We stopped to get some gas.*

TRY

We use *try* + *-ing* when we talk about doing something to see what will happen.

> *I tried turning the key the other way, but I still couldn't open the door.*

We use *try* + infinitive with *to* when we talk about making an effort to do something.

> *I tried to open the door, but the lock was broken.*

Verbs with *-ing* and *to* infinitive

USE

When one verb follows another verb, the second verb is either the *-ing* form or the infinitive, with or without *to*.

Verbs that are followed by the *-ing* form include: *adore, don't mind, hate, love, like, can't help, can't imagine, can't stand, enjoy, fancy, feel like, involve, (don't) mind, miss.*

> *I don't feel like going out tonight.*

Verbs which are followed by the infinitive with *to* include: *agree, aim, appear, arrange, choose, expect, hope, learn (how), offer, plan, refuse, tend, want, wish.*

> *We've arranged to meet on the 25th.*

Verbs which are followed by object + infinitive with *to* include: *advise, allow, ask, authorize, encourage, expect, forbid, need, remind, teach (how), tell, want.*

> *They encouraged me to do it.*
> *I'm teaching my cousin to play the drums.*

Make and *let* are followed by object + infinitive without *to*.

> *My boss never lets me leave work early. He always makes us stay until 5:30.*

Help is followed by object + infinitive with or without *to*:

> *Can you help me cook/help me to cook dinner?*

Other uses of *-ing* form

USE

We use the *-ing* form in a number of ways. These include:

- as subject or object of a sentence.

> *Running is my favorite hobby.*
> *I hate washing dishes.*

- adjective/noun + preposition + *-ing* form.

> *I'm tired of working here.*
> *Are you interested in coming with us?*

- time conjunctions such as *before, after, since,* and *while* + *-ing* form. This is only when the subject is the same in both clauses.

> *All course participants must sign out before leaving.*
> *I fell asleep while watching TV last night.*

We use the *to* infinitive in a number of ways. These include:

- adjective/noun + *to* infinitive.

> *Is the software easy to install?*
> *It was nice to meet you.*
> *Come on. It's time to go.*

- noun + *be* + *to* infinitive.

> *My advice is to work harder.*
> *I'd say your best option is to start again.*

- *something/nothing/anything,* etc. + *to* infinitive.

> *I don't have anything to do.*
> *Come here. I've got something to tell you.*

- *too* + adjective + *to* infinitive.

> *It's too hot to sleep right now.*

 GO ONLINE for the complete grammar reference.

Unit 7

Defining and non-defining relative clauses

USE

We use relative clauses to connect a sentence to a noun phrase. There are two types of relative clause:

- a defining relative clause defines a noun. It identifies who or what we are talking about.

> Do you know anyone **who designs websites**?
>
> Have you seen the DVD **I bought yesterday**?

- a non-defining relative clause gives us extra information about something already identified.

> James Reed, **who is a Harvard professor**, will be the main speaker at the conference.

A relative clause normally begins with a relative pronoun. We use *who* for people and *which* for things. We use *whose* for possessions. We can also use the adverbs *where* and *when* for places and times.

> The speech **which** the politician made was very powerful.
>
> I've never been to a place **where** you can't buy coffee.
>
> My friend Anna, **whose** husband is away on a business trip, is coming to stay for a week.

In a defining relative clause, we can replace *who* or *which* with *that* for both people and things.

> There are many people **who/that** have never used a computer.
>
> I need some software **which/that** can edit songs.

In a defining relative clause, we can leave out the relative pronoun when it is the object of the relative clause.

> This is the person I was telling you about. OR This is the person **who/that** I was telling you about.
>
> Is this the laptop you got for your birthday? OR Is this the laptop **which/that** you got for your birthday?

We can generally put a preposition at the end of a relative clause or before the relative pronouns *whom* or *which*. When we put a preposition before *whom* or *which*, it sounds formal or old-fashioned. Note that we cannot put a preposition before *that*.

> I know the man you were waiting **for**.
>
> I know the man **for whom** you were waiting.

Participle clauses

USE

A participle clause begins with a present participle (e.g., *leaving*, *taking*) or a past participle (e.g., *left*, *taken*).

A participle clause replaces a clause that includes a subject + verb and allows us to include information more concisely in a sentence. We generally use participles in this way in more formal contexts.

> *Being* from the area, Jose knew his way around. → *Because he was* from the area, Jose knew his way around.

> *Not knowing* the area, we got lost. → *Because we didn't know the area*, we got lost.
>
> *Born* in the 1960s, he is part of the baby boomer generation. → *As he was born* in the 1960s, he is part of the baby boomer generation.

We use *having* + past participle to talk about the past.

> **Having missed** the bus, he was again late for work.
>
> Increased life expectancy means that **having been** born in the 1990s, these children may well live in three different centuries.

We can sometimes use a participle clause in place of a relative clause. The past participle has passive meaning and the present participle has active meaning.

> People **born** between the early 1960s and the early 1980s are known as Generation X. (= "who were born")
>
> Do you know the man **standing** next to the window? (= "who is standing")
>
> We stayed in a room **overlooking** the town square. (= "which overlooked")

Would rather

FORM

Would rather is followed by an infinitive.

> I'd **rather watch** a DVD at home than go out.
>
> If you're not interested in Paris, where **would you rather go**?

USE

We use *would rather* + infinitive without to to say that we prefer something. We usually use the contraction *'d* for *would*.

> We'd **rather speak** to him in person.

If the alternative to our preference is not clear, we use *than* to state the alternative. We can use *much* for emphasis.

> He'd **rather read** a book **than** watch a movie.
>
> Young people **would much rather** send a text **than** call.

We often use *would rather* in questions to ask about preferences or to give options.

> **Would you rather have** beans or peas?
>
> What **would you rather do** tonight? Watch a movie at home or go to the movie theater?

 GO ONLINE for the complete grammar reference.

Unit 8

Reporting verbs

FORM

Reporting verbs are followed by a number of different structures.

- **verb + *to* + infinitive:**

agree, ask, demand, offer, promise, refuse, threaten

> *Jana **agreed to come** with us.*

- **verb + person + *to* + infinitive:**

advise, ask, convince, encourage, invite, order, persuade, remind, tell, warn

> *Xavier **advised me to talk** to my boss.*

- **verb + (preposition) + *-ing*:**

admit, apologize for, deny, insist on, suggest

> *He didn't **apologize for being** late.*

- **verb + person + preposition + *-ing*:**

accuse... of, blame... for, congratulate... on/for, praise... for, thank... for, warn... against

> *Did you **thank Claire for helping** you?*

- **verb + (*that*) + clause:**

add, admit, argue, claim, complain, deny, explain, mention, predict, promise, suggest, think, warn

> *Helen **promised (that) she wouldn't** be late.*

- **verb + person + (*that*) + clause:**

assure, convince, inform, promise, reassure, remind, tell, warn

> *She **reassured me that everything** was OK.*

When we use a reporting verb followed by a (*that*) clause, we usually change the verb in the clause by moving it back one tense.

> "The room is too small." → He complained that the room *was* too small.

> "I think they*'ll* win 2–0." → He predicted they*'d win* 2–0.

USE

We often use the verbs *tell*, *say*, and *ask* to report what people say. However, we can also use other reporting verbs to report offers, apologies, promises, etc.

> "I'll help you with your homework, if you like." → He *offered to help me with my homework.*

Reported questions

FORM

To report a *yes/no* question, we use:

***ask* (+ object) + *if/whether* + clause with affirmative word order.**

> Did you fix your wi-fi? → He *asked (me) if/whether* I had fixed my wi-fi.

To report a *wh-* question, we use:

***ask* (+ object) + question word + clause with affirmative word order.**

> Where is your camera? → He *asked (me) where* my camera was.

USE

We can report questions using verbs such as *ask*, *want to know*, and *wonder*. We generally use a personal object after *ask*.

> *She wondered **why they had left** in such a hurry.*

Note that the word order of the reported question is different from direct questions. It is the same as in affirmative statements: the subject comes before the verb, and we do not use the auxiliary verb *do*.

> '"Are you going to take the job?" she asked. → She wanted to know whether *I was going to take the job.*

When we are reporting, we generally use the past tense of the reporting verb, e.g., *asked/wondered*, and we usually change the reported verb by moving it back one tense into the past:

present tense > past tense

past tense/present perfect > past perfect

will/can/must > *would/could/had to*

> "Why *haven't* you *replied* to my email?" → I *asked* Oliver why he *hadn't replied* to my email.

If what the person says is still true, relevant, or important, we often do not change the tense.

> *Eva **asked** me what time the movie **starts**.*

Reported speech

USE

We use reported speech to report what someone has said. We often use the verbs *say* and *tell*.

> *He **said** he never watched TV.*   *He **told** me he never watched TV.*

We can use *that* after the reporting verbs.

> *She **said (that)** she was hungry.*

> *She **told me (that)** she was hungry.*

When we are reporting, we generally use the past tense of the reporting verb, (e.g., *said/told*), and we often change the verb by moving it back one tense into the past.

> I*'ll be* there at 6:30. → He told us he*'d be* there at 6:30.

If what the person says is still true, relevant, or important, we often do not change the tense.

> I *don't like* action movies. → She said *she doesn't* like action movies.

We can also use the reporting verb in the present. When the reporting verb is in the present, we don't change the tense.

> I*'m going to be* a bit late. → Sarah *says that* she's going to be a bit late.

We sometimes need to change time references. (e.g., *yesterday > the day before/the previous day, tomorrow > the next day/the following day, next week > the week after*).

> I spoke to Alex *yesterday*. → He said he'd spoken to Alex *the previous day*.

 GO ONLINE for the complete grammar reference.

Unit 9

Structures with infinitive

USE

Verbs which are followed by the infinitive with *to* include: *agree, aim, appear, arrange, choose, expect, hope, learn (how), offer, plan, refuse, tend, want, wish*.

> *We've arranged to meet on the 25th.*

Verbs which are followed by object + infinitive with *to* include: *advise, allow, ask, authorize, encourage, expect, forbid, need, remind, teach (how), tell, want*.

> *They encouraged me to do it.*
> *I'm teaching my cousin to play the drums.*

Make and *let* are followed by object + infinitive without *to*.

> *My boss never lets me leave work early. He always makes us stay until 5:30.*

Help is followed by object + infinitive with or without *to*:

> *Can you help me cook/help me to cook dinner?*

> **Tip**
>
> We can use *not* with verbs followed by the *-ing* form or the *to* infinitive.
>
> *I love working abroad, but I miss not seeing my family.*
> *They agreed not to charge us for the first night.*

Infinitive constructions

USE

We use the *to* infinitive:

- after certain adjectives or nouns (e.g., *easy, difficult*), *too* + adjective, *something/nothing/anything/anywhere/nowhere, time*.

> *I always find it difficult to speak to strangers.*
> *I'm finding it too cold to work in here.*
> *Come on, it's time to go.*
> *Do you have anything to eat?*

- after some nouns + *be*.

> *My suggestion would be to paint it all blue.*
> *The plan is to get going tomorrow.*

Purpose clauses with infinitive

USE

We use purpose clauses to talk about the reasons why someone does something. Purpose clauses answer a "why" question. We use phrases such as *in order to* or *so as to* + infinitive to give the reason for doing something. *In order to* is generally considered more formal.

> *They went to the drugstore to buy some more painkillers but it was closed.*

> *We went to Paris so as to learn French, but spent most of the time speaking English!*
> *In order to obtain your driver's licence, you have to pass a theory and practical test.*

We use *so as not to* and *in order not to* to make the negative form.

> *So as not to hear them, she turned the music up!*
> (NOT *So as to not hear them...*)
> *In order not to miss her appointment, she used four alarm clocks.* (NOT *In order to not miss...*)

But we can't use *not to* on its own.

> *She turned up the music so as not to hear them.*
> (NOT *She turned up the music not to hear them.*)

> **Tip**
>
> We can also use *so (that)* + clause to talk about the reasons for doing something.
>
> *She stood up so (that) she could see better.*
> *Why don't you call them so (that) they know you're interested in the project?*
>
> If we put the purpose clause first, it sounds more formal.
>
> *So (that) I could hear him better, I asked him to sit closer. (More formal)*
> *I asked him to sit closer so (that) I could hear him better.*

 GO ONLINE for the complete grammar reference.

Unit 10

Passive reporting verbs

FORM

We can use reporting verbs in the passive with the subject pronoun *it*:

It + be + past participle of reporting verb + (that)...

> *It is thought (that) the virus will spread.*

We can use reporting verb in the passive after other subjects:

Subject + be + past participle of reporting verb + to infinitive...

> *Singing is known to relieve stress.*

When we are reporting on something that happened in the past, we use a perfect infinitive.

> *The director is reported to have taken off with company money.*

USE

We use reporting verbs such as *believe, claim, consider, know, report, say,* and *think* in the passive to talk about general beliefs and ideas. The subject of the sentence can be the main noun (or pronoun), or *it*. These structures are common in news reports and formal written English.

> *It is believed that no one has been seriously injured in the attack.*
> *In some cultures, coins are considered to bring you good luck.*

Passive future

FORM

We form the future passive in various ways:

will future
> *The chairs won't be needed for the reception.*

be going to future
> *They are going to be taken out to dinner for their anniversary.*

future perfect
> *The house sale won't have been completed by the end of the month.*

We form questions with the future passive in the same way we form active questions: by putting the auxiliary verb *will* or *is/are* before the subject.

> *Will he be sent to prison for his crime?*
> *Is the shopping going to be delivered this afternoon?*

USE

We use the future passive in the same way we use other passive tenses. We use the passive to say what happens to someone or something, especially when we do not say who or what does the action. This is often because the person or thing is not known, is already obvious or is not important in the context.

> *Surely you don't believe that life will be found on Mars!*

Passive—perfect forms

FORM

We form the passive perfect with:

the present or past perfect of *be* + participle of the main verb.

> *The audience had been made to wait too long.*

We form questions by putting the auxiliary verb *have/has/had* before the subject.

> *Has the leaflet been printed yet?*

We do not usually use the passive perfect in the continuous form.

Passive voice

FORM

We form the passive with *be* + past participle. Passive verbs can be in the same tenses as active verbs.

> *Billions of text messages are sent every day.*
> *The computer mouse was invented in the late 1960s.*
> *I wasn't sent the email.*

We use the passive infinitive (*be done, be opened,* etc.) after modal verbs, *be going to* and verbs followed by *to* (*need to, have to, want to,* etc.).

> *It can be done, but it's not easy.*
> *The software needs to be updated.*

USE

We use the passive to say what happens to someone or something.

> *The sign was knocked over in the storm.*

We most often use the passive to avoid saying who or what does the action. This is usually because this person or thing is not known, or is obvious or unimportant.

> *The mixture is heated to over 100°C.*

Tip

If we want to say who or what does the action, we use *by*.

> *The modern computer mouse was invented by Douglas Engelbart.*

When a verb has two objects, there are two possible passive structures.

> *The wrong person was sent the email.*
> *The email was sent to the wrong person.*

 GO ONLINE for the complete grammar reference.

Unit 11

Have/get something done

FORM

We form the structure with:

have/get + object + past participle.

> *I had my apartment valued last week.*
> *I am getting my car serviced tomorrow.*

HAVE/GET SOMETHING DONE

We use *have/get something done* to say that someone does something for us, usually when we have arranged it. We do not say who does the action. We generally use *get* for more informal situations.

> *I had my report proofread – there were loads of mistakes in it!*
> *Where do you get your hair cut?*

We can also use *have something done* to say that something unwelcome or negative happens to us. We do not use *get* in this way.

> *I've had my car broken into.*
> *Sarah's had her bike stolen.*

Intensifying adverbs

USE

We often use the words *so* and *such* to give extra emphasis or intensity. We use other adverbs to express degree of emphasis or intensity.

SO

We use *so* before adjectives and adverbs.

> *I got so bored listening to that speech.*
> *She plays the piano so well.*

SUCH

We use *such* before a noun, with or without an adjective. We add the indefinite article *a/an* before singular countable nouns, but not before plural nouns and uncountable nouns.

> *The festival was such a success.*
> *They're such professionals.*
> *He gave me such good advice.*

ADVERBS

We can use an adverb before an adjective to say "to what extent" or "how much." The adverb makes the adjective stronger or weaker.

Gradable adjectives describe qualities that you can measure, e.g., *intelligent, tedious, interesting.* We can say a person is more or less intelligent. With gradable adjectives we use gradable adverbs, e.g., *a little, a bit, particularly, very, not at*

all, *rather.* We usually use *a little* and *a bit* before adjectives that talk about a negative idea.

> *Our tour guide was very knowledgeable.*
> *I was a little disappointed by the response I got at my presentation.*

Non-gradable adjectives describe qualities that are absolute or extreme, e.g., *ideal, awesome, overwhelming.* They cannot be used as comparative adjectives. We cannot say that something is more or less ideal: either it is ideal or it is not. With non-gradable adjectives we use non-gradable adverbs, e.g., *utterly, absolutely, completely.*

> *Your suggestion is absolutely ideal.*
> *The movie was utterly terrible.*

> **Tip**
>
> The adverbs *quite, really, pretty,* and *fairly* can be used with both types of adjectives.
>
> *Quite* means "very" when used with gradable adjectives, and it means "to the greatest degree" when used with non-gradable adjectives.
>
> > *I thought the movie was quite good.* (= "very")
> > *The experience has been quite overwhelming.* (= "completely")

Conjunction clauses

FORM

When talking about the future, conjunctions such as *unless, in case,* and *as long as* and time conjunctions such as *when, as soon as, while, before,* etc. are followed by a present tense. They are not usually followed by a future tense. The main clause can be a present or a future form.

> *You should take your umbrella in case it rains.*
> *Unless I call you, I'll meet you at 6:30.*
> *I'll be waiting for you when you arrive.*
> *As soon as you arrive, we'll have some food.* (NOT ~~As soon as you will arrive,...~~)

USE

When talking about the future, we can use conjuctions such as *unless, in case,* and *as long as* and time conjuctions such as *when, as soon as, while, before,* etc. to link two ideas in the same sentence.

> *Don't touch the animals unless you want to get hurt.*

When talking about the future, we can use time words like *until* (up to a point in time), *as soon as* (at the moment when / immediately after), *by the time* (one event will be completed before another), *while* (during a period of time), *before, after,* and *when.*

> *I'll look after your things until you come home.*
> *By the time you read this, I will be in Paris!*

 GO ONLINE for the complete grammar reference.

Unit 12

Second conditional versus third conditional

FORM

In the second conditional, we form the if clause with:

if + **simple past.**

We form the result clause with:

would/wouldn't + **infinitive without** *to.*

In the third conditional, we form the if clause with:

if + **past perfect**

We form the result clause with:

would/wouldn't have + **past participle**

SECOND CONDITIONAL

We use the second conditional to talk about an imaginary or unlikely situation and its imagined result. It can describe present and future situations.

> *If we had more time, we'd stay a bit longer.*

It's possible to use other modals in the result clause.

> *If they saw the evidence, they might believe us.*

We can also use *unless* in second conditional sentences.

> *She wouldn't move unless she won a lot of money.*

We can use *were* instead of *was* in the if clause after *I, he, she,* and *it*, especially in formal style.

> *If the Minister were able to arrive by 6 p.m., we'd hold the press conference before the dinner.*

THIRD CONDITIONAL

We use the third conditional to talk about unreal situations in the past. The condition is imaginary because it didn't actually happen. Consequently, the result is impossible. *Unless* is never used in third conditional sentences.

> *If you had studied, you would have passed the exam.*

It is possible to use other modals in the result clause.

> *If you'd mentioned it earlier, I might have been able to do something about it.*

> **Tip**
>
> Note that we often contract *would* and *had* to *'d,* and in speech we often contract *have* to *'ve.* Also note that the if clause and the main clause can go in either order.
>
> > *If I had more money, I'd get a bigger apartment*
> > *I would've told you if I'd known.*
>
> Where the if clause is first, we need a comma. If it is second in the sentence, we do not use a comma.
>
> > *If I knew the answer, I would tell you.*
> > *I would tell you if I knew the answer.*

Mixed conditionals

FORM

To talk about an unreal situation in the past which has a present result, we use:

if + **past perfect** + *would* + **infinitive.**

> *If I hadn't switched my alarm clock off, I wouldn't be late now.*

To talk about the possible past result of an unreal situation in the present, we use:

if + **past tense** + *would have* + **past participle.**

> *If I had more money, I would have bought it.*

USE

We used a "mixed conditional" sentence when the time reference in the if clause is different from the time reference in the main clause. Mixed conditionals are a mix of second and third conditionals. They describe an unreal situation: either a past condition with a present result, or a present condition with a past result.

> *I'd be able to chat with my Spanish parents-in-law if I'd worked harder at Spanish in school.*

We can use other modal verbs in the main clause, especially *could* and *might*.

> *If you'd been listening, you might know what to do.*

I wish...

USE

We use *wish* to say that we want things to be different from how they are or were.

To talk about the present, we use *wish* + past tense.

> *She wishes she was a bit older.*

To express regrets about the past, we use *wish* + past perfect.

> *I wish I hadn't eaten so much.*

We use *wish* + person/thing + *would* to talk about things we want to happen or change in the future. We often use this structure to express annoyance or dissatisfaction.

> *I wish it would stop raining.*

Note that *would* cannot have the same subject and object.

> *I wish I was richer.* (NOT *I wish I would be richer.*)

We can use *if only* instead of *wish* in all these situations. *If only* is generally more emphatic than *wish.*

> *If only we had more time.*

We can also sometimes include a second clause after *if only.*

> *If only it wasn't raining, we could go for a walk.*

 GO ONLINE for the complete grammar reference.